Work/Life Balance For Dummies®

Starting Your New Work/Life Changes Now

You can improve your work/life balance in many ways, starting today. Follow this guide as you work out how to make your longer-term working arrangements more flexible.

- **Find out what your work place already offers.** If you're unhappy at work, don't hand in your notice until you check what flexible working arrangements your employer has in place. They may exist but aren't being practised.

- **Have a holiday.** You're entitled to a certain number of days a year to take as holiday, so take them. You're not indispensable and you need time away from work to rest, recuperate, and refresh yourself.

- **Look beyond your current job.** Find out whether opportunities exist for you to work in another department, to shadow a person, to learn new skills, or to offer to share your expertise with newer staff members.

- **Look beyond your current employer.** The online and newspaper job advertisements – as well as your own contacts – are full of job vacancies. Don't be afraid to apply if some really interest you.

- **Reject perfection.** Feeling a bit overwhelmed and tired is okay. You can live in a less-than-sterile home and use personal time to relax instead of cleaning. Being perfect is unachievable, and may be very boring.

- **Support your partner.** Tell your partner how much you appreciate the support you get. Find more time to spend together, such as meeting for breakfast or coffee, or lunch. Use email to chat during the day. Book a weekend away a couple of times a year without kids, work, electronic gadgets, or lengthy travel times.

- **Value your family.** Get home in time for dinner. Find 15 minutes to talk to your partner, read to your child, and turn the TV off at least one night a week.

- **Work out your goals and values.** What do you want in order to be happy in life? Do your own personal brainstorm on paper to find out what really motivates you.

- **Use electronics for errands.** In your lunch hour, use the Internet to order your groceries online, do your banking, buy gifts, or search for trades people. Send emails to friends and family who you struggle to phone after a hard day's work.

Stress-Busters to Make Your Life Easier

Are you paid to get stressed? No. So why get stressed when there's no reward at the end? Instead, pamper yourself at work by following these easy tips:

- **Be the first to leave at five.** If you've done your hours, go home. You may find it daunting at first to be the first to pack your bag and leave the office, but your move can encourage others to follow.

- **Be unavailable sometimes.** Turn off your palm device, mobile phone, and laptop when you're at home. When you make yourself available 24 hours a day, seven days a week, then your boss expects that of you – your work place can run without you.

- **Have a say in when and how you do your work.** Negotiate with your boss a starting and finishing time that suits you both. You can also negotiate flexible conditions, such as compressed hours, working from home, working part-time, or taking leave to pursue further study or personal interests.

- **Look at your emails only twice a day.** Check emails mid morning when you need a break from your other work and again once mid afternoon. You run your emails, they don't run you.

- **Take your lunch break.** Your body and brain need a rest on a busy working day. Get some fresh air at lunch time, eat outside, or go for a walk. Apart from your lunch, the rest is healthy and free.

For Dummies: Bestselling Book Series for Beginners

Work/Life Balance For Dummies®

Cheat Sheet

Stress-Busters to Make Your Life Easier (continued)

✔ **Use your diary.** Plan your work tasks into manageable chunks of time by using your electronic and paper diaries. Book in at least one hour of specific work (such as a project) first thing each morning before reading your emails.

✔ **Work out that your job isn't the whole you.** Change your attitude to work when you find stress and anxiety eating into your personal life. You have friends and family who care about you, a home you like, and interests outside of work.

How Balanced Is Your Whole Life?

The following figure shows several major life areas that you're likely to want to focus on to improve your work/life balance. Use the figure as a quick reference for seeing how balanced your life is by rating each area on a scale of 1 to 10 (10 being the highest) according to your levels of satisfaction and happiness. Ideally, you want to see high scores in all the important areas of your life and if that's not the case, Chapter 5 in particular can help you reset priorities and goals.

Remember, you can personalise this guide – each life area has its own definition – and you can change any of the headings to make it fully represent your unique ideal balanced life.

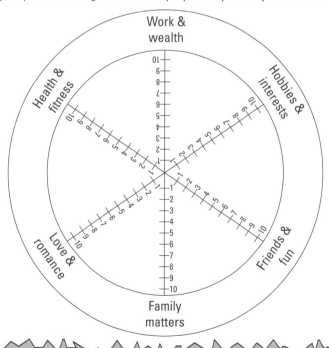

Wiley, the Wiley Publishing logo, For Dummies, the Dummies Man logo, the For Dummies Bestselling Book Series logo and all related trade dress are trademarks or registered trademarks of John Wiley & Sons, Inc., and/or its affiliates. All other trademarks are property of their respective owners.

Copyright © 2009 John Wiley & Sons, Ltd. All rights reserved. Item 1380-8.
For more information about John Wiley & Sons, call (+44) 1243 779777.

Work/Life Balance

FOR

DUMMIES®

by Katherine Lockett and Jeni Mumford

A John Wiley and Sons, Ltd, Publication

Work/Life Balance For Dummies®

Published by John Wiley & Sons, Ltd
The Atrium
Southern Gate
Chichester
West Sussex
PO19 8SQ
England

E-mail (for orders and customer service enquires): cs-books@wiley.co.uk

Visit our Home Page on www.wiley.com

Copyright © 2009 John Wiley & Sons, Ltd, Chichester, West Sussex, England

Published by John Wiley & Sons, Ltd, Chichester, West Sussex

For general information on our other products and services, please contact our Customer Care Department within the U.S. at 800-762-2974, outside the U.S. at 317-572-3993, or fax 317-572-4002.

For technical support, please visit www.wiley.com/techsupport.

Wiley also publishes its books in a variety of electronic formats. Some content that appears in print may not be available in electronic books.

British Library Cataloguing in Publication Data: A catalogue record for this book is available from the British Library

ISBN: 978-0-470-71380-8

Printed and bound in Great Britain by Bell and Bain Ltd., Glasgow

10 9 8 7 6 5 4 3 2 1

WILEY

About the Authors

Katherine Lockett works at the University of South Australia and helped to establish the Centre for Work & Life Research Unit.

Kath holds a degree in Arts (English) and graduate diplomas in Education (Secondary) and in Business (Management). In addition to working in the education and finance sectors, she has worked in a variety of federal and state government agencies in a range of jobs and subsequently had many opportunities to view people striving to achieve work/life balance in these situations.

Kath has also lived and worked in the United Kingdom and in several states in Australia. She now lives in Adelaide and is married with one daughter (and a very friendly dog).

Jeni Mumford is the author of *Life Coaching For Dummies* and is a professional coach and facilitator. Much of her work with clients centres around helping them to get the right balance across all areas of their lives.

Jeni had a 16-year corporate career as a director with the Hays group prior to becoming a coach, and knows from first hand the perils and joys of juggling life and career priorities. She found time a few years ago to complete a Master's in Human Resource Management and continues to love learning as a way of enhancing her skills and personal effectiveness.

Jeni's passion is helping people to work out what makes them happy and successful. For herself, she derives a great deal of happiness from making a difference to her clients, travel, having fun with the people she loves, and spending quality time with her two cats, who don't really give a hoot about that but play along with her out of sheer grace and favour.

You can contact Jeni via her website www.reachforstarfish.com.

Dedication

From Katherine: To my husband, Dean, and my daughter, Carly – thank you for giving me all the 'life' I need in my work/life balance. I love you both!

Authors' Acknowledgements

From Jeni: I would like to thank Katherine for writing this book in the first place and Wiley for giving me the opportunity to take on a new and challenging role as an adapting author.

From Katherine: Work/life balance is such an enormous topic. People around me are trying their best to work, develop a career, run a house, be a decent family member, participate in their community, and simply find more time to just live. All this, while trying not to feel guilty about what they feel they should be doing, instead of what they are doing.

There are literally thousands of ways to gain more work/life balance – so much more expertise than just one author can offer. Academics, human resources professionals, employers, business leaders, workmates and parents at the school gate, and many more people are developing, testing, and adopting new ways of working and living. These experts and real-life people have enabled me to carry out the necessary research for this book. Their passion, practicality, common sense, and lateral thinking have been very inspiring.

Writing this book has been a challenging and rewarding experience. Many people can attest to being interviewed and questioned over just why they look so relaxed compared to the rest of us, why their employees stay with them for many years, or why they've changed jobs from software programming to cafe catering. I'd like to thank them all for graciously allowing me to pick their brains and for generously sharing their experiences.

I am also extremely grateful that Charlotte Duff at Wiley Publishing Australia gave me the opportunity to write this book and sustained me throughout the challenges with many words of encouragement. As did my editor, Carolyn Beaumont, whose skill made this book a much better read.

I am also grateful to my colleagues at the Centre for Work + Life at the University of South Australia for their support and friendship: Helen Masterman-Smith, Jude Elton, Pip Williams, Natalie Skinner, Ali Elder, Catherine Earl, Jenny Linney, and Sigrid Christiansen. You guys inspire and interest me every day.

Publisher's Acknowledgements

We're proud of this book; please send us your comments through our Dummies online registration form located at www.dummies.com/register/.

Some of the people who helped bring this book to market include the following:

Acquisitions, Editorial, and Media Development

Project Editor: Steve Edwards

Content Editor: Jo Theedom

Commissioning Editor: Samantha Spickernell

Publishing Assistant: Jennifer Prytherch

Copy Editor: Anne O'Rorke

Proofreader: Helen Heyes

Technical Editor: Katherine Tulpa

Publisher: Jason Dunne

Executive Editor: Samantha Spickernell

Executive Project Editor: Daniel Mersey

Cover Photos: © Henrik Trygg/GettyImages

Cartoons: Ed McLachlan

Composition Services

Project Coordinator: Lynsey Stanford

Layout and Graphics: Nikki Gately, Melissa K. Jester, Sarah Philippart, Christin Swinford

Proofreader: Dwight Ramsey

Indexer: Cheryl Duksta

Brand Reviewer: Rev Mengle

Contents at a Glance

Table of Contents

Introduction

● ●

*W*elcome to *Work/Life Balance For Dummies*. This book is designed to help you adopt a lifestyle that allows you to feel better than utterly shattered and exhausted at the end of each working day. Are you looking for ways to have more say in how you want to structure your work and non-work life? Then this book is for you.

When you get home from work, slump through the door, drop your bag and keys, and kick off your shoes, and you're met by household noise, mess, and kids needing attention, having any kind of work/life balance seems an impossibility. Sure, changing your situation is a challenge. And like all the vitally important challenges in life, for you to achieve your particular work/ life balance is going to take some effort. Don't despair. You can make literally hundreds of changes, from the minuscule to the major, and enjoy the genuine improvements in your approach to work, life, family, and fun.

Your decision to improve your work/life balance – or should we say lack of work/life balance – has come at a very opportune time. Employers, managers, academics, Human Resource (HR) professionals, and even forward-thinking government agencies are sitting up and realising that work-place arrange-ments need to change if people are to be encouraged to remain in the work-force. Employers these days know the benefits of having employees who are refreshed and energised enough to contribute their best to their work. At the same time, they're beginning to appreciate that employees need time and energy left for a fulfilling life outside of their careers. You're going to be pleasantly surprised to discover just what tools are already available to help you achieve more balance in your life, and to help you influence others to support your new ways of working and living.

Don't get us wrong; we're not advocating that you turn your back on your glittering career and try to become a sustainable market gardener from your courtyard home instead of filing into an office every day. On the contrary, this book is about recognising the pressures you're already under – from your workload, career ambitions, health, fun, and family. Just finding time for you alone can put pressure on your life. The time has come to be assertive and find out what you really want in your life. Some of your dreams may be simpler to achieve than you think. We're glad you're interested in finding out more about improving your work/life balance. After all, isn't happiness and contentment what you deserve?

About This Book

You're probably reading this book because you're tired, fatigued, worn out, weary – in fact, exhausted. You know that the increasing demands on your job are making it difficult for you to find enough time for non-work responsibilities, such as taking care of your health and wellbeing, maintaining your home, contributing to your community – and that's before you get around to enjoying your life with the people you care about. In this book you can find tips, suggestions, real-life examples, and information with tools you can use to help change your daily work-home-sleep routine.

Don't always think of the two most important words in this book – work and life – as separate entities, one easily distinguishable from the other. Human beings aren't that easily generalised. In this book, we cover pretty well every part of your life, except for religion! The compound *work/life* is all-encompassing and covers issues that affect your work place, your boss, your partner, your brain (yes, you do have one, even though you may think that it's gone completely AWOL right now) and your body (exercise and sexercise). We look at what tools and policies already exist for you and how to ask for and get what you want, while valuing family time, contributing to your community, looking for new jobs and careers, doing further study, or moving up and out altogether. Get the idea?

A key part of this book is about actions you can take to improve life for yourself. Despite the demands of employers, shareholders, bosses, families and under-staffed schools, the decision to make positive changes to your work/life balance rests with you. This book gives you all sorts of information, as well as tips and advice. After that, the decision about which aspects of your work/life balance need changing is up to you.

As much as we'd love you to read this book from cover to cover (no tests afterwards, we promise) you can turn to particular sections to find the information you need for an issue you want to deal with right now. We know from personal experience that you can't change everything about your life overnight and you're going to need a fair bit of courage to make even the tiniest changes. So, bear in mind that sometimes the smallest steps can lead to the biggest results.

Conventions Used in This Book

To help you navigate through this book, we use the following conventions:

- ✔ *Italic* is used for emphasis and to highlight new words or terms that are defined.

✔ **Boldfaced** text is used to indicate keywords in bulleted lists or the action part of numbered steps.

✔ Monofont is used for website addresses.

What You're Not to Read

This book is a hands-on guide to achieving a work/life balance. If you're pushed for time, you don't need to read everything in the book from cover to cover. In particular, you can skip:

✔ **The text in sidebars:** the shaded boxes that appear here and there contain extra information or stories and anecdotes – fun to read but not essential to the topic in hand, so you can safely skip them if you're not interested.

✔ **The stuff on the copyright page:** unless you absolutely adore reading through legal notices and reprint information, you'll find nothing here of interest!

Foolish Assumptions

All authors must make some assumptions about their audience, and in writing this book we've made a few assumptions about you:

✔ You want to enjoy your life to the full and manage all your priorities.

✔ You're hardworking and conscientious.

✔ You often feel that your job or career sometimes takes over space that you'd like to devote to other things that are important to you.

✔ You may often feel frazzled and a bit burnt out by the intensity of your work and the challenges of making quality time for relationships, especially the one you have with yourself!

✔ Most importantly, you are ready to make changes, develop different behaviours, and try out new things in order to get the balance that you want in your life and work.

How This Book Is Organised

Work/Life Balance For Dummies is divided into six parts, with each part focusing on a different aspect of work/life balance.

Part I: Stand and Deliver: Your Job or Your Life

This part explains what work/life balance actually means. Find out why more and more people are struggling to find the right balance in their lives and why employers are recognising the need to help you contribute at work and have a more fulfilled and replenishing life outside of work. You'll get an understanding of the different types of flexible working that are available for you to consider.

Part II: Looking After Yourself First

This part uncovers the pressures that make you feel as though you have to work harder and harder in order to be considered a 'success'. This part also provides you with tips on how to say 'No', helps you avoid the destructive powers of guilt, and guides you to look after your mental and physical health.

Part III: Size Isn't Everything: Small Changes That Work

Part III explains that achieving work/life balance can involve making changes to your current role at work – so that throwing in your job and starting all over again isn't the only solution. The chapters in this part give you tips on how to more effectively use your time at work and how to avoid distractions that can eat into your day, making you less effective. In addition, simple tips ensure that you take proper breaks during your work day so you can remain refreshed and productive.

Part IV: Preparing to Work for Work/Life Balance

Time for the nitty-gritty. This part guides you into applying the flexible working arrangements and practices that are already available to you, and how you can get your hands on them. The chapters discuss how to do research to help your manager see the value in your request for more flexible working hours, and how to prevent your work/life options being eroded. This part also helps you see the importance of holidays, as well as making the most of family time, community volunteering opportunities, and caring for your children.

Part V: The Bigger Picture: Getting What You Want, Long Term

The changing nature of the workforce – with its impending opportunities as the baby-boomer generation reaches retirement – means that you no longer need to feel trapped into staying in your current job. If, despite your best efforts, your job isn't providing you with the work/life balance you need, then Part V is for you. Here we discuss how to look for and win new job opportunities, how to access study for new skills and career directions and even how to decide to be your own boss. You also get some insights into that increasing trend – downshifting and lifestyle changing for better balance.

Part VI: The Part of Tens

Work/Life Balance For Dummies wouldn't be a *For Dummies* book if it didn't have these short chapters that you can turn to for quick reference and useful tips. We provide you with a list of ten quick ways to reduce stress, ten ways to motivate your workmates, and the best work/life skills you can teach children.

Icons Used in This Book

We use icons in this book to help you find particular kinds of information that may be of use to you:

With a subject as personal and integral as work/life balance, often the best way to highlight an option or arrangement that may appeal to you is to hear a real-life story from a person who's already had that experience. This icon points to real stories from people who've made genuine efforts to produce better work/life balance in their lives.

This icon relates to fairly in-depth information. You may want to flick past these paragraphs or stay there and find out more. When the information can be applied to your work/life balance, you may find the information encouraging you to undertake further research into the subject.

Sometimes, a little pearl of wisdom is important to remember. This icon helps you to file away information that may help you achieve a better work/life balance when the opportunity arises.

Warning icons are serious and exist to ensure that you don't do anything harmful or without sufficient professional advice and assistance. Please read and consider these warning points carefully.

Tips are small steps you can take to improve your work/life balance. Tips are designed to be simple and achievable, so keep your eye out for anything that can help you make the changes you want.

Where would life be today without the Internet? The *World Wide Web* is an incredibly handy source of information and pretty well any topic you can think of has one or more websites attached. Whenever you see this icon you'll find websites that help you find information and develop ideas that are included in this book.

Where to Go from Here

Work/Life Balance For Dummies covers each topic in its own chapter. How many books provide you with details on cleaning up desktop clutter and introducing time management in one chapter, and the importance of having dinner with family in the next?

Some of you may know enough about some topics and not want to read everything we've written about the issue. Fair enough. You may be more interested in making changes at work, rather than at home, or vice versa. The point is that you can skim the Table of Contents at the front of the book and go straight to the chapters that most interest you.

If you consider yourself to be a complete work/life balance beginner, and you want a bit of general background on the topic, then we suggest you go straight to Part I and begin your reading there. You can then read through the following chapters and remaining parts at your own pace, with a growing understanding of why the subject is useful to you.

Part I
Stand and Deliver: Your Job or Your Life

In this part . . .

Most people agree that despite having access to the latest electronic equipment, household appliances, and domestic services, our lives feel busier and more stretched than ever. The reality is quite the opposite to what most people are looking for – more 'life' in their work/life balance.

Work/life balance is not restricted to people with children or partners. Life outside work can range from child care to housework, to sport, leisure, and self-development activities such as study or exercise programmes – virtually anything.

This part explains what work/life balance means, how long working hours can affect health, family, and relationships. And the good news – what measures some employers are taking to recognise that employees have lives outside of work.

Chapter 1

Defining Work/Life Balance

. . . .

In This Chapter

▶ Understanding work/life balance

▶ Realising why families are important

▶ Finding out how to be flexible

▶ Balancing so that everyone's a winner

. . . .

The failure to achieve real work/life balance means that your personal life can suffer, affecting your physical, emotional, and mental health. The huge increases in illnesses such as chronic backache, clinical depression, heart disease, blood pressure, type 2 diabetes, and obesity indicate that the current work/life balance is way out of whack.

This chapter shows you just why work/life balance – or the lack of it – is so vital for the future wellbeing of you and your loved ones. The statistics don't paint a pretty picture when it comes to managing the work/life balance. Yet the signs are increasing that both employees and employers are realising how a better work/life balance can benefit everyone. Working smarter, not harder (read longer), is the way to go for individual and organisational benefit, and that starts with knowing the balance points.

So Just How Hard Are Brits Working?

If you stop someone in the streets of this green, pleasant, and rather rainy land in which we live and ask them if work/life balance is an issue for them, it's a safe bet they'll say a resounding yes. We'd also bet that if you had to guess who in the world is putting in the longest hours at work, you'd say that the UK is way up there. And to a degree, you'd be right. We are a pretty hardworking nation, and that's only likely to increase in our 24/7 society where customers are ever more demanding and shareholders seemingly even more so.

Still, you may be surprised to discover that working hours in the UK have actually fallen in the last century. One hundred years ago the average working week was more than 50 hours. During the '70s this fell to around 35 hours as higher productivity and more part-time options came into play. But the downward trend started to reverse in the 1980s as people got caught up in the 'make it rich' frenzy of that decade. In addition, those in managerial and professional roles stepped up a gear with longer hours becoming a strong part of the unofficial culture of many organisations.

According to the Office of National Statistics (ONS) Annual Survey of Hours and Earnings 2006, full-time workers in the UK average 39.5 hours a week and part-time workers come in at 18.4 hours. Which sounds OK, doesn't it? However, just over a fifth of people in employment work more than 45 hours a week, a high figure compared to other countries in Europe. Additionally, UK workers have less paid leave than their EU counterparts. On the positive side, this is a lot better than countries like Japan, the United States, and Australia.

So it's not a totally bleak picture. Legislation in the UK (mostly following EU directives) has made a big positive difference in opening up more flexible options, especially for working parents, and increasing numbers are taking advantage of that. And work is part of life, right? Many of us enjoy the financial rewards, the challenge, and the sense of achievement we get from 'going the extra mile'.

All of this would be fine, if it weren't for the hidden costs. The Work Foundation's 2006 survey *About time for change* found that, although average working hours may not be as long as they used to be, the sheer intensity of today's demanding work place means that everyone's trying to cram much more into their working day. And a recent report by the London School of Economics found that over a quarter of men and 29 per cent of women said that their jobs left them feeling exhausted most of the time.

Finding a Balance between Work and Your Personal Life

Work/life balance is the phrase of the moment. You've no doubt come across the phrase everywhere – in magazines, on TV health shows, in advertisements, and on the lips of anyone who cares about achieving the right work/life balance for themselves, in their personal relationships, and with work colleagues. If you're like me, you may even picture a set of old-fashioned brass scales with 'work' on one dish and 'life' on the other. The official definition we use in this book for *work/life balance* is the need of all individuals to achieve and maintain a balance between their paid work and their life outside of work. The word *balance* doesn't necessarily imply an even divide between work and life; instead, balance means successfully managing all the responsibilities you have in both areas of your life.

How well do you balance your life?

For the last couple of decades, there's been a strong focus on work/life balance issues. The Government, academic researchers, professional bodies, and family organisations all have something to say about it. Here are some findings from recent reports:

✔ **The Centre for Business Performance:** A 2004 report on flexible working and work–life integration in the accountancy profession recognised the strong business case for flexible working to ease work stress and to attract young chartered accountants into the profession. Yet it highlighted serious conflicts between the willingness to adopt formal policies and the strong belief in the necessity of long hours in order to advance careers.

✔ **The Department of Trade and Industry:** The DTI's Second Work Life Balance Survey of employers shows strong support for work/life balance and notes that more organisations are adopting policies of flexible working, with positive benefits on labour turnover, motivation, and employee commitment. It also points out that there's still a way to go to increase awareness and adoption of best practice, and highlights that the best solutions are those that match business needs.

✔ **The Work Life Balance Centre:** A 2008 survey of a representative cross section of people working in a range of businesses in the UK highlighted that the reasons people choose to work above their contracted hours were the sheer volume of work, and the increasing pressure of deadlines. Even so, more than four in ten people said that they actively chose to work longer hours.

✔ **The Work Foundation:** *About time for change (2006)* shows that many people find it very difficult to balance their whole life responsibilities and that this isn't confined just to parents.

Work/life balance is not restricted to people with children or partners. Life outside work can range from child care and looking after older family members, to housework, doing sport, leisure and self-development activities, such as study or exercise programmes – and to virtually anything else.

The aims of work/life balance

Achieving work/life balance is about being given the opportunity to have some control over when, where, and how you work so that you can perform at your best and also have time to recuperate and enjoy pursuing your own interests outside of work.

Although the debate continues over whether 'balance' is the right term, the general consensus is that you achieve work/life balance when you achieve your right to a fulfilled life inside and outside of work, and this achievement is respected by your employer.

Many people believe that work/life balance means a quieter life, working fewer hours, and achieving a much clearer separation between work and your personal life. Academics now suggest that this view of work/life balance isn't, in fact, what most people want. Instead, most employees and self-employed workers, although willing to work hard and long hours in a job they love, want to have some control over where and when they work. It's about figuring out the right balance for you and creating the best working arrangement possible so that everyone benefits. Chapter 2 gets you started by setting the context for work/life balance and helps you to begin identifying which flexible options are right for you.

So work/life balance means more than just being given the flexibility to leave work early to pick up the kids or having a medical appointment and being able to replace the lost hours by working later or on other occasions. What's just as important is the control you have over your working life. Currently only a tenth of the UK workforce decide their own working time according to their individual priorities. And getting more control shouldn't have to mean that you sacrifice interesting work or your career aspirations. We're hoping you're nodding in agreement.

Time is the enemy

The Work Foundation's 2006 survey identified that many people in the UK feel desperately 'time poor'.

- Two-thirds of respondents want to spend more time with family and friends, regardless of whether or not they have children. Those feeling the squeeze most were, not surprisingly, people in full-time work, even where they were not working excessively long hours.

- Over a third of all respondents agreed that in the evenings they were so tired they just fell asleep on the sofa and lacked time for social and leisure activities. At an even more basic level, a high proportion of folk reported that they didn't feel they had time to eat properly, relying instead on takeaway and convenience foods.

- Although two-thirds of UK couples with dependent children are now both out working and earning, that doesn't seem to have made a big difference to who takes on the main burden of housework. The survey indicated that domestic tasks haven't been redistributed equally and most women in this situation effectively do a 'double shift' – or if they can afford it, they hire domestic support. Because women now make up 45 per cent of the labour force that's a lot of extra hidden effort, which doesn't help the balance picture.

The reality of work/life balance

At work, you may think that if you 'prove' – to yourself, your boss, and your colleagues – how hard you work and how productive you are, then rewards and recognition are going to fall automatically into your lap. When the rewards don't arrive, you work harder and longer in an effort to be noticed. You keep telling yourself that as soon as everyone realises how great a worker you are, then you'll have your chance to ask for a salary increase and ask to leave earlier one day a week to take your child to swimming classes, or focus on your out-of-work passions. You probably feel a tad nervous about asking for the time off but you reckon by this stage your boss appreciates you so much that asking for an early mark won't be a problem.

Can you spot the fundamental flaw in this? Working harder/longer won't necessarily make you more productive and often just sets up expectations that you have to work even harder to get results. Chapter 6 looks at the key basics that you can control to help you work smarter (not harder) – like tackling time effectiveness and beating procrastination – and Chapter 7 offers tips for making the most of work breaks like your lunch hour to enable you to find more daily balance.

The home/life balance

The 'life' in work/life balance doesn't automatically mean time spent at home. For some people, home can, in fact, mean more work. Many people perceive home as the site of their unofficial second job: caring for children, supervising homework, cooking dinner, walking the dog, hanging out washing, loading the dishwasher, organising bath and story times, and sitting at the laptop to catch up on work emails long after the children have gone to sleep.

The pressure of stress

Understanding what happens when you're forced to cope with additional workloads and changes in your work place – such as downsizing or being offered contract or casual work over permanent employment – is important. Stress can build whenever you have no say or control in where, when, and how you do your job. In these situations, you can expect a downturn in your standard of health. Stress makes your heart pump faster and speeds up your breathing. Your body pumps out adrenaline and cortisol to keep you on high alert. If stress continues, your hormone levels stay elevated and can start to cause illness. Chronic stress is linked to heart disease, lowered immunity, higher blood pressure, and even cancer – and chronic stress is now showing up in workers' compensation claims.

Long hours – are they productive or not?

The 247 Work Life Balance Survey 2008 (by the Work Life Balance Centre) showed that the pressures of work intensity and of long hours created stress that led to errors on the job. Of those people surveyed who said that they'd made a serious error, 61.9 per cent said that they were stressed all, or almost all, of the time due to intensity or pressure of work.

Examples of these 'serious errors' ranged from direct costs to the business – one respondent admitted a £60k cost due to a funding error when stressed and overworked – to tales of driving into the back of another car at traffic lights after having put in a 12-hour day at a weekend following a full working week.

According to the survey, when you feel extremely stressed at work, it doubles the risk of you making a serious error that impacts on business or your own wellbeing.

The cost of work-related stress is on the increase in the UK. In the decade up to 2003 it increased by 45 per cent and now sits at around £12 billion per annum. The time spent off work is much longer for stress claims than for physical injury claims (with some sufferers never returning to paid employment). Stress claimants also have significantly higher expenses for medical, psychiatric, and legal services. All estimates consider that these claims are likely to continue increasing in cost and in time lost at work. In addition, these workers' compensation claims create additional staff-training and replacement expenses for employers. (Take a look at Chapter 3 for the lowdown on stress and how you can avoid it leading to anxiety and depression. You could also flick through Chapter 4 for lots of tips on looking after your health in your balanced life.)

Whittling work/life balance away

Many people today believe that they need more money and more possessions in order to feel happier. Even in the richest 20 per cent of households, almost half of the people agreed that 'You cannot afford to buy everything you really need'. This statement is rather startling when you consider that people in the UK today have incomes that are three times higher in purchasing-power terms than incomes in the 1950s.

The awful affliction of affluenza

The excessive consumer culture that afflicts the Western world has been tagged 'affluenza'. The US website (www.affluenza.org) defines *affluenza* as 'The bloated, sluggish and unfulfilled feeling that results from efforts to keep up with the Joneses . . . An epidemic of stress, overwork, waste and indebtedness caused by a dogged pursuit of the American dream and an unsustainable addiction to economic growth.' You don't have to buy into the concept of the American dream to recognise that the same thing has very definitely reached our shores in it's own British way too!

A nation of holidaymakers? Not likely

The two-week summer holiday may be traditional, but alarmingly large numbers of people in the UK don't take all their annual entitlement. The 247 survey found that 26 per cent rarely managed to squeeze it all in and almost 1 in 5 had cancelled holidays or cut them short due to the demands of work.

And when we do get away, it takes quite a while for us to wind down, so much does work prey on our minds even when we're not there. The survey found that 87.5 per cent of respondents didn't look forward to getting back to work because of the thought of the extra workload waiting for them!

Affluenza may contribute to medically recognised depression. Consider the fact that the World Health Organization predicts major clinical depression to become the second largest disease burden in the Western world by 2020. This scary prediction makes the adage 'Money doesn't buy happiness' sound very true.

Chapter 5 discusses the money and consumption-driven lifestyle further and shows you how to look beyond what you may think you need for what you really value.

Recognising the Importance of Family Life

Family means more than just children. Family includes your spouse or partner, parents, brothers and sisters, and other relatives who don't have immediate family to care for them. Your family responsibilities can involve caring for children, partners, and other family members, including the elderly or relatives with disabilities or illnesses, or those who need special care and attention, whether they live with you or not.

Balancing work and family is important not only for people with young children. Family responsibilities continue to affect your work/life balance throughout your entire working life. Even if you don't have family responsibilities, you still need family-friendly work practices on occasion, such as flexibility to study, travel, participate in sport, or to undertake volunteering or community activities. Everyone must have opportunities to rest and rejuvenate themselves.

The number of women in paid employment is almost certain to increase in the future because of property prices that necessitate two incomes to meet the mortgage payments. And the trend to favour private schooling over the state system means more costs for many families. Labour shortages and opportunities for women to access study and new skills are other factors encouraging women into paid employment.

Men, too, feel increased pressure to be better parents and to take part in their children's lives, as well as being the major breadwinner when their partners are on maternity leave.

The work/life pressures don't end there. Our ageing population means that many workers face responsibility for caring for their elderly relatives, as well as raising children. (Chapter 10 helps you plan family activities and time together so you really can feel that you have a life outside of work.)

Why part-time work is not always a solution

The most common way to try to claw back some 'life' time is to reduce work hours to part-time. But reducing work hours doesn't guarantee that work/life balance can be achieved. In fact, working part-time can have the opposite effect. Women who work part-time are more likely to have worse work/life balance than men who work full-time or part-time – or even women who work full-time. In fact, part-time working women appear to be the 'personal shock absorbers of work/life interference'. These women have to put up with less free time as a result of their part-time work and their domestic loads.

Fathers doing the 'walk of shame'

Overwhelmingly in the UK it's men who report working the longest hours. In fact, fathers in Britain work the longest hours in Europe, with two-thirds working into the evening and six out of ten at the weekend.

Some fathers clearly need assurance from their employers that taking up more flexible working arrangements isn't a backward step career-wise. Fathers need to be able to use leave, or to reduce their work hours, when their children are sick and need their care or when they have to go to school events.

Tim, a father of two and a former IT professional, said, 'When I left work at 5 p.m., I felt as though I was doing the "walk of shame" because I was the only one who showed any signs of leaving at finishing time.'

Younger generations of fathers also believe that when men and women both work, they need to share domestic and child-care responsibilities.

In addition, women working part-time receive less help from their partners and report having to deal with increased expectations from schools and community groups who see them as available volunteers because they don't work full-time.

Other studies show evidence that many women who choose part-time work to fit in with the family often have to work in industries that specialise in unskilled part-time jobs such as hospitality, retail, and in factories, which offer traditionally low pay. Taking these part-time jobs sometimes means that mothers move away from the careers they pursued before having children. The results are:

- ✔ Loss of previous qualifications due to lack of continual training in their former career.
- ✔ Reduction of future opportunities to return to their earlier career.

How working affects the family

The difficulties in achieving the goal of work/life balance for working parents negatively affect their relationships with their children. Balancing work and the hours and attention you pay your children is possibly the hardest part of achieving a successful work/life balance.

Whereas work responsibilities can be fairly consistent – regular hours, schedules, meetings, and so on – the needs of children can vary erratically depending on their health (a cold can keep you away from work), school functions (schools give fairly short notice of day-time outings, concerts, and so on) and behaviour (all children at some stage require spontaneous parent/teacher discussions during school hours).

Focusing on Work-place Flexibility

Achieving work/life balance must involve reducing stress levels, increasing job satisfaction and personal fulfilment for the employee, and improving business outcomes for the employer. What's now becoming widely accepted is that both employers and employees can achieve significant gains from recognising and accommodating family responsibilities with flexible working arrangements. These family-friendly initiatives involve flexible work policies and practices that can cover types of employment, hours of work, paid and unpaid leave, work-place facilities, and supportive management practices. All these options give employees a bigger say in how they work in order to balance the demands of their employment and family responsibilities.

Studies show that workers want the following conditions from their employers:

- Flexible working arrangements that see workers get the same opportunities for new and challenging work, training, and promotion as full-time workers. Flexible working doesn't always mean less hours – at the extreme ends of the age spectrum people tend to want more, or at least full-time, hours, whereas those in mid career, if they have particular responsibilities or goals, may at various times want reduced or flexible patterns. The point is, employees want different arrangements to be treated no less fairly than traditional ones.

- Some control over how their working hours are determined, whether that be straightforward starting and finishing times, or a more complex arrangement designed around their life circumstances.

- Specific leave available to all workers to care for a sick child, partner, or parent without time deducted from their own sick leave or recreation/holiday leave, or without being forced to take leave without pay.

- The ability to take career breaks from time to time that can be treated as 'career lay-bys' rather than 'career cul-de-sacs'. If you've built up expertise and skill in a job, you want that to be recognised so that following any kind of break, you can come back at the same level as before your break.

At many stages of the work/life cycle – such as study, birth of a baby, child-rearing, leave without pay, and caring for elderly relatives – enlightened work-place conditions are the best ways for employers to keep skilled workers and at the same time increase morale and productivity in their workforce. Smart employers realise that beneficial conditions can provide relatively cheap ways to attract the best workers, reduce absenteeism, and retain productive staff for longer periods.

That's all very nice, you may be thinking, but what type of flexibility can employers with sales targets and shareholders to satisfy actually offer their employees? A broad range of family-friendly work practices for employees is available to employers to offer. These work practices include the provision of:

- Flexible employment arrangements (part-time, full-time, job sharing, working from home).

- Flexible hours arrangements (starting earlier or later to incorporate school runs or after-school commitments, holding family-friendly meeting times during core hours, compressed hours).

- Flexible leave arrangements (purchased additional leave, carer's leave, or time off in lieu)

- Other work and family initiatives (sabbaticals, training opportunities, or volunteering days)

In Chapter 2, we explain more about what types of flexible working arrangements are available and in Chapter 8 you can discover how to prepare your *business case* – the argument you use to convince your manager to adopt improved work/life balance policies.

Having these types of policies in place is useless when senior managers and supervisors don't actively support their use. The solution seems simple but employers don't always see the advantages. Put simply, a business's productivity and profitability depend on the quality and commitment of staff. When workers have difficulties with the demands of their jobs and life outside work, their productivity and motivation can suffer.

Experts say working long hours is not sustainable. The result is that people resign from their jobs when they aren't able to balance work and family responsibilities. In addition, flexible working arrangements don't work when employers cut staff numbers and expect the remaining employees to produce the same work and productivity as the larger staff produced.

If employers don't notice the long hours their staff members work, they may soon sit up and take notice when they see the effect on their profit margins if staff leave. This is because high staff turnover leads to the loss of skilled employees. And a loss of staff members dramatically increases advertising, recruitment, replacement, and training costs.

Making Work/Life Balance a Win–Win for Everyone

Work and family initiatives do have positive results. Increasing agreement across the board says that family-friendly policies can improve organisational performance when employers:

- ✔ Are recognised as an 'employer of choice'
- ✔ Improve employee morale and commitment
- ✔ Reduce staff turnover
- ✔ Reduce absenteeism
- ✔ Increase the ability to attract and recruit staff
- ✔ Recognise and improve occupational health and safety outcomes
- ✔ Reduce stress and improve productivity

Organisations and employers that have introduced work and family arrangements have found that the benefits far outweigh the cost and effort of making changes, particularly in attracting and retaining skilled and productive employees.

Employees can find benefits that include:

- ✔ Flexible working arrangements resulting in reduced stress.

- ✔ Increased focus, motivation, and job satisfaction knowing that their personal and work commitments are being met.

- ✔ Increased job security and commitment after employers show they value and support workers with family and other non-work responsibilities.

Chapter 9 gives you ideas to help you maintain flexible arrangements through assertive communication and spreading the word within your organisation. If your current employer isn't supporting you in this important area, though, you might feel the need to make a career move, either within the same professional field or to something completely different. Chapters 11 and 13 give you some important steers in these directions.

And don't forget the importance of building your skill in order to put yourself in the best possible position for securing the most benificial arrangements for you. Chapter 12 shows how committing to lifelong learning can really help you to achieve balance and personal satisfaction.

When all is said and done, your balance strategy will be unique to you. Hopefully, this book will inspire you to look at the big picture of what you really want in your life, whether that is radical simplifying, downsizing, or moving out of the city to a calmer way of life, and to find the best win/win for you. Chapters 14 and 15 can help you plan for that exciting adventure.

Flexible working hours are catching on

The DTI's Second Work Life Balance Survey shows real progress amongst employers. Nine out of ten employers believed that people work best when they can strike a balance between work and the rest of their lives, and that represents a significant increase in perception from the first survey taken in the early years of this century.

Two-thirds of employers felt they were responsible for helping people to achieve this balance by offering appropriate policies and options, although almost all respondents admitted it was not always easy to do this.

A resounding 74 per cent believed that flexible working should not affect promotion prospects adversely.

The best news is that these perceptions were borne out by practice – those employers who were most positive about work/life balance were the ones who tended to provide the widest range of practices.

Chapter 2

Work, Life, and You

Despite the increased talk and use of flexible working practices, such as reduced hours, part-time work, telecommuting, or voluntary leave, 'dinosaur' managers still lurk in the work place. These old-fashioned managers are the breed that still insists that their employees stay at their desks in the office from 9 a.m. to 5 p.m., or even longer!

The irony is that dinosaur work places are suffering as much as their employees are suffering because these workplaces are the ones with 'revolving doors' syndrome as people start to work there, receive expensive training, and then become burnt out and leave.

In this chapter we set the context for the importance of work/life balance, introducing you to the hard facts about the changes in the labour force, and to the increasing costs and challenges of caring for children and elderly relatives. We look at issues like *presenteeism* – the old-fashioned work-place culture that makes so many people put in longer hours than they need. We also give you an easy-to-follow overview of legislation that has a bearing on creating a work/life balance, and consider some of the flexible working options available.

The Waning Workforce

The UK's population is ageing. By 2010, the 50–64 age group will be larger than at any time since the 1970s and many workers are expected to retire or reduce their working time in the next few years. The work place today has fewer younger workers with experience, training, and skills to replace those who are planning to retire or who are ready to retire. In addition, with parents having their first children in their thirties, more and more workers need to combine caring for their elderly parents with raising their own children.

Companies are recognising that they have to provide more up-to-date working arrangements to attract and keep good staff. Work-place studies show that work/life balance initiatives improve employee morale, productivity, retention, and recruitment. So you should be drowning in an ocean of choices, shouldn't you? No?

Challenging the child-care misconception

The belief still exists that people are ill advised to have children unless a partner can stay at home full-time to care for the children. In this era of increasingly unaffordable housing prices, high mortgages, and interest rate increases, the 1950s ideal of the happy mother at home, doing unpaid housework and preparing three meals a day, has almost disappeared. Instead, many families and couples now rely on two salaries to meet the mortgage payments.

Although the situation is starting to change, many senior board executives tend to be male and still have traditional family structures. Their understanding of the pressure felt by workers with children to look after is distanced by the fact that senior executives are extremely well paid and can afford to have a wife remain at home as the 'support', to deal with all aspects of child care, social life, home life, and so on.

These managers are also the types of bosses that stressed and anxious parents lie to when their child is too sick for child care. Instead the parents say that they are the ones who are sick and need to take the day off. These managers more than likely have partners at home to take care of their sick children, check on their elderly parents, and take care of the household duties.

These managers simply are not aware that their prized employees are trying to work full-time and find a suitable care home for a frail parent as well as time to support their kids' after-school activities. These dinosaurs help create work places where employees believe that they can't take any kind of flexible leave without kissing their longer-term career prospects goodbye.

Media stories about top-performing women who choose to drop out of the workforce in order to raise a family or to simplify their stressful lives don't always help either. Although this choice may be achievable for a CEO or lawyer who earns a high salary and has a big rainy day fund, this choice isn't so affordable or stress free for the average UK working woman (or man).

Reading and hearing about these kinds of 'success stories' can be frustrating when you want to contribute more at work and at home but can't because you need help with child care or elderly care. Increasingly, the call is for more flexibility and control over start and finish times at work, and opportunities to work outside of the office to balance the needs of the family and the need to earn a living.

The increasing cost of child care

The decision about returning to work after having a child is almost as big a decision as whether to have a child, because some parents need two incomes to support their debt commitments or simply to bear the normal cost of living. Alternatively, a woman wishes to resume a career that she put on hold for the birth of her baby. And don't forget the many single parents out there who may not have a choice about returning to work, simply because they are the sole breadwinner.

The question is, how do you factor in the additional cost of child care and balance that with the extra income brought in? The Daycare Trust gives the following statistics (based on prices during 2007/8):

✔ The typical cost of a full-time nursery place for a child under 2 is £159 a week in England – that's over £8,000 a year. Costs are slightly higher in London, and slightly lower in Scotland and Wales.

✔ The typical cost of a full-time place with a childminder for a child under 2 ranges throughout the UK from £139–£153 a week.

✔ The highest cost of a summer play scheme identified in 2007 was £390 a week or £2,340 for the six-week summer holiday period. That number did not include costs for meals, trips out, and visits.

✔ Help with child care is available through the tax system, with the current average award through the child-care element of the Working Tax Credit of £48.45 a week. This applies for up to three children.

When considering the big picture of 'return to work or not?' it's clear that many families need to consider carefully how much additional pressure child-care costs put on the family income, and for what benefit.

For more information on holding on to your work/life balance arrangements in the work place, see Chapter 9.

Providing care for the elderly

When you think of the caring responsibilities of workers, child care is what immediately springs to mind (see preceding section). However, as the working population ages, care for the elderly has begun to emerge as another caring issue affecting employees and their work.

Distinct differences exist between caring for children and caring for elderly parents or relatives. Not all workers have children, but many employees have living parents, and therefore have the responsibility to provide or coordinate the provision for their care at some stage. Unlike child care, care for older people is an unpredictable, variable event that can occur suddenly or occur gradually as a parent or relative's health and functioning declines. Care for older relatives requires continual monitoring and flexibility to respond to a relative's care requirements and a great deal of flexibility by the employer and the employee.

Child care mainly concerns children who live with you, but care for the elderly involves a range of degrees of involvement with your relatives' affairs to deal with sometimes complex financial and legal arrangements, changes to living arrangements, and various health issues and services. These services may be difficult for you to access if you live in a different location to your parents or other relations. You may often need to negotiate and arrange services by telephone during work hours.

The additional factor that can make a situation particularly stressful for employees – especially if they also have children to care for – is that their relationship with their parents changes over the years. In some cases, the parent–child relationship can become reversed as the elderly parent or relative becomes more and more dependent. Unlike child care, caring for older people doesn't necessarily have a positive outcome, so you may begin to feel emotionally drained and need support both at work and at home. The process can involve a number of an elderly person's children and other relatives and friends providing assistance to them at different times – for example, shopping at the weekends, visiting doctors, organising nursing care, and so on – or the burden of care may all fall on one person if no other relatives live nearby to help.

Finding a solution to this challenge relies on exactly the same principle as working out how to manage your child care responsibilities if you have children – you need to make a case for a flexible arrangement that helps you to cope. Check out the different options later in this chapter and then skip to Chapter 8 for lots more detail on how to make your business case.

Employers and mature workers together need to face the issues regarding care for the elderly

Retaining mature-aged workers and providing flexible arrangements for their non-work needs – caring for elderly relatives as well as children – is becoming a key issue for UK organisations.

Career UK gives the following statistics about the role of carers:

✔ The UK has 3 million working carers, of which 56 per cent are women.

✔ Research suggests that 3 out of 5 people will care for a parent or elder relative at some stage in their lives.

✔ Many carers find themselves forced to give up work due to a lack of care services or flexible employment – in a recent survey by Carers UK it was found that 7 out of 10 carers under 50, and 8 out of 10 carers aged 50–60 had given up work to care for elderly or long-term sick relatives.

Changing work-place culture

Some employers believe that implementing non-traditional working arrangements, such as working from home (telecommuting), is expensive. Other examples of non-traditional working arrangements include flexible starting and finishing times, and job sharing. These arrangements require the employer to put together new policies that support people with busy lives outside the work place (that is, *every* worker).

Even when supportive work-place policies and arrangements are in place, a new factor – *work-place culture* – emerges. This is the 'feeling' in a work place that can affect the hours you work, the expectations you feel, and so on – the 'atmosphere' in an office that can make it hard for you to attain work/life balance.

Smart managers recognise that working long hours actually decreases productivity. Working eight hours in an organised and efficient manner can produce better work outcomes than lingering for twelve hours and spending a fair portion of it on private emailing, or moaning to workmates in the tea room.

Managers can assess work effectiveness by quality and output per hours worked. That way, part-time workers get assessed fairly too, and can be given work as complex as full-time workers. In addition, employers are likely to retain their best workers by adapting work practices to suit employees needing time off for parental leave and part-time work on their return. This flexibility enables skills and experience to be retained, and money to be saved from advertising, recruiting, and training replacement staff.

REAL-LIFE STORY

Refusing to work long hours

Here's an example of the damage work-place culture can bring. Radiation scientist Patrick ran into the brick wall of work-place culture when he started a new position in the health industry.

'Officially, the job had flexible starting and finishing times, manageable work shifts, and days off for time in lieu. Once I started and asked about a flex day, I was told by a colleague that flex days didn't happen. I also started work at 8 a.m. and rarely got away before 7 p.m.'

After months of long work days, unwieldy workloads, and very little time spent seeing his children awake on week nights, Patrick decided a change was due. 'I just asked for what was my right. I started keeping a timesheet and asked for a day off in lieu of overtime worked.'

Patrick's stand encouraged his colleagues to do the same. 'At least the hours are now being recorded. Having a day off – even though I feel I do three extra days' work for that one day – is a step in the right direction.'

Eradicating outmoded thinking

Employers and managers who implement accessible work/life balance policies sometimes discover that workers are reluctant to slow down or take personal leave, feeling that the changes may mean the worker can't handle the workload.

In this case, corporate and management executives need to step in and openly embrace the flexible way of thinking and working. The volume of studies and results from best-practice employers in the UK, the United States, and worldwide show that when a high percentage of their professional workforce is using work-place options, the flexible option becomes a 'normal' part of the work-place culture.

Seeing a manager or supervisor who 'walks the talk' by working at home every Friday, or electing to 'buy' an extra four weeks leave is one of the most effective ways for executives to encourage workers to actively adopt flexible working options. (See Chapters 9 and 10 for more on this topic.)

Battling 'presenteeism'

You've heard of absenteeism – having lots of days off from work due to issues other than illness. Presenteeism is considered even more of a concern these days. Presenteeism occurs when workers are present in the work place but not performing at their best. Not performing includes time-wasting due to illness or lack of motivation, not working on priority jobs, decreased work quality and quantity, and poor communication with colleagues.

Presenteeism is linked to obesity, stress, back and neck pain, migraine, allergies, and lack of physical activity. Presenteeism is also linked to the perception that workers must be in the office for long hours to prove their worth. This inevitably leads to illness, burn out, or resignation, and high staff turnover means high costs for employers.

Legislating for change

Legislation in the UK has gone a long way to reducing working hours. The main regulations governing hours are the Working Time Regulations 1998, which set out the minimum conditions relating to weekly working time, rest entitlements, and annual leave, and make special provisions for night workers. These have been significantly amended and supplemented in the last decade.

Your basic rights under this legislation are:

- A limit of an average of 48 hours worked a week over a 17-week period.

- A limit of an average of 8 hours work in 24 hours when night workers are available to work.

- A right to 11 hours' rest a day and a day off each week.

- A right to a work rest break if the working day is longer than 6 hours.

Currently UK employers can apply an 'opt-out' clause so that if they want, and you agree to, different (read longer) working hours, then they are able to do so. The opt-out is widely used – and it's not always a case of employers being heavy handed here – as the research shows, many people are more than willing to put in long hours, either because they've always done so, because they need the extra cash, or because they feel responsible for delivering results in ever increasingly demanding markets. And don't forget the many people who actively enjoy and thrive on their work, and choose to make it a big priority in their life.

As ever with work/life balance, legislation is a guide to good practice. Good habits start with you, the individual, and knowing how you want to run your balanced life.

In addition to the Working Time Regulations, legislation has improved the rights of parents and carers as follows:

- Maternity leave in the UK can be up to 52 weeks in total. Fathers are entitled to 2 weeks of paid paternity leave which can be taken within the 56 days following the birth of the child.

- Working parents can claim up to 13 weeks unpaid parental leave at any time up to the child's fifth birthday.

- Parents with children under 6 (or age 18 if disabled) and those with caring responsibilities have the right to request flexible working.

Any application for flexible working hours can, of course, be refused by an employer on business grounds. For example, a tax accountant asking for the whole of April off – when each financial year comes to an end – as part of a flexible working arrangement is likely to go down like a lead balloon! This is another reason why thinking of the big picture at all times helps you put your own business case successfully!

Taking Advantage of Flexible Working Options

A huge variety of different patterns is evolving in the UK when it comes to flexible options. Although not all of these are widespread, the options listed in Table 2-1 can help you get a feel for some of the models that may work for you and your organisation.

To secure flexible working, you need to be flexible yourself – you've a far better chance of getting the very best deal if you're willing and able to see and accommodate the business and customer perspective.

Table 2-1	Flexible Work Arrangements
Option	*What It Is*
Part-time working	Working less than the standard basic full-time hours, usually less than 30 hours a week.
Flexitime	Choosing when to work outside core hours. This can be a formal or informal arrangement.
Job sharing	Full-time post is split across (usually) two workers who agree to share hours between them.
Term-time working	Permanent contract where workers can take time off (paid/unpaid) in school holidays.
Annualised hours	Hours are calculated annually, with shifts allocated. Workers can be called in at short notice to work the remaining hours.
Family contracts	Members of immediate family can also cover shifts. This unusual approach is applied by McDonalds in the UK but won't apply to all types of roles or companies.
Working-time accounts	Hours worked are banked and may be saved or withdrawn, just like with a bank account.
Homeworking/telecommuting	All or part of the week spent working from home or off premises.
Shift swapping	Workers arrange shifts between themselves provided all hours are covered.

Option	What It Is
Self rostering	Staff nominate their preferred shifts and are allocated to them as far as possible.
Time off in lieu (TOIL)	Time off to compensate for extra hours worked.
V-time working	Hours can be reduced for a short period of time (usually several months) on the basis that full-time hours will be resumed at the end of the period.
Sabbatical/career break	Extended period of time off (paid/unpaid).
Compressed hours	Cover total working hours in fewer days.

So there's no shortage of options available that have already been tried and tested by someone out there!

Getting a flexible working option in place doesn't guarantee an immediate improvement in your work/life balance. Of course, your own attitude as to how you do your work is equally, if not more, important.

Making the Most of Your Time at Work

The following tips can help you remain career-minded at work but also have a better personal life balance as well:

- ✔ **Decrease your distractions.** A recent US survey found that the average full-time worker loses about two hours a day to office distractions, such as informal queries and meetings with colleagues, telephone calls, and being bogged down reading non-essential emails. To reduce interruptions, place a sign on your door or desk that says you're busy and why you're busy. Saying why gives people a reason and they can then respect it. Other ways to reduce interruptions include booking a specific time in your day to meet up with colleagues to discuss queries and projects.

  Select certain times during the day to check all your messages at once. Instead of letting your email, palm device, or mobile phone SMS interrupt you all day, book a specific time in the morning and once in the afternoon to check, read, and respond to all important messages. Also, turn off any beeping sounds or envelope pop-ups that can tempt you to stop the work you're doing to read what's been sent to you. And tell colleagues what you're doing so that they allow you that clear uninterrupted space to get on with your other tasks.

✔ **Stay home when you're ill.** You're not doing yourself – or your colleagues – any favours by dragging your sick carcass into the office when you should be seeing a doctor or staying at home in bed. Instead, avoid the temptation to stay in the office after hours and the risk of spreading your illness to everyone else in your department. Taking time off to recover means that you regain your productivity and interest more quickly than by remaining in the office and producing no, or low-quality, work for longer time periods.

If you feel ill late in the day – and leaving early is an impossibility – try to handle tasks that don't take too much mental or physical energy, such as updating your diary, responding to brief emails, or tidying your desk space. You should also update your work list so that your boss or colleagues can see where you're up to and what needs to be done if you end up on sick leave the following day.

✔ **Eliminate inessential work.** List your projects and ongoing responsibilities by importance in your diary and work schedule, and estimate how long you expect each to take. You can also identify the low-value and unnecessary tasks and remove them from your list of responsibilities.

Combining several reports into one can cut time too. Ask your colleagues whether particular emails or memos are still required or whether there are more effective ways of communicating. Put it this way: you won't know what you're 'allowed' to get rid of unless you ask.

✔ **Know your peak periods.** Many professionals are more productive at certain times of the day than others. Recognising just when you work at your best is easy. I'm (Katherine) a morning person so I schedule my more challenging writing tasks (including writing this book) before lunch. I do the less cerebral tasks, such as returning calls and emails and filing, after 2 p.m. when my energy begins to wane. My colleague, Sigrid, on the other hand, tends to fire up in the afternoons and gets her best research work done in the early evenings.

✔ **Record your hours.** If you're an early bird who tends to start and leave earlier than your workmates, you may want to – every now and then – send an email to your manager or a colleague shortly after arriving at your desk. Sending this email can be a subtle way of showing that you're working your full eight hours, especially if you're worried that the boss 'walks the floor' at 5.30 p.m.

If your work place doesn't have a flexible-hours policy, consider holding a meeting with your boss to discuss implementing one. Such a policy lays to rest any concerns that early starters or late finishers have about being 'seen' to be doing their fair share of the workload. These policies can also be used to determine staff availability for meetings, future projects, and implementing a time-in-lieu scheme for motivation and recuperation. (Chapters 8 and 9 provide details on what flexible working arrangements are commonly used and how to implement them in your work place.)

✔ **Set deadlines.** Use your online or paper diary to block out chunks of time. These time periods can range from 15 minutes to two hours and you use them to complete key work projects and duties. This plan ensures that your work day is not eaten up with informal meetings or interruptions. People who use this approach to plan their working times have found it a successful way of completing work within a strict time frame.

One way to do this is to tell the boss or client that you can deliver project X by a certain time, which forces you to stick to the deadline and ensures that you book time in to complete the job. (See Chapter 6 for more details on how to use your time more effectively.)

✔ **Transform your travel time.** Technology's wide reach isn't all bad news. Mobile phones, wireless laptops, and palm devices mean you can check and respond to emails while on the train into work (or you can read a good book, play a computer game, or listen to a relaxing CD on your headphones to refresh your mind and be ready for work). The catch is to make sure that when you work on the go, you only deal with non-critical issues, such as checking your daily schedule, responding to brief emails or catching up on team reports. If you drive, you can listen to podcasts via your iPod or car MP3 player or make hands-free phone calls.

Key trends for the future

The Work Foundation's report, *Changing Demographics,* paints an interesting picture of how the UK will look in 2010, one in which flexible working and work/life balance issues will be just as important, if not even more so, than they are now:

✔ The workforce will have grown by 300,000 from the year 2004. And 80 per cent of this growth will be women.

✔ 1 in 5 UK workers will be mothers.

✔ 25 per cent of all families will be single parent families.

✔ Up to 10 million people will be caring for elderly relatives.

Checking Whether Your Long Hours Are Healthy

Some of you reading this book may be feeling frustrated. You work long hours because you own a small business that needs all of your energy and time. And you love what you do. We can hear you saying: 'What's wrong with that?'

The answer is nothing, albeit with a caveat or two. If you find yourself in the working-long-hours trap, but feel energised and enthused about your work, you can still ask yourself the following questions:

- ✔ Am I healthy in body and in mind?
- ✔ If married or co-habiting, do I attentively listen to the needs and goals of my partner and 'do my share' in the partnership?
- ✔ If single, do I make time to develop nurturing friendships?
- ✔ Do I make enough time to spend with my extended family?
- ✔ Do I sleep well and wake up refreshed – or dreading the new day?
- ✔ Is 'taking time out' to be alone and not work part of my schedule?

If your answers are positive, you're one of the very rare few and you can put the book down now and go back to working. Most people find that it's not possible to answer all of these questions without at least some guilt or reservation. If your partner is supportive of you working long hours, is that because your partner believes that the long hours are going to end soon and your work is going to slow down? Or is your partner resigned to you working 60-plus hours with no let-up? Would you really like to have more friendships in your life but find that the main people who you associate with outside of work are the ones who are as busy as you, and therefore put up with your cancelled dates?

Is breakfast a service station sandwich grabbed on the way to a morning meeting? Do you grab leftover biscuits from the boardroom for lunch and struggle to remember the last time you did some exercise? Even workaholics who are successful in terms of career, status, and money need to look after themselves. (Visit Chapters 3, 4, and 5 to find out ways you can have more 'non-work' health and balance in your life.)

Cutting down business travel

In the 1980s and 1990s, business travel – in the same way as the work-funded laptop and mobile phone – was seen as a career status symbol. You were important if your company was prepared to send you overseas to represent its interests.

These days, however, professionals realise increasingly that business trips and being away from home are not so glamorous after all. And in any case, sophisticated teleconferencing and video link facilities cut out the need for so much face-to-face contact.

Talking Yourself Out by Tea Time

Have you ever felt too tired to talk? Have you ever trudged home after a long day in the office spent on the phone, dealing with workmates, holding meetings with clients, and responding to never-ending emails, and found that by the time you're home, the person you love most in the world just isn't going to get any decent conversation from you? Even though your level of exhaustion is understandable, in the longer term such tiredness may well damage your personal relationships.

Although some workers have jobs that deal with unpleasant situations – for example, child abuse, drug dependency, crime, and poverty – and understandably don't want to discuss the day's events with their partners or children over dinner, most people find that feeling 'talked out' is a call for a brief respite between the demands of the office and the demands at home.

Remaining silent at home is a way of gaining a bit of 'head space' when there's no existing quiet room or spa sanctuary available. You may hope for a Pause button to press as you walk through the front door, but your lack of conversation risks hurting your partner.

Another good way to build a gap between work and home is by exercise. Not only does activity benefit your health but exercise is also a form of meditation or a way of getting your mind to focus on something other than work or home. Exercise can help you feel surprisingly refreshed and energised afterwards. Craig walks the mile home from work each day. 'I listen to music or just notice the lovely old houses in neighbouring suburbs and the gardens. It's a nice half an hour to have time to myself.' See Chapter 4 for more information on looking after your health and wellbeing through exercise.

When home needs to be a sanctuary

Initially Natalie saw Craig's silence at home as a sign that he was sick of her, or cross with her for some reason. 'I'm the type of person who likes to come home and sort of "download" the events of my day onto Craig,' Natalie said.

It was only after Craig explained that he needed about 15 minutes of quiet time after a hard day that Natalie stopped taking it personally. 'Now, if Craig gets home after me, I give him a chance to get changed and wind down a bit. He's then in a better frame of mind to talk, so the change really works for us,' she said.

Sometimes, however, Natalie just has to tell Craig something as soon as he walks in the door, or his daughter is bursting with news about something that happened at school. 'I then ask my 8-year-old about her day and get to avoid talking and just listen', he says. 'Focusing on my daughter reminds me that there's more to life than work, and that whatever was bugging me that day stays in the office after I've left for home.'

Part II
Looking After Yourself First

'I must admit, over the last few months
I've noticed a change in Arthur since
he started working from home.'

In this part . . .

*E*ating sensibly, exercising regularly, sleeping well, finding relaxation time, and revving up your love life helps give you more energy and time outside of work. Common sense? Maybe, but in times of stressful over-work, seeing the 'sense' among the deadlines, home chores, and empty junk food containers can be difficult.

Getting to know the true you means finding out what really motivates you at work and in your personal life. In this part, we show you how to make more time for your loved ones – and yourself – and how to set goals that achieve what you want.

Chapter 3

You Can't Have It All and Nor Would You Want To

....

In This Chapter

▶ Facing up to your life instead of the advertiser's image

▶ Examining the super hero myth

▶ Recognising and reducing stress

▶ Thinking in different ways

▶ Making family and friends your allies

▶ Understanding the signs of depression

....

Most people want to live satisfying and successful lives that involve families and friends, and provide rewarding jobs that fund a comfortable lifestyle. Unfortunately, external forces often challenge that simple ambition and can make us feel as though we're not doing enough, don't own enough, and are not fast enough.

In this chapter, we show you why images portrayed by advertisers and celebrities are only constructed to entice you to buy more than you may need and to feel incomplete when you don't live up to the popular image. Many people are surprised to discover that trying to 'have it all' can result in stress, which can seriously damage their physical and mental health. This chapter helps you recognise the signs of stress and depression, and provides some quick ways to reduce stress and change the way you think and react to pressure.

Saying 'No' without guilt can be difficult. In this chapter, we also cover why setting boundaries enables you to realise the importance of having some time alone, as well as a good laugh and the support of your family and friends.

Don't Believe the Glossy Magazines

'I do not read advertisements – I would spend all my time wanting things.'

– Frederick Donald Coggan, Archbishop of Canterbury.

In the 1970s and 1980s, even the very traditional women's magazines were telling young readers that the future for their children was going to be better. Their children's fathers would help more around the home, all families would have easy access to child-care services, and work and parenthood would be a choice for all. Adults from the padded-shoulders era and beyond could 'have it all' – if only they were able to 'think smarter, not harder', 'master multi-tasking', 'put their best foot forward', have a 'hands-on approach', be 'yummy mummies' and know how to 'juggle competing priorities' . . . arrghh!

What those magazines didn't tell their readers (and often still don't) was how to juggle their commitments: how to genuinely feel as though their lives were under control – all aspects of their lives – and not feel exhausted, over-whelmed, and under pressure to look successful.

Whether you're a stressed-out parent feeling guilty about the time you steal from your home life, or you're a work-hard singleton wondering how to fit in the play-hard to your over-committed schedule, you have every right to feel a little cheated by these rose-tinted, lifestyle promises.

Selling an image to create a need

Glossy magazines make money by selling an image or a lifestyle. Often the product on sale has nothing to do with you striving to achieve a work/life balance. Instead, what you're more likely to find between the pages are poor-quality, low-nutrition instant meals, environmentally unsound 'no scrub' cleaning products, junk foods, and brand names. Time-saving devices adver-tised to deliver instant cleanliness, tasty refreshments, and sophistication – qualities the magazines claim are going to gain you the envy of your friends – are, quite honestly, stuff you don't need. The packaging and marketing of all these items aim to make you *think* that you need them. But no visitors in my house have ever left in disgust because we didn't have a plug-in air freshener in every room. They came to enjoy our company.

Often, this advertising targets women directly. Marketers the world over have known for years that women have the largest say in grocery and minor household purchasing decisions. Therefore, marketers portray women as smart and organised, coping with dumb husbands. Advertisements show, time and time again, clueless males who are unable to remember their kids' schedules and yet are saluted as heroes when they walk in with takeaway food for the family, and who smile adoringly at their wives' skills in sorting out the coloured washing from the white loads.

And it's not much better for the supposedly 'lucky' single person who's portrayed as living the good life – decked out in designer clothes, driving fast cars, and eating in fancy restaurants, with a new date every night of the week. Most solo people are far too busy single-handedly sorting out their cleaning, finances, or that burst pipe under the sink.

Recognising the unreality of Hollywood

A couple of years ago, celebrated English actor (and mother) Kate Winslet caused a stir when she angrily criticised a high-profile magazine for not only air-brushing her cover shot, but also digitally stretching her legs to make them appear longer and slimmer. Around the same time, I (Katherine) remember seeing an image of Madonna on a fashion cover and not being able to recognise her – the visual editing department had gone overboard in erasing any identifying feature, such as laugh lines or wrinkles. Even supermodel Cindy Crawford once said that she doesn't look like Cindy Crawford before her photograph is enhanced, and many male actors have clearly had their eyes or jowls 'done' to appear more youthful.

And yet fashion magazines, A-list stars, and paparazzi photos continue to make many millions of dollars; people want whatever products the stars are using. This marketing technique is successful because it tells people that if they wear the same shade of lipstick as, say, Cate Blanchett, they'll also become beautiful, successful, and adored. (And if Tom Cruise is seen wearing the black-lens sunglasses, so should everyone else.)

You don't need to give another second's thought to wondering if your Hollywood idol manages to combine his or her career with a happy love life, or whether your favourite supermodel or footballer's wife is successful in maintaining her work/life balance . . . you already know the answer, which is that in reality, they probably aren't. And if *they* can't manage it with the aid of publicists, personal assistants, dieticians, personal trainers, nannies, bodyguards, limo drivers, housekeepers, gardeners, and chefs, why should you feel guilty when you can't?

Advertising equals unreal expectations

Standards set by advertising and marketing ideals can create guilt in people who feel they're not as good as the people portrayed in the advertisements. Advertising increases the pressure on people to 'perform', be successful, be happy, and have a lot of material possessions.

Work/life balance expert Barbara Pocock calls this the 'advertising equals spending' cycle. Spending means more work, and more work means less family time. Less family time leads to guilt, which leads to more spending in a never-ending cycle.

Having It All Means Doing It All

Having it all sounds like a lot of fun, doesn't it? This is not necessarily the case.

Have you found yourself returning home from work, running a bath for your son or daughter, defrosting some chicken, feeding the dog or the cat, and putting on a load of washing while shuffling through the junk mail? While you've been busy doing those things, your other half has picked up your child from after-school care, put out the rubbish, started peeling the vegetables for dinner, paid some bills online, and is busy planning the next stages of your home renovation and keeping an ear out for your child's violin practice.

During dinner, you scoff down your meals, make brief conversation before the kids get into pyjamas, clean their teeth, play with the dog, and pack school bags for the morning. You wipe down the kitchen, load the dishwasher, make the school lunch, hang out another load of washing, and water the pot plants. Your other half waters the front garden (by hand), answers some work emails, reads the next chapter of *Harry Potter* to the kids in bed, and returns some phone calls.

By 9.30 p.m., you both slump on the sofa, too tired to speak, and wonder just when you can find the time to remove the green mushrooms growing on the mould in your bathroom before getting up at 6 a.m. for exercise, breakfast, commuting, school, and work, and doing it all over again. This is how much fun 'having it all' feels like.

Does this sound too frighteningly familiar to you? You're not alone in living a life like the above scenario. You probably feel as though you're constantly on the move – mentally and physically – as you toil with the conflicting demands of your job, child-care arrangements, housework, finances, and phone calls, and wonder just where your so-called 'free time' has run off to.

Super Hero, Super Myth, Super Sham

Whatever lifestyle choice you've made, the one thing we'd like to make clear right now is that the notion of super hero perfection in all aspects of your life is one that's certain to de-rail you into frustration and distress. You may be working full-time, part-time, juggling two demanding careers with your partner, caring for children, or trying to squeeze meaningful friendships into a jam-packed work schedule. *All* these scenarios involve hard work and precision planning and can leave you exhausted at the end of the day, wondering just when life is going to be easier, let alone fun. What may be holding your lifestyle back is that, despite wanting to find the answer to your work/life balance, just like everyone else, you may instead be wasting time and energy in judging others and yourself, instead of supporting other people around you.

Thirty years on from hard-won freedoms of planned parenthood, equal pay, and anti-discrimination legislation, many people continue to create more road blocks for themselves.

Stay-at-home mothers feel that working mothers hate them for being docile, boring, unfulfilled, and unchallenged. Working mothers feel as though they're blamed for selfishly choosing work over play time or money for love, and fret when they drop their kids off at child care. Stay-at-home fathers still feel as though they have to answer that 'Oh that's nice, but what *else* do you do?' question, yet for men, the self blame doesn't end there.

Career-focused singletons worry that they can't find the time or make the effort with important people in their life, whereas those that do put their life priorities on their employer's table and reduce their work commitments, may feel that colleagues judge them for not pulling their weight – after all, isn't it selfish to want more leisure time when you only have yourself to be responsible for?!

It's this kind of muddled thinking that causes you to mistake what being a *true* super hero in your own life really is – deciding what your core priorities are, what you honestly want for yourself and the important people in your life, and having the courage to speak up against the trends and the media myths to design a balanced, happy, and successful way forward.

The best super heroes are fundamentally human beings with special powers, and, trust me, the pursuit of perfection isn't one of them!

 If you're a parent, remember that many studies show that quality and not quantity of time spent with children is what's most important. Children don't always want you 'hanging around' them after school, but when you do get home they want to be able to talk to you and get your undivided attention. Reading stories at bedtime is a classically effective way to get important one-to-one time together without it being too mentally or physically draining at the end of the day.

Understanding Stress

Today's ever-increasing working demands – and hours – mean that you may be continually fighting for time. This struggle to fit in family life and personal commitments around work agendas creates high levels of stress in many UK households.

All stress – good and bad – originates from the *fight or flight* response built into all animals. Yes, this includes you. Animals react to threat via their central nervous system that immediately gets them ready to fight or flee. Your body produces cortisol, adrenaline, and other hormones, which speed up your heart rate, slow digestion, and move blood flow to major muscles in order to give your body a big burst of strength.

This response also applies to more dramatic, or the most untimely situations you may face, such as narrowly avoiding a road accident, catching a dropped vase, or coping during a particularly stressful period at work. When the threat goes (for example, the car's driven off, you have the vase in your hand, or you've handed in the final report on time), your body reverts to its normal rested state. Your breathing returns to normal, your heart stops pounding out of control, and your muscles relax.

Although 'fight or flight' stress affects you physically, it can work in a good way. Good stress is sometimes known as *eustress* (from the ancient Greek 'eu' meaning good). Eustress can help you work to a deadline and achieve things due to the adrenaline rush, urgency, and thrill of it all. Common examples of this include winning a competition, successfully meeting a challenging deadline, earning a promotion, getting married, being pleasantly surprised, buying a house, going on a much-anticipated holiday, or just a spine-tingling, roller-coaster ride.

As funny as it sounds, however, you can't always cope with too much of even this 'good' stress – it's meant to be occasional and balanced with periods of rest and relaxation, or the body just gets overwhelmed. Remember too that what is good stress for one person may be someone else's anxiety attack, so pay attention to your own unique physical and emotional responses.

The stress you may experience most often is the negative type that can affect you physically, emotionally, and psychologically. In your everyday, modern life, you rarely have to decide to stay and defend yourself from an angry mammoth or run from a lion, yet your body still reacts to stressors in the same physical ways.

If the stress causing the heightened physical response doesn't go away, your body remains on 'red alert', taking a toll on your health and your mind. Physically, you may notice these effects:

✔ Churning stomach or 'butterflies'

✔ Diarrhoea or constipation

✔ Loss of sexual desire and/or arousal

✔ Neck aches, backaches, and headaches

✔ Poor sleep patterns

✔ Sweating, or dry mouth

Eliminating stress from your life completely isn't realistic but you can manage it and avoid the worst effects. You do this by thinking differently about setting such high expectations for yourself, engaging with positive self talk, and getting support from friends and family.

Changing the Way You Think

You don't have to be forced into feeling a failure just because you don't fit the advertisers' unrealistic prototypes. The following sections show you ways to forget the unrealities of glossy advertising, Hollywood hype, and being a 'super' anything, and help you turn negative phrases into positive ones. Remember that it takes 30 days for a new method to become a habit, so you may need to read some of these lists out loud to yourself every day for a month to help change the way you think and act.

Accepting the truth behind your front door

Forget Hollywood. Look at what your home is really like and try to accept the following:

- ✔ **Home is for you and your family.** A lot of people have a tendency to be overly critical of themselves, their skills, and their homes. Housework perfectly portrays these unfounded criticisms. Is your home happy, safe, and comfortable? Sitcom mothers-in-law are portrayed as evil witches running their fingers down stair banisters in search of dust, but today's mother-in-law is more likely to be looking after grandchildren to give you a night off, and wondering just how she's going to fit in her power walk with her part-time job. And even if mum-in-law is the critical type, ask yourself 'whose home is it anyway?'. You are in charge of your lifestyle, however you choose to run it.

- ✔ **Honesty works.** The best and most rewarding friendships – old and new – have been made when one party admits to feeling terrible; is not coping; or would love to sit down, have a good cry, eat bad food, and smash the phone. Honesty opens doors to other people's experiences that you can learn from and *everyone* loves hearing that they're not the only one who feels the way they do. This goes for men too, many of whom may still be a work-in-progress when it comes down to sharing confidences with someone other than their wives.

- ✔ **Nobody has it all.** Stop admiring people who have it all. They don't – not even the rich, the famous, or the super intelligent.

- ✔ **Nobody cares about your floors.** At no stage in your lifetime are you going to be forced to suck spaghetti off your floor. However, despite what advertisers say, your floor does *not* have to have every single microbe known to mankind eliminated from it. Ironically, scientists are now finding that the homes of today are too clean, which contributes to increased rates of asthma and allergies because people's bodies can no longer properly fight off germs. Remember too that no one notices the mess but you. When was the last time you tut-tutted at the dust under your friend's sofa, or wondered how often her shower screen was scrubbed? Stay within the sensible boundaries of what is hygienic and healthy for you and yours and forget about trying to live up to some impossible standard of perfection.

✔ **Work/life balance isn't a competition you have to win.** Despite what the media tell you, you don't have to do it all, nor have it all. No one does and no one can, not even the very rich and famous – look at the gossip mags if you think that this statement is incorrect. Instead of focusing on the next pay rise, the gorgeous mother at school drop-off, or your next car, think about what you *can* do to help the community – simple stuff like donating clothes for a car boot sale or taking home school library books to cover while you're watching TV.

Ways that a working parent can connect with their children

Often, where there's a main or solo 'breadwinner' in a family unit, that person comes home from their stressful job and finds it difficult to 'wind down' and enjoy time with his children, who are relaxed and ready to play. However, most parents know that spending time with their children, however brief, can influence a child's emotional development and ability to interact with others. Here are some ways to ensure some quality time with kids:

Converse: Don't rely on your partner or caregiver to pass on messages to your child. Your child is interested in you, not facts about you via someone else. Even just a few minutes of conversation with you (in person or via the telephone) means more to your children than any information relayed second hand.

Create pictures: If you go away for work (whether it be regularly or suddenly), purchase two digital cameras – one for you and one for your child. While you're away,

take pictures that show where you are and what you're doing and have your child do the same. When you get home, make time to share your photos with each other. If you have to go away for longer periods, set up a free online account where you and your child can post images to each other for quick updates. These online albums can give you and your child a visual update to look forward to when you're travelling.

Eat out: If arriving home in time for dinner is an impossible task, invite your child out to breakfast at the weekends. Take your child out – on his own – to your local café and enjoy the experience of both choosing your own breakfast on the menu (you can still choose and encourage a healthy breakfast). By giving your child your undivided attention away from home, he feels important. Opening up and sharing conversation and thoughts with your child doesn't take long. If you have more than one child, rotate weekends.

REAL-LIFE STORY

The happy meal

David and Sonia insist on having dinner together with their two sons every night, during which time each person must list these three things about their day:

- ✔ What was the best thing about your day?

- ✔ What was the worst thing about your day?

- ✔ What was the funniest thing that happened today?

Going through this list can take less than five minutes, but this family routine then becomes an experience they enjoy. David remarked that it was a unique way of finding out just what interested his 6- and 4-year-old sons and that their answers were a combination of being extremely revealing, very funny, and endearing.

Rejecting perfection

Hand in hand with being able to 'have it all' is the image of perfection. Or, more precisely, how you believe that *other* people have achieved the pinnacle of success and that you need to work harder to stop 'failing', to keep up, or do better. Perfection is unachievable, lonely, and exhausting, and you're much better off realising what you're already doing well. Besides, what one person defines as success may be someone else's own worst nightmare.

Here are some good reasons why forgetting about being perfect is a good idea:

- ✔ **Achieving perfection is impossible.** Look up the word perfection in the dictionary and you find descriptors such as 'the state or quality of being or becoming perfect', 'the highest degree of proficiency, skill, or excellence', 'a perfect embodiment of something' or 'a quality or feature of the highest degree'. But in seeking perfection, you miss out on experiences with your family and friends because you're too busy, too tired, or too cranky from your efforts. Even at less extreme levels, many people are so often focused on crossing things off their 'to do' lists that they forget to look up, see what's important to them, and just appreciate life. Just 'be'.

- ✔ **Being perfect is un-fun.** How can being perfect be 'fun'? Do the perfect parents on TV ads going into ecstasies over new SUVs and stain removers look as though they'd be fun to spend time with? In contrast, laughing at your mistakes and life's minor hiccups along the way can be a lot of fun. So your young son puts his shoes on the wrong feet and is now late for the bus and you're a tad late for work. Instead of getting upset, help your son to learn to giggle at the small stuff.

- ✔ **Striving for perfection is a very lonely experience.** Often it's only *you* who's seeking perfection and wearing yourself out trying to achieve it. No one else around you notices or cares about the impending restructure at work, the unfolded T-shirts or the never-ending lists. You're never going to win the battle for the perfectly run home – not unless you freeze-frame your family and clean up around them, which in itself would be a rather futile and lonely success, wouldn't it?

- ✔ **Trade in the quest for perfection and you can still be a 'winner'.** Just do the best you can. Even world-class athletes who don't win a race but beat their 'personal best' are thrilled with the result because it's the *best* they've ever done. The same goes for a relatively happy family with a drawer full of clean underwear.

Maryanne's mother has a very dear old friend who is 90 years old. She learned long ago not to care about what other people think. In fact, instead of cleaning the house from top to toe before visitors arrive, she sits back and says, 'No one notices the dust after a glass of sherry.'

Stepping out of the super hero suit

There's no need for you or your partner to slave at being a super anything in your hectic life, so give the whole idea the brush-off. You can do this by:

- ✔ **Agreeing to disagree.** You don't always have to agree, but taking three deep, long, and slow breaths calms you down to enable you to think of a better way to phrase things, that's more preferable to using judgemental statements, such as 'How come you never' or 'I can't ever rely on you for anything', which only increase anger and lack of understanding on both sides. Acknowledge the *good* things your partner does – they may seem minor (for example, she picks me up from work on Wednesdays; he goes to the corner shop for the paper and milk) but everyone wants their good deeds to be noticed. This positive approach also allows your partner to become more willing to let you know what he or she appreciates about you, too.

- ✔ **Ending the 'who's the most tired' argument.** Everyone's tired! It's vital to stop keeping score with your partner or loved ones on this point, because this only increases the stored resentments and makes you (or them) say things that you regret later.

- ✔ **Refraining from over-stimulating your children to ease guilt about time constraints.** My grandmother considered 'I'm bored' as the two most offensive words in the English language. By all means involve your children in selecting two extra-curricular activities to do per week, but no more. Children need time to rest, be with their families, read, reflect, and use their own imaginations. Feel proud to answer those two awful words with, 'Well, go and find something to do.' You don't have to be their full-time Entertainment Coordinator.

✔ **Supporting each other.** Think of this in terms of being each other's understudy. Find out how to start the mower, file the accounts in the filing cabinet, acquaint yourself with the fuse box, or cook triple the amount of your delicious Bolognese sauce to freeze later. These are the tasks that most people only notice when they're not done.

✔ **Talking and working together.** Acknowledge the work that your partner does by saying something like, 'I'm dealing with a lot at work and/or home right now and it would really help me if you can . . .'
It's better to adopt a considered approach rather than trying to nag, blame, or shame your partner into doing something that he is then going to feel resentful about and throw back at you later: 'What about the time when you *made me* . . .'

Turning 'I can't do' into positive self-talk

Change your self-defeating internal thoughts to constructive ones. Table 3-1 lists a few classics that may be familiar to you. The trick is to replace the negative self-defeating thought with positive thinking. Go on, give it a try: take a few breaths, think, and then rephrase your automatic thought. Before long, you're going to discover that you're smiling.

Carving out time for yourself

A relative of mine is a busy, career-focused singleton who aims to work just as hard at keeping in touch with her supportive network of friends and extended family. As a result she's often someone her friends turn to in times of minor personal crisis and she's usually very glad to be there for them. She realised recently that she was taking it to extremes when she took a call from a friend at 8 p.m., having just walked in the door from a challenging business meeting, and was still on the phone to her at midnight, feeling hungry, tired, and anxious in anticipation of another early start the next day.

Although she didn't resent the time given to her friend, the issue that was keeping them both up into the small hours was one that undoubtedly would look quite different in the fresh light of day. Looking back, she felt that she could have helped her friend get some perspective by putting some personal boundaries in place.

She now makes sure that she carves out some 'me-time' immediately on getting home from a long or challenging day and she has a couple of hours to herself over a peaceful, simple, home-cooked meal. She makes sure that she lays the table and makes the effort because the rituals help her unwind, and feel cared for. And most importantly, she takes the phone off the hook for that short period of time!

Table 3-1	Replacing Negative Thoughts	
Self-Defeating Thought	**Analyst's Couch**	**Constructive Thinking**
'They think I'm nowhere near as good as . . .'	Is that right? You're a mind-reader, are you? This is a negative thought that automatically springs into your head and, like any good habit, takes some practice to stop. 'No one's perfect and if I'm worried, I'll go and ask my colleagues how they think I'm doing at work.'	
'Things never work out for me . . .'		What, never? How have you survived this far? Who got you educated, dressed properly, who got you your job, your family? Your self-defeating thought is called catastrophising, or thinking that everything in life that occurs to you is, well, a complete catastrophe. Your rational mind knows that this isn't true, but this 'I never . . .' thought is a regular visitor. 'This is something different for me. I may as well give it a try. I haven't got anything to lose if it goes wrong.'
'I'm hopeless at this . . .'		Where is the panel of judges that gave you zero out of ten? Who are you comparing yourself to – someone real, someone enormously talented, or someone airbrushed in a magazine? Are you mistaking this automatic thinking for fact, instead of feeling? 'I'll give this a try. There's no law that says I must be brilliant at everything.'

Self-Defeating Thought	Analyst's Couch	Constructive Thinking
'No one really likes me . . .'	You haven't met everyone in the world yet and this is your preconception working against you instead of letting your actions speak for themselves. 'I don't have to have everyone's approval all the time. I'm happy with myself and can see that I'm doing my best.'	

Hoping that everyone likes you all the time doesn't make this happen. But as Eleanor Roosevelt once said, 'No one can make you feel inferior without your consent.'

Erasing all negative thinking can be a very difficult task and one that's impossible if signs of clinical depression (when dark or negative thoughts linger for more than two weeks and physical symptoms such as insomnia or lack of appetite occur) are evident. If you feel that your negative feelings have been with you for too long, read the section on depression at the end of this chapter.

Setting boundaries and saying 'No'

It's one of the smallest words in the English language, but 'No' is one of the hardest things to say. From an early age, most people are trained to say 'Yes' in order to please, be polite, and to be seen as friendly.

Saying 'No' to anyone other than a child is often one of the most difficult words to utter in everyday work and social and home life. The many reasons people say 'Yes' instead of 'No' can include guilt, feeling backed into a corner and unable to think of a good enough reason to refuse, or not wanting to be the bad guy. Learning to say 'No' can be one of the biggest steps you take because it can reduce stress levels and give you time for things that are more important.

Here are some pointers to help get you started:

✔ Be firm (not defensive or overly apologetic) and polite. This gives the signal that you're sympathetic but won't change your mind easily if pressured.

✔ If asked for an explanation, remember that you really don't owe anyone one. 'I can't fit it into my working hours/diary/schedule' is a fair answer.

✔ If you decide to tell the person you'll get back to them, sound very matter-of-fact, and not too promising.

✔ If your boss makes a request that looks difficult to fit in, respond with 'I'll show you my schedule and we can decide what other task needs to be dropped in its place.'

✔ Remember that there are only so many hours in the day. Whatever you choose to take on reduces your ability to do other things. Even if you *can* squeeze something else into your work day, if it's not more important than the things you would have to give up to do it (including going home at a decent time and relaxing), then the answer is still 'No': you don't have time and can't do it.

Having Family and Friends on Your Side

Often, the simple act of trying to carve out some time just for yourself can seem impossible, almost selfish. But remember, you're not being selfish: you need time for yourself, you deserve your own space, and you must stop allowing others preventing you from attaining some time for yourself. And don't forget the importance of a good laugh – a hearty laugh makes life seem so much easier.

Your family and friends (and colleagues) enjoy your company, they like you, and identify with you more if you're prepared to admit your shortcomings, talk about them, and have a laugh. But that's not all. Your family and friends, and again colleagues, can be your allies as you seek out ways to achieve your work/life balance. To ensure their support, here's the best approach:

✔ **Explain that you're working towards making changes.** Tell them you're planning to make some positive changes to your life. This expression of what you're doing allows them to see that you're not being irritable or unhelpful. You're concerned about your work/life balance and need their understanding and support to help you make some genuine changes.

✔ **Relate your plan.** Tell them about the changes you're planning to make, what and how much you intend to take on, what you put in your diary, what time you finish work and so on.

✔ **Seek help.** Tell your family, friends, and colleagues what you expect from them in order to help you and keep you on track.

✔ **Show appreciation.** Don't forget to thank them for listening and appreciating that you're serious about making changes that will improve your health, mood, work life, and the time you spend with them.

Giving guilt the heave-ho

Guilt tends to be a never-ending cycle for most people. You feel guilty when you work; you feel guilty when you stay at home; you feel guilty if you're not busy all the time; and you feel guilty when you're relaxing and trying to do nothing. Achieving your work/life balance is much easier if you can let go of guilt.

Ask yourself some honest questions about guilt:

- Am I responsible for the problem?
- Am I taking on someone else's responsibility?
- Am I trying to stop someone else from feeling guilty, or stressed, or uncomfortable?
- Can someone else help me?
- Does this problem have more than one solution?
- How much does my guilt help the problem?
- How much guilt do I feel about this problem?
- What am I doing to make this problem worse for myself?
- What problem is really troubling me?
- What would my problem feel like if I had no more guilt?

When you give in to guilt, you make yourself feel as though you don't deserve much, and you can waste a lot of needless time and mental energy worrying about what you *did* versus what you think that you should've done. Because you want to do the very best at work, for your partner, and your children, you may feel that you're doing something wrong in thinking of yourself first.

On the plus side, guilt can motivate you to change for the better. When you constantly feel guilty and hate the additional stress it causes, you can use it as a benchmark to measure what needs to be changed in your life.

Treating yourself to time-out

Even with loved ones on your side willing to help you make positive changes to achieve your work/life balance, every person needs some time on his or her own. For some people this may only be some time out for privacy in the bathroom; others may need chunks of days or hours. Whatever the amount you need, it's vital that you plan and schedule the time you need – so that you actually get to enjoy it.

Time-out isn't a punishment, nor is lying in bed with a stomach ache or migraine considered a rest. Time-out is time devoted solely to you, to do whatever you like in whatever manner you choose. This should be respected by your family, colleagues, and friends – especially if it's a regular, scheduled event.

Knowing how much time-out you need

Think about it: time-out gives you time to think. Planning the type of time-out you need is an important decision because you want to make the most of it. Here are some suggestions to help you know your time-out preferences:

- ✔ **Away time-out:** Away from your usual work and home space to rest, think, and play. Plan this space with enough time to consider your partner, kids, work commitments, and finances. For example, my friend Paula, a full-time accountant with two children, books herself into a five-star hotel for a weekend of pampering once a year. Dave, another friend, is locked into a work schedule and his finances don't stretch that far, so he picks up his son from school three afternoons a week so that he can play a round of golf on Saturday mornings.

- ✔ **Creative time-out:** Time to think and to feel free to come up with, and explore, ideas yourself. This can be two minutes away from your desk, a five-minute walk, a nap, or having the house to yourself for a couple of hours.

- ✔ **Fun time-out:** Time for whatever you like! A gym workout between the end of work and the trip home, a movie, an afternoon off to go fishing. Make time in your diary as you would for any other event, because this time is just as important.

- ✔ **Quiet time-out:** Away from noise, distractions, and the telephone to think, rest, relax, and recharge. No radio, television, computer, or mobile phone – just you.

- ✔ **Working time-out:** Taking five minutes per hour to look up from your computer, stand up, and stretch your arms, shoulders, head and neck muscles, walk around the office, or take the stairs instead of the lift.

Laughing your way to happiness

Laughter and humour actually benefit your health and reduce stress. The sad fact is that many adults laugh on average only 15 times a day, whereas children laugh up to 400 times a day. Another interesting fact to note is that when people list the qualities they look for in a partner, a sense of humour is always near the top.

You've just gotta laugh . . .

Humour can also be used by you to get a message across in a subtle way or to change the mood. In just one day, Jan discovered that one son had been hospitalised; the other had broken up with his partner and mother of his child; her ex-husband had recently remarried; she had just been made redundant and realised that she didn't have enough money in her purse for the bus ride home.

'As I stood there by the side of the road, I thought that things had really hit rock bottom in my life when – splat! – a bird dropping landed right on top of my head. I felt as if I was a clown in a bad movie plot and just stood there, laughing and laughing. It felt so wonderful to be able to find the funny side in what was the worst time of my life. It still makes me smile now and that day was ten years ago.'

If you think that you're too insignificant to make any changes in your non-glamorous life, remember how painful it is when a tiny stone gets caught in your shoe. That's one of my own analogies and it's meant to show that even a small step – such as forcing a smile – can actually make you feel better.

Amazingly, even fake laughter results in a similar physical stress-release response by your body. As many experts from many different fields say, 'Fake it until you make it.' Try stretching your lips across your face – this is commonly known as a smile. Any customer service trainer can tell you that if you answer the phone with a smile it can be 'heard' in your voice. As with fake laughter, try smiling even if you don't feel like it. You feel tension release immediately.

When people are laughing together, they feel more positive towards each other and more positive about themselves. Like breathing exercises and small five-minute 'time-out' sessions, having a good laugh brings fantastic short-term physical change, for example laughing:

- ✔ Eases muscle tension and stomach aches

- ✔ Increases the immune system

- ✔ Lowers stress hormone levels, heart rate, and blood pressure

- ✔ Stimulates the heart and lungs, also known as an 'internal workout'

Laughs are all around us, just waiting for someone to notice them and invite them in. Easy tips for finding humour in life include:

- ✔ Find something simple like a favourite cartoon and hang it on the back of your loo door, in your office, or keep it in your wallet.

- ✔ Find the funny side of your situation.

✔ Have fun – find it, appreciate it, and realise how important it is for your health and wellbeing. Remember how good it felt to go on the swing? To throw basketballs in the hoop? That's it – now you have the idea!

✔ Seek out the funny people in your life – listen to their stories and laugh with them. Don't interrupt them with an anecdote of your own; just listen, relax, and enjoy.

✔ Surf the TV channels until you find a good sitcom. Sitting on the sofa laughing until coffee spurts out of your nose is brilliant and free, and is also something you can do with your partner – who *doesn't* want to have a big chuckle with their other half?

✔ Take a closer look at your children, mates, and pets – such as the best of the funny-home-video programmes on television and online. When you take a moment to sit back and observe them they're fantastic sources of humour. Seeing my dog standing up on her hind legs to delicately pick and eat the ripe grapes from our lone vine in the garden is very amusing to witness.

✔ Try the World Wide Web because it offers a constant source of wicked humour, topical humour, classic humour, and creative humour. Websites such as (www.utube.com), (www.neatorama.com) and thousands of 'joke of the day' sites, provide so many options for you to choose from. It never ceases to amaze me that such clever people are out there creating wonderful material.

✔ Write or find the humour in you – everyone has a funny incident, thought, or experience. Write it down or tell someone. It's so much more fun to laugh with someone else and see how they appreciate your quirky view. Sometimes a mere raise of the eyebrow or grimace timed at the right moment can crack everyone up and diffuse tension or show them that you empathise with their situation.

Recognising the Signs of Depression

There may be times and circumstances when, despite all efforts to make positive changes to improve your work/life balance, things still feel lousy and out of your control. Everyone has a rough day every now and then, but when these feelings don't go away after a couple of weeks and begin to interfere with your ability to work properly, feel pleasure at home, and affect your sleep or appetite, it's time to examine things more closely.

This book is not intended to replace the education and skills your doctor or psychologist can provide, but we can give you some important questions to ask yourself – and anyone close to you – who may be suffering from depression:

✔ Have you been feeling sad, miserable, or hopeless most of the time?

✔ Are you feeling overwhelmed, worthless, and guilty without being able to pinpoint a specific reason?

✔ Are you having problems sleeping, or are you sleeping too much?

✔ Are you increasing your use of alcohol and other (legal and illegal) drugs?

✔ Do you feel tired and lacking in energy all the time?

✔ Do you want to avoid socialising or seeing people, and feel very fragile?

✔ Has your appetite disappeared or increased?

✔ Have you been having thoughts about death, self-harm, or 'getting out of everyone's way'?

✔ Have you lost interest in doing the things you usually enjoy doing?

✔ Is it difficult to finish routine tasks at work, home, or school?

✔ Is your physical health suffering – churning stomach, neck aches and bowel disturbances?

If you have ticked or nodded to half of these or more, you may have a depressive illness and should contact your doctor immediately. Ignoring depression and hoping it goes away doesn't work. In fact, your depression is likely to get worse.

Understanding how depression works

Despite increased public awareness campaigns about depression and the fact that many studies indicate that at least one in four people in the UK suffer from the illness, the condition is still not something people want to yell out from the rooftops or announce to strangers at dinner parties.

However, one thing is worth realising: depression is a serious illness that results from chemical imbalances in the brain. You would readily seek medical help for a kidney infection, and treating your mind is no different.

If not treated properly, depression can lead to increased absences from work, inability to make considered decisions, and withdrawal from family, friends, and colleagues. There's no need to hide from depression. Your GP can help you, or refer you to a psychologist, psychiatrist, or social worker, all of whom have many ways of treating depression in a professional and confidential manner.

Seeking help without fear

The following websites offer practical information on depression:

- **Mind** (www.mind.org.uk): The leading mental health charity in England and Wales. Mind advocates positive attitudes in the support and treatment of mental health. It provides a confidential helpline as well as a network of local associations that offer a range of services including counselling and befriending. Mind is a key driving force in campaigning for fairness and equality at work for individuals with mental health issues.

- **Depression Alliance** (www.depressionalliance.org): A UK charity that provides information and support for people with depression. It works to raise awareness amongst the general public about the realities of living with depression and provides numerous publications that describe the causes, symptoms, and treatments available.

- **Samaritans** (www.samaritans.org): Well-known as the pioneering UK organisation that provides 24-hour helpline support for individuals who are experiencing distress and despair. The work of the Samaritans has expanded in recent years to providing valuable information and solutions on work-place stress. Along similar lines, SANE (www.sane.org.uk) seeks to improve the quality of life for anyone affected by mental illness, including partners and families of individual sufferers. Both websites carry lots of information and resources to educate, inform, and support people in times of life crisis.

Chapter 4

Your Body Is Your Temple and Not Your Local Dump

*E*verybody knows the adage 'You are what you eat'. Yet with busy lives, many people tend to absentmindedly reach for high-fat, low-nutrition snack foods, grab frozen meals and instant sauces from the supermarket on the way home, or throw their bags on the kitchen bench and order a curry. Heart disease, obesity, diabetes, and mental health are the biggest health problems facing UK workers today, with more people than ever neglecting diet and exercise regimes. In this chapter we get to the heart of the matter – your body and your health.

Admittedly eating healthily is an area I (Katherine) continually struggle with – I can get my daughter a healthy breakfast, sort out her school uniform, make her a packed lunch, drop her off at school, and arrive at work on time, only then to have *my* breakfast courtesy of the vending machine. On the same day, I meet my family for dinner at one of the nicest restaurants on our side of town – straight from work of course.

And it's official – the nation is getting fatter! The Office of National Statistics reported in 2006 that 67 per cent of men and 58 per cent of women are over-weight in the UK (compared with 58 per cent of men and 49 per cent of women ten years ago). Diet is only part of the problem. Humans also need fresh air, rest, and exercise. This chapter shows how, by starting some simple exercises, you can soon make them part of your daily routine, making you feel healthier, sleep better, and enjoy time with your friends and loved ones.

Getting Active

Spending long hours at a desk in front of a computer screen is damaging to your body. Human bodies are just not designed to sit still for long periods of time. Exercising regularly becomes even more crucial to combat all of this sitting.

Always check with your doctor before starting any new exercise programme, particularly if you're overweight, over 40 years of age, haven't exercised in a long time, or have a chronic medical condition.

But if you become active and stay active, your body and mind benefit. Undertaking regular moderate activity can:

- ✔ Build and maintain healthy bones, muscles, and joints
- ✔ Help with weight management
- ✔ Promote psychological and emotional wellbeing
- ✔ Reduce feelings of depression and anxiety
- ✔ Reduce the risk of developing heart disease, diabetes, colon cancer, and high blood pressure
- ✔ Reduce the risk of dying prematurely

Regular exercise can also help to improve your quality of life, manage these health conditions, and prevent their recurrence.

Often, small is the best way for a new or reluctant exerciser to start an exercise programme. If you can find just 10 minutes a day, you'll find it easy to gradually increase exercise time to the recommended 30 minutes needed for optimum health benefits. Keeping exercise activities simple and inexpensive also helps make the start easier.

Finding easy activities to begin

Choosing an activity that appeals to you, is affordable, and fits in with your lifestyle can help you stay motivated. Finding a friend to exercise with you can also be an effective way of sticking to an exercise plan.

Walking is known to be an extremely effective form of exercise and many opportunities arise in day-to-day life when walking can replace driving. Such opportunities include:

✔ Parking the car as far away as you can from the office or shop's entrance to fit in a mini-walk.

✔ Walking to the corner shop instead of driving.

✔ Walking to the bus, tube, or railway station, and catching public transport all the way to work. Commuting can also be a less stressful method of travel because you can look out of the window, rest, and read.

✔ Walking to the bus, tube, or railway station, getting off one or two stops short of your destination and walking the rest of the way.

✔ Washing and vacuuming the car yourself instead of taking it to a car wash.

✔ Walking a dog. Dogs are remarkably good at training humans to walk at least once a day.

Cycling is also a good, low-impact way to get started on your fitness journey. And you don't have to have any pretensions to be the next Lance Armstrong to think about how you can incorporate a cycle ride to and from work or social activities on a more regular basis. Increasingly, new cycle lanes are opening up and there's even an initiative to help fund the cost of a bike.

Finding the time to work – at work and at home

Just because you work all day doesn't mean you need to forego exercise. Work situations provide many opportunities to take the long way around – not only for a few minutes' break from the desk, but also for some free exercise. These opportunities include:

✔ Getting up and walking around for a few minutes every hour – take the longest route to get your next cup of tea, glass of water, or to go to the toilet.

✔ Stretching at your desk – five minutes every half an hour is enough.

✔ Taking the stairs instead of the lift.

✔ Using at least half of your lunch break for a power walk (preferably out of doors), even if you have only 10 to 15 minutes.

✔ Walking to talk to work colleagues – talk face to face rather than phoning or emailing them. You may find this practice also eases some communications that may have required several emails to sort out.

30 minutes a day is enough

Health experts advise adults to be moderately active for 30 minutes every day. If the activity is more intense, you can do it for less than 30 minutes and still receive the health benefits. Some examples of moderate physical activity are:

✔ Cycling 4 miles in 30 minutes

✔ Gardening for 30 to 45 minutes

✔ Running 1 mile in 15 minutes

✔ Swimming laps for 20 minutes

✔ Walking 1–2 miles in 45 minutes

Apart from the health benefits, breaking up your schedule like this actually boosts your overall creativity as your brain is better able to process things in small chunks, so don't worry about 'wasting time'. You'll find you get much more done in the shorter periods of intense work.

And when you're at home, you probably have a little housework to do. As you have to clean the house, keep the garden tidy, amuse the kids, and exhaust the dog, you can make these tasks much more enjoyable and find great ways to combine them with exercise:

✔ Add more physical activities into your family's fun time. Walk with your children (or borrow your neighbours') to the park or kick a ball around the garden.

✔ Burn fat calories by pushing around the hoover, broom, and mop.

✔ Get stuck into your garden. Mowing, raking leaves, re-potting overgrown plants, and mulching flower beds make great exercise.

✔ Listen to your favourite music and dance around the house while sorting papers and dusting. (Go on – no-one's watching you!)

✔ Play actively with your children or friends. Try hide-and-seek instead of video games. Consider joining a team for your favourite sport.

✔ Walk the dog more often, or make your usual walk ten minutes or so longer.

Always set yourself realistic goals. For example, aim for four short exercise sessions a week rather than planning a whole morning out running the equivalent of a half marathon. Accept that regular exercise is a lifelong commitment, not a short-term whim. If you're trying to lose weight, aim to lose between ½–2 pounds of body fat each week. Half a pound might not seem a lot, but it makes a difference astonishingly quickly, and lots of research suggests that a slow consistent weight loss is healthy and allows you to retain skin tone and elasticity. Remember too that muscle weighs more than fat, but bathroom scales can't tell the difference, so you may want to think about a different way of monitoring your progress – perhaps dress size or actual 'vital statistics'.

Maintaining the Motivation

Starting an exercise routine is the easy part – I know, I've done it dozens of times. Sticking to the exercise routine is the challenge.

People exercise for different reasons. Think about why you're exercising to help you during the times when you don't feel like doing any exercise. You may be exercising regularly to:

- ✔ Feel more energetic
- ✔ Improve joint mobility
- ✔ Keep up with the kids
- ✔ Lose weight
- ✔ Manage depression or anxiety
- ✔ Reduce back pain
- ✔ Sleep better

It's easier to stick to an exercise routine when you can see the benefits. Make the commitment as you would for anything else that's important, such as work meetings, kids' sports schedules, and so on. Try these tips:

- ✔ Avoid boredom by setting yourself challenges like walking a bit faster, changing your route, jogging with a friend.
- ✔ Consider getting up 30 minutes earlier to exercise if the rest of your day is packed with events.
- ✔ Keep at-home exercise options accessible, for example, exercise DVDs or a stationary bike.
- ✔ Keep a training diary to help you to spot every little improvement you make. You'll feel immensely satisfied to read, over a few weeks, that your walking sessions have increased from half a mile to eight miles.
- ✔ Pay attention to the way you feel. Do your clothes feel a bit looser? Can you keep going at the gardening for a longer period? Are you able to laugh off an annoyance today? Taking the time to recognise these little improvements can increase your motivation to exercise.

✔ Remember that unexpected events arise from time to time and disrupt your exercise routine. Don't let this worry you. Instead, make a date in your diary for your next available exercise session.

✔ Reward yourself whenever you reach a fitness goal. For example, when your aim is to walk every night after work and you achieve your goal. Rewards can range from a massage to a movie. Choose a reward that's meaningful to you and is seen as a real reward. It goes without saying that the best rewards are the ones that support your health goals, so that gooey chocolate cake may not be the best way to treat yourself if you're aiming to lose fat!

Eating Sensibly – Not from a Vending Machine

At what stage of modern life did sensible eating stop and vending machines take over? When you think about it, vending machines pop up just about everywhere you go, from the railway station, to work tea rooms, to school grounds, hospital corridors, and shopping centres. Is there nowhere these temples of temptation have missed?

It's time for sensible eating to come back and the first place to start is with breakfast.

Bringing back breakfast

Going to work on an empty stomach may save ten extra minutes, but missing breakfast also means that your body hasn't had anything put into it for up to 14 hours. At this stage, blood sugar and energy levels hit rock bottom. Then the body tries to counter this effect by producing the hormones adrenaline and cortisol. The latter makes you feel edgy and you find concentrating very difficult. Many studies show that students who eat breakfast think clearer and faster than those who do not eat before beginning the day's work.

Skipping the first meal of the day can lead to over eating for the rest of the day and usually bad choices of foods. Becoming over hungry can lead to a lack of control and may result in taking in more calories, fats, and sugar than you eat when you have a proper breakfast.

Breakfast muesli recipe

Here's a scrumptious and healthy breakfast that's quick and easy to make and provides breakfast for one adult for an entire week (if you add the apple to your serving each day). Try this yummy recipe:

2 cups of oats (quick cook or normal)

1 cup natural fruit juice (orange or apple juice work well)

2 apples, coarsely grated

1 cup blueberries (fresh or frozen)

1 tablespoon honey

250 grams natural yoghurt

½ cup slivered almonds

In a large, sealed container, add the fruit juice to the oats and leave to soak while preparing the other ingredients. Grate the apples and add to the oats. Add the rest of the ingredients. Mix well and leave in the fridge overnight.

By breakfast time, the muesli is soft and ready to eat. This muesli can keep you satisfied until lunch time.

Ideal breakfast foods include:

- Low-fat cheese. Melt cheese on wholegrain toast, a bagel, or a muffin.
- Eggs. Poached, boiled, or scrambled are the healthiest ways to cook eggs. You're even better off serving the eggs on wholegrain toast.
- Fruit smoothie. Your favourite fruit and low-fat milk whizzed in a blender make a perfect breakfast.
- Porridge. A really sustaining breakfast and even more delicious if you sprinkle dried fruit or nuts on top. Go easy on the salt, for those of you with a savoury tooth!
- Pancakes. Use a non-stick frying pan or add a touch of oil spray to make thin pancakes. Top with fresh fruit and honey.
- Toast. Use wheat or wholegrain toast or a muffin.
- Yoghurt. Serve with fruit or nuts.

If you find yourself skipping breakfast because you're too rushed, try preparing your breakfast the night before. You can eat it before or after the rush starts, or take it to work with you.

Never say 'diet'

The word diet technically means the foods you eat in the normal course of life. However, the word diet has become something akin to penance – that is, a punishment for wrongdoing in the food sense. Whenever you give something up you're likely to want the thing even more, so focus instead on the healthy new foods you're choosing to eat.

What people mean by using the word diet is, in reality, a lifestyle change. Your new lifestyle is meant to make you feel satisfied, and to help you be someone you intend to continue to be for many years to come. You shouldn't be eating a certain way 'just until I lose 10 pounds.' The eating habits you adopt need to be maintainable over a lifetime.

Adding super foods to your daily routine

All foods have some nutritional value but ten foods are now known as super foods because they're extremely beneficial for your health and considered to contain the essential vitamins and nutrients needed for continued good health. The bonus is that each of these foods rated 'super' is commonly available and affordable:

- **Apples.** Always available, apples are full of antioxidants. One apple provides a quarter of your daily requirement of vitamin C as well as pectin, which can help to lower blood-cholesterol levels. Apples have low *glycaemic index* (GI), so are digested slowly. Low GI foods may help with weight control, as well as improving the long-term control of blood sugar levels for people with diabetes.

- **Baked beans.** Packed full of protein, fibre, iron, and calcium, baked beans contain low GI carbohydrates. The tomato sauce covering baked beans in the tin is a good source of lycopene, another powerful antioxidant shown to help prevent heart disease and prostate cancer.

- **Bananas.** Bananas are slightly higher in energy than other fruits but the calories come mainly from carbohydrate, which is excellent for refuelling before, during, or after exercise. Bananas are a good source of potassium, which can help lower blood pressure, and they contain vitamin B6 for healthy skin and hair.

- **Brazil nuts.** All nuts contain essential vitamins, minerals, and fibre and a small handful of different nuts eaten four times a week may help reduce heart disease and satisfy food cravings. Brazil nuts are one of the few rich sources of selenium that may help protect against cancer, depression, and Alzheimer's disease.

- **Broccoli.** Just two florets of broccoli – raw or lightly cooked – count as one vegetable portion. These little green trees, as Australian children call them, contain antioxidants, including vitamin C and also folate

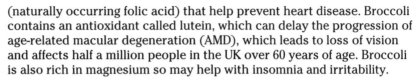

(naturally occurring folic acid) that help prevent heart disease. Broccoli contains an antioxidant called lutein, which can delay the progression of age-related macular degeneration (AMD), which leads to loss of vision and affects half a million people in the UK over 60 years of age. Broccoli is also rich in magnesium so may help with insomnia and irritability.

✔ **Olive oil.** Studies suggest that the mono unsaturated fat in olive oil is good for the heart. Olive oils can lower bad cholesterol levels, increase good cholesterol levels, and they contain plenty of antioxidants.

If you're trying to lose weight, remember a tablespoon of oil equates to the same amount of fat as the butter you generously spread on a large slice of bread.

✔ **Salmon.** All fish species are sources of good-quality protein, vitamins, and minerals. Oily fish, such as salmon and sardines, also contain omega-3 fats, which reduce blood clotting and inflammation. Studies show that eating oily fish dramatically reduces the risk of having a heart attack, even in older adults. Omega-3s also help prevent depression, and protect against the onset of dementia. My mum was right: fish is true brain food.

✔ **Tea.** The caffeine content of tea helps stimulate alertness, mood, and motivation. And tea counts towards your recommended eight cups of fluid daily, which is the minimum to avoid dehydration. Whether black or green, tea provides a good source of catechin that may protect artery walls against damage that causes heart disease. The antioxidants in tea may also prevent the formation of sticky blood clots. As little as one cup of black tea a day can provide some protection. Green tea, which is higher in antioxidants, is even better for you. So put the kettle on!

✔ **Wholegrain seeded bread**. Breads containing seeds and wholegrains have low GI and provide an excellent source of dietary fibre, which keeps the gut working efficiently. Seeded breads contain essential fatty acids. Studies show that including four slices of soy and linseed bread a day can supply a dose of phytooestrogens, thought to relieve hot flushes in menopausal women.

✔ **Yoghurt.** Yoghurt, especially the natural, lower fat kind, is an easily absorbed source of calcium and a useful milk substitute for people who can't digest large amounts of the milk sugar, lactose. Yoghurt benefits the health of the large intestine and helps relieve gastrointestinal upsets.

Losing Sleep over Losing Sleep

Busy workers frequently complain of feeling tired and having low energy levels during the daytime. Energy levels relate to the amount (and quality) of sleep you get each night, as well as the time of day, the foods you eat, when you eat, and your general health.

A good sleep generally means around seven or eight hours for an adult. However, some adults can get by quite happily with less than that whereas others need nine hours. Many studies suggest that more than ten hours sleep is too much, creating more lethargy. The conclusion: sleep can be an individual need. What's important to realise is that whatever sleep you get is better than no sleep at all.

Sadly, *insomnia* (chronic lack of sleep) increases over time. Sleeping late at weekends doesn't allow you to catch up on the sleep you need. Instead, a sleep-in may make it more difficult to sleep the next night because your body's sleep rhythms have been disturbed and you no longer feel sleepy.

Common reasons for lack of sleep include:

- **A snoring partner:** the noise of snoring is always difficult to ignore.
- **Cramped or aching legs:** this painful condition can make sleep difficult.
- **Sleep apnoea:** breathing stops for a period of time during sleep.
- **Sleep starts:** muscle jerking or a falling sensation can awake the sleeper with a jolt.
- **Jet lag:** coping with different time zones can slow your internal body clock. You can expect to spend a few days getting back to normal again.
- **A busy mind:** a good night's sleep results when the sleeper is able to switch off the thousands of thoughts, reminders, worries, and silly sayings inside their heads, and relax.

Insomnia is most often caused by worrying that doesn't stop after the light's been turned off.

To reduce night-time niggles, try these easy tips:

- **Breathe:** Breathing is the most simple and the most effective way to relax. Breathe in slowly and deeply for five seconds, and then breathe out for five seconds. Concentrate on nothing but your breathing and the feeling of your muscles gradually relaxing. Try five breaths to start, and repeat the cycle if and when you need to during the night.
- **Find 15 minutes of worry-window time before you go to bed:** Outside of your bedroom, sit down quietly and have a run through all the subjects swirling around your mind. Tell yourself that you won't deal with them now, and simply acknowledge each one. Write down the big items in a notebook so that you can assure yourself that you can deal with them the following day or at an appropriate date.
- **Keep a pencil and pad by your bed:** Sit up, write down the details, and turn off the light straight away when a new or persistent worry is keeping you awake. By doing a brain dump, you pay attention to the worry and then remove it from your mind. In the morning, look at the notepad to remind you of how you're going to deal with the issue.

✔ **Relax:** Turn off the television, or put your thriller novel down, 30 minutes earlier than usual. Find a comfortable chair, or lie down in your bed. Working up from the tips of your toes to the top of your head, consciously relax each muscle group while breathing in slowly and deeply. This exercise makes you aware of just how tense your body is, even when you think that you're already relaxed.

Obeying your body clock

Experts describe habits that help you have a good night's sleep as *sleep hygiene*. Many people form bad sleep habits that are reinforced over weeks, months, or even years.

To find the right amount of energy to deal with the waking hours, the body needs to have sleep. Try these tips:

✔ **Don't ignore your body clock.** When your body feels tired, go to bed. Your body makes the decision as to when rest is needed, not your mind.

✔ **Don't make yourself go to bed if you don't feel tired.** You only increase your worry and frustration when you lie in bed awake. In time, you associate bedtime with insomnia and discomfort.

✔ **Get up at the same time every day.** Sleeping in at weekends makes sleeping the following night even harder. If you get up at the same time at weekends as you do in the week, your body feels sleepy at the same time every night.

Watching what you eat

Although many people take the trouble to feed their bodies the right food for energy, many forget about avoiding the wrong foods for sleep.

✔ **Avoid caffeine.** Ideally, don't drink coffee, tea, cola, or energy drinks after mid afternoon. Instead, stick to water for the remainder of the day and even try a glass of warm milk. The old wives' tale is a true one – milk contains an amino acid that has been scientifically proven to enhance sleep.

✔ **Don't smoke.** People who can't stop smoking are better not smoking before bedtime. Nicotine is a stimulant that makes a person stay awake longer. Smoking can accelerate heart rate and increase blood pressure.

✔ **Refuse the booze.** Alcohol is a depressant that may make you drop off to sleep – but you won't feel truly refreshed in the mornings. Alcohol robs the body of much-needed fluids and can wake you in the night for toilet trips.

Beautifying your bedroom

Your bedroom is where you spend eight hours out of every 24-hour day. Therefore, you deserve a bedroom that encourages you to rest and recuperate for the next 16 hours of work and leisure. Try these tips:

- **Buy a decent mattress.** Use the Goldilocks mattress rule: not too hard, not too soft.

- **Darken the room.** Avoid streetlights or moonlight coming in through gaps in the curtains and blinds because these become fluoro tubes in strength when you're lying awake and can't sleep.

- **Designate your bedroom for sleep (and sex).** If the room is also used to watch television, hold telephone conversations or, heaven forbid, work on the laptop, then you can expect trouble when you try to associate the same space with sleep and rest.

- **Keep your bedroom quiet.** Buy a comfortable pair of earplugs if the neighbour's late-night arrivals, the sound of barking dogs, the snoring of your partner, or nearby traffic noise is too invasive.

- **Make sure that the room is at the right temperature.** Preferably, keep your bedroom temperature on the coolish side, then choose covers to reach your ideal level of snugness. Sleeping snugly and warm is much better than tossing and turning in the heat. Open a window for fresh air if the night is mild.

Throw away the clock

Insomnia causes a great deal of frustration which, even more annoyingly, causes sufferers to stay awake, fretting about staying awake when they should be sleeping. This is the time when you need to tell yourself to stop worrying about not sleeping and stop counting down the hours.

Many people look at the glowing dial on the clock radio and instantly calculate, 'It's 2.30 a.m. now and the alarm's going off in four hours. How am I going to be able to function properly at the staff meeting today?' Put your clock radio on the floor and out of sight. Better still, invest in a smaller clock that doesn't automatically glow in the dark. Your biggest visual stressor is now gone from sight. And that grandfather clock that chimes on the quarter hour and twelve times at midnight is right out – unless your entire household can sleep through it.

Music to sleep by

Cate's new position as the manager of a busy claims team meant that she had real problems getting the sleep she needed. 'My mind was constantly buzzing with tasks I'd forgotten to do that day, stuff I needed to do tomorrow, and issues that were not so important but kept popping up unwanted in my brain,' she said.

After seeing her family doctor, Cate changed her sporadic exercise routine to a regular one just before dinner and ensured that she did not work on her computer or watch TV for at least one hour before bedtime. She even gave up her much-treasured Saturday and Sunday afternoon sofa naps in order to train her brain to wake and feel sleepy at the same time, seven days a week.

'Cutting out my afternoon energy drink also helped, even though I thought I needed it to stay alert,' she says. Cate also likes to listen to music when the lights are out, and selects some of her more relaxing CDs to put on. 'Nowadays I don't even remember hearing the last few songs.'

Meditation for Real People with Busy Minds

Meditation is the art of quickly relaxing the body and calming the mind and is very easy to do. It is increasingly popular due to its simplicity and its ability to provide many benefits, including:

- ✔ Helping you to gently bring your mind back to meditation whenever it wanders off
- ✔ Allowing you to let go of other thoughts and distractions
- ✔ Enabling you to relax quickly
- ✔ Gaining a sense of wellbeing and health
- ✔ Improving clarity of mind and concentration
- ✔ Reducing anxieties

Many meditation techniques can take as little time as two to ten minutes. These mini meditations can help you relax and return to a more balanced state at any time of the day. Now, who can't find two minutes?

Modern forms of meditation teach you how to relax the body but still keep the mind alert. This doesn't mean alert in the 'get ready to run' sense. It means being able to notice and listen to what is happening around you, to take in sounds, sensations, or the endless thoughts and worries that buzz continually in your mind.

To make the most of meditation, you can enrol in a class and discover how to meditate with an expert. Inquire at your local health centre or ask your doctor for a recommendation.

If you prefer a more go-it-alone approach, you can find a wide range of books on the subject of meditation. Browse through your local bookshop's shelves or use your favourite book search sites to check the latest publications. You can also find a range of CDs and DVDs to get you started. Often, these aids are a better way to begin than buying a book on the topic, because they guide you straight through what you need to do, and you don't need to read and digest anything first.

Meditation can help you choose how much and how often you want to actively think about your problems. Nothing needs to be dwelt on 24 hours a day. Instead, people who do meditation commonly develop more control over what thoughts need to be concentrated on and what thoughts can be pushed aside as irrelevant.

Finally, don't get bogged down in 'doing it right'. Just taking a few moments to be still, to focus on your breathing, to notice your thoughts and imagine letting them go . . . All these things are the essence of any meditation practice and the more you do it the more it works for you in the way that is best for you.

And don't get hung up on a label either! Anything that stills your conscious mind's chatter is a form of meditation, so a lovely walk in the park where you pay attention to your surroundings and listen to the sounds of nature can be just the thing. Alternatively, gazing at a beautiful painting or listening to soothing music can give you the same effect. The key is to really focus on what you're looking at or hearing and gently allow other thoughts to drop away.

Reviving Your Sex Life

Sex is as natural to the body as food, water, and sleep. Yet, for many people, sex in a committed, long-term relationship is no longer about the physical act of intercourse. Barriers to good sex – or any sex at all – can be linked to work stress, tiredness, resentment, depression, or feeling unable to communicate openly with a partner.

Reviving a dormant sex life can be made easier by finding time to talk openly about sex with your partner because the problem is not going to be solved by itself. Solutions to a poor sexual relationship can also involve scheduling sex as an ongoing appointment – after all, you use your diary for important work meetings, events in your children's lives, dinner parties, and so on – so why not sex?

In the first 6 to 18 months of a relationship, sex can feel effortless, spontaneous, and wonderful for both partners. Sex feels like the act depicted in movies and novels – steamy, exciting, and frequent. As life goes on though, time for sex and the desire for sex can dwindle and be overshadowed by work, children, financial concerns, lack of time, or physical illness.

Discussing sex with your partner

Starting up a conversation about sex, while standing fully clothed in the kitchen, can be a very difficult and stressful discussion to have. Accusing your partner, or your partner accusing you, of being abnormal for not having sex is not going to help improve the situation. Neither is a permanent refusal to discuss it going to do anyone any good.

Sex – it can be as easy as one, two, three

Enjoying a fulfilling sex life – or indeed any sex life – after children can seem like another chore to add to the never-ending list. Here are three stages that you may try, depending on time and energy levels. Each stage is fun and can strengthen your intimacy with your partner.

✔ **Time for a quickie.** When you have small children, a busy household, and work commitments, having a 'quickie' can be simple, comforting and, yes, quick. Having a 'quickie' generally means that you grab a quick minute with your partner when the opportunity arises. Talk to your partner about quickies and then watch out for an opportunity. You'll enjoy the spontaneity of the moment, which is about as long as it takes.

✔ **Friday night sex.** Regular weekly sex always feels the same and feels satisfying. You may be feeling tired at the end of a working week so what better way to revive yourself for the weekend than with Friday night sex with your partner. Be proud of your Friday night arrangement – nothing's boring when you look forward to being together and enjoying yourselves.

✔ **Honeymoon sex.** This means doing whatever you feel like! When the kids are staying at Nanna's or having a sleepover with friends, seize the opportunity. Unfortunately, what most parents tend to do is waste this time in front of the telly or computer. Turn off the TV and go to bed.

The first step to reviving your sex life is to acknowledge that you're each *different* people with *different* levels of desire. After all, you don't like exactly the same foods, books, hobbies, or TV programmes. So having a parallel libido is unlikely too.

As with everything else in your waking hours, maintaining a sex life that suits both of you relies on negotiation. Yes, a business-like word is very much applicable to sex. Most people negotiate all day long – when to get up, what to eat, who's doing what household chores, child care, work and tasks to be completed, after-school involvements, meal times, TV programmes, rubbish bins, you name it.

Therapists are now suggesting that sex too needs to be negotiated. If you do find yourself exhausted after the day's routine, then make a time to drop the chores and enjoy your relationship with your partner. This can be something as easy as going to bed an hour earlier. Surely that's more important than putting out the garbage.

Rejecting rejection and embracing anticipation

To borrow a phrase from a very successful sporting company, *Just Do It*. A very common misconception about sex is that desire and lust must be present in order to have sex or in order to enjoy sex. Experts – yes, people do actually study sex for a living – are now finding that desire and lust aren't necessary. Expert opinion says that if a couple always waited for their desires to match, some people would never have sex again!

Instead, therapists are urging the partner with the lower sex drive to give out some goodwill sex. For the higher-drive partner, the recommendation is to focus on the sex she's getting, rather than on what she's missing.

Having sex can be enjoyable for the lower-libido partner because it shows the feelings of kindness, respect, and love that are already in the relationship. Both partners see the experience of sex as an act of love rather than a mere physical performance.

Sex is never acceptable when forced or done without consent. Sex is an action that is intended to make people feel truly loved and appreciated.

Friday night nookie: a great start to the weekend

Adam and Penny, like many people, found their sex life threatened by long working days and household chores. Here's their story of sex survival:

Adam. After the arrival of our second child, my wife returned to work four days a week and she was exhausted by bedtime. She just wasn't interested in resuming our sex life. I felt rejected and hurt and started getting irritable and cranky at her for other reasons. I can see now how this hurt her too. She was annoyed at me for not doing my share around the house or helping out with the kids.

Penny. It was hard for me to instantly find some burning desire for Adam after a long day. And I felt that when I got home each evening there was this issue between us, always there, in bed with us, every night. I didn't want to reject Adam, but I was worried that I'd lost my sex drive completely.

Penny confided her concerns to a close friend, who recommended scheduling in a weekly sex night. This is now referred to by them both as Friday night nookie.

'It's worked really well,' Adam says. 'It relieves the pressure of me always asking and getting knocked back, and Penny knows that she can get into the mood for Friday night.'

Penny agrees. It means that we don't have that tension in bed between us any more. I'm finding that I love Friday nights. I really look forward to it and make an effort by lighting candles and turning off the telly early. Afterwards feels great because the weekend's ahead of us, we feel more relaxed, and have time to cuddle and talk.

Re-establishing a connection

Reminding ourselves that sex can be comforting, affectionate, funny, enjoyable, help you sleep, release tension, make you feel closer and more able to communicate with your partner is very important.

Sex with a long-term partner may involve a lot of repetition but you can always find ways to keep sex interesting:

✔ **Build up excitement.** Leave a note somewhere, an item of clothing or even a phone message: 'Wait until you get home tonight.'

✔ **Don't compare your sex life to anyone else's.** Ignore what the magazines say. Do you really believe that people always tell the truth when they're surveyed about their sex lives? Experts acknowledge that some magazine-style surveys are worthless. Either that or there's a very busy lady in one suburb who's satisfying the entire male population in her postcode!

✔ **Don't let the gap between sex get too long.** Stick to your agreed sex schedule and remember that sex is as important as everything else in your calendar.

✔ **Female libidos can be more easily dampened.** Minimise distractions by timing sex earlier in the evening. Helping with the last chores of the day and telling her how much you love her is a great way to start an exciting night.

✔ **Tell each other what you like, want, and what you don't want.** He's not going to know if you don't gently guide or tell him and yes, he does want to please you. She's not going to know unless you tell her either.

Don't blame, ignore, or resent each other for your inconsistent sex life. Seek help from a professional if you're unable to change and improve your sex life on your own.

Chapter 5

Getting to Know You

· ·

· ·

*O*ften people struggle to keep up with what they think society expects of them. They don't feel as though they've time to sit still and think about what they'd really like to do. Before you can make any long-term plans for improving your work and life commitments, you need to work out what you'd ideally like to be doing and what you're going to do to achieve your goal.

This chapter helps you create the best conditions for the important connections with people in your life, whether that be with an existing partner, or with someone new that you're yet to meet. Finding out about what you really want and need to live a fuller life also extends to your current job situation and the importance of recognising the positive – as well as the negative – aspects of your job. This chapter also gives you tips on generating creative ideas for your life plans, visualising your goals, and setting about achieving them.

Satisfying You

Regardless of what's going on outside of work in your family life and social life, your satisfaction with your job is based on the actual job itself. Therefore, when you're making career decisions, you need to think about yourself first. No, we're not saying that you drag your city-loving family to the Amazon rainforest for you to fulfil a far-flung career fantasy, but that you consider what kind of job can satisfy you at work. Ask yourself this question: what job would I like to do that can make me want to go to work and that also won't disrupt my home life?

Blissful blogging

Taking the time to sit down and jot down your thoughts – whether they're humorous, serious, a list of chores, or opinions about world events – is an easy way to give you some 'me time' and an opportunity to think about subjects other than work and family commitments. It is also a brilliant way to discover your 'voice' – in fact, some bloggers have gone on to write books and secure publishing contracts as they realise what a talent for words they actually have.

A blog is the term used for web logs or online journals that people with a modem can view, comment on, or create themselves. They can be set up with restricted access for writers who wish to keep their thoughts largely to themselves, or opened up to the entire online community.

A blog entry can take a few seconds if you choose to write a one-liner or upload a photo. On the other hand, it can be a long, involved essay that calls on contributions from other bloggers. Many bloggers (myself included) report feeling more creative, more willing to share experiences and develop increased confidence in their writing and communicating skills after they enter the blogging arena. Recent research shows that people who make regular entries in a journal or blog are more likely to feel satisfied with their family life and an even greater number are more likely to feel that their individual opinions matter in their lives.

Here are some websites and tips to start your own blog:

✔ www.blogger.com: This is a very user-friendly site for people brand new to blogging. The site gives you explanations, a tour of what you can do and many types of blog skins, or visual designs to choose from. Even the most inexperienced blogger can manage to use this site.

✔ www.typepad.com: Also incredibly user friendly, making all this new technology really accessible and easy to use.

Finding out what work you love to do starts with finding out more about who you really are. There's a lot more to discover in yourself than you may ever have thought!

Collecting your own case studies

A useful way of inspiring yourself to continue working out what you value is to hear, read, or seek out the success stories of other people. In addition to the famed sports heroes, musicians, and celebrities that you normally hear about, the case studies we're referring to relate to the real people you know who are able to make positive changes to their lives and achieve their goals with little fanfare.

You tend to notice these people because they're like you. You see them at school fairs, in the lunch room, at the sports club, or at a friend's party barbecue. And yet these seemingly ordinary folk seem less stressed, less worried about how they appear to others, and seem quietly contented. These are the people we suggest you sit down and talk with, and ask a few very simple questions: 'How did you achieve your goals? What changes did you make so that your life became more fulfilling?'

One Saturday, Anne found herself looking through the employment section of the paper. 'I was thinking, why are you reading through here?' Anne had always considered herself lucky to have a well-paid job as a public service health manager with 12 staff and a budget of £100 million, even though she had to start work at 7 a.m. and found it difficult to leave at 5 p.m. and took work home with her.

And then a job in the newspaper caught her eye. A respected academic was advertising for an assistant. The pay on offer was half what she was currently earning but the job meant more time at home in the evenings, less time commuting, and work in a field that interested her. Anne and her partner John did their sums and realised they were able to meet the mortgage and household costs on a smaller income.

Anne took the job. Twelve months later, she no longer wakes during the night, she stops work when she leaves the office, and never takes her laptop home. 'I've contributed to research that's now sought by overseas experts, which tells me I'm doing work that makes a difference.'

Checking your cerebral health

How many times have you seen a workmate at a desk reading and instantly thought, 'Oh, she's just reading so she's not busy and I can interrupt her now'? Or, perhaps you see your partner sitting, staring out of the window in deep contemplation and assume he's just daydreaming? What you assume these people are doing is not necessarily what they *are* doing, so choosing the right time to interrupt their reading or thinking time is important. In fact, it's better to wait so you don't interrupt them at all.

Thinking time is important. The chairman of an environmental agency used to say to his employees, including me: 'Find half an hour each day for thinking time. Lock yourself away if you have to, but do it.'

Quick reads to inspire the true you

Many people enjoy reading books that help them improve their lifestyles – after all, you're reading this book. Here are some handy reads that may also inspire you to discover and to become your very best self:

✔ *Feel the Fear and Do it Anyway* **(Vermilion):** By Susan Jeffers, this book is written in a very friendly, conversational style and encourages the reader to admit their fears and recognise that they're likely to always be fearful of change and of trying new challenges. The book then helps you to attempt these changes and face new challenges.

✔ *Jonathan Livingstone Seagull* **(Harper Collins):** By Richard Bach this book is an inspirational fable which encourages you to follow your heart and soul and find the purpose of your life, despite the challenges

of wanting to fit in with the easy options and to follow the rules set by society.

✔ *Dandelion* **(Totally Unique Thoughts):** By Sheelagh Mawe, *Dandelion* is another easy-to-read story about a misfit horse who discovers how to value his own uniqueness and trust his true gifts in life.

✔ *Who Moved My Cheese?* **(Vermilion):** Dr Spencer Johnson's little morality fable concerns mice coping with their cheese supply being moved. The book can be read in an hour and makes some very valid points about how to avoid simply coping with change and instead how to anticipate and enjoy change. Its brevity means the book can be read over and over again whenever you need to remind yourself of the need to embrace change.

Most people spend far too much time running around reacting to situations, putting out fires, worrying about the next big meeting and when an issue will be resolved. They then sigh in relief and mess around a bit as a way of winding down. What they don't do is sit and think about what they learnt, how they can do better next time, and decide how best to plan for the future.

In order to achieve the kind of work/life balance you seek, you need to take some time to really think carefully about what you want long term, medium term, and short term – or even just for the following day.

Ideastorming without a flip chart

An easy and effective way to start finding the goals lurking within yourself is via ideastorming. This technique has been widely used in the workplace for years as a useful means to get a group to produce creative solutions together. Any ideas that pop into someone's head are allowed to be yelled out and written down on a flip chart or whiteboard, no matter how crazy they may seem. Ideastorming with a group of people can often generate a large amount of useful and varied ideas, which can then be evaluated at leisure.

Take some time now to ideastorm on your own and put your own goals down on paper. Don't panic. Even if you don't yet know what your goals are, this little exercise can help you. Find a clean sheet of paper and a decent working pen and sit somewhere quiet. For the next 60 seconds, write down anything and everything you want to happen within the next 12 months. Don't edit your list or cross out any items or ridicule yourself out of writing them – just get the ideas out of your head and on to paper. This process is an easy way to take the first step towards working out what dreams, ideals, and values you have, and how to work towards using these to set goals for your future.

Now go and make yourself a hot drink or get a glass of water and then come back and look (with fresh eyes) through what you wrote. Circle the ideas that are most important to you. Try not to select any more than five; if you have too many on the list, your mind tries to talk you out of attempting any of the ideas. Alongside these goals, draw another column and make a list of your values and reasons. What's really important to you regarding goal number one: You? Your family? Your career? Your home? Your hobbies? For example, your job might feed your value of 'freedom' or of 'making a difference'.

By deciding what your most important values in life are – and lining them up against each of your goals – you can get a clearer idea of what you're pre-pared to do, and not do, to achieve them. Table 5-1 shows an example of an ideastorming list of personal goals.

Table 5-1	**A Sample Goal-Setting List**
My Goals for the Next 12 Months	*Why I Want to Achieve These Goals*
A pay rise or promotion	Get experience acknowledged; help out more with mortgage; enable partner to study part-time
Get fitter and eat healthier	Feel better about myself; be more energetic, show more enthusiasm; set good example for the kids
Reduce my overtime	Improve family time; eat dinner together; help part-ner more with the kids; set example for workmates
Two weekends away each year with partner	Value time alone with partner; rekindle romance; let partner know feelings and show appreciation
Start hobby with daughter	Learn something new with daughter; discover what we find mutually enjoyable

Now that you've written down your goals, you have something real to look at. Use your list to remind you of your goals in the following ways:

- ✔ Imagine what achieving your goals will look and feel like.

- ✔ Keep the list of goals on a small card within reach – by your bedside, in your diary planner, on your desk.

- ✔ Look at what you've written and adjust the words if you need to.

- ✔ Read and reread your words.

- ✔ Read out loud and say the goals and the reasons behind them every day for a week.

- ✔ Train your mind to focus on your goals to develop a strong desire to put your plans into action.

Using visualisation to set your goals

Visualisation is an extremely effective and simple way to keep your goals fresh in your mind and to be able to 'see' the end results of achieving them.

A friend of mine, Mary, writes fictitious newspaper articles around the goals she's set, penning them as noteworthy achievements. She reckons these fun little articles help her 'see' what success looks and feels like, even if the goal is as minor as losing half a stone over winter or reading five non work-related books for no reason other than enjoyment.

Many time-management and life-planning experts use this method of writing down achievements to help set goals. What Mary is doing is beginning her goal with the end result in mind. She's looking into the future to get a better sense of what the achievement of her goal is going to feel like. Time and again we've read of successful people 'walking the walk and talking the talk' of success before they have reached it.

The founder of IBM, Tom Watson, used this method when he started the company. First, he created a clear picture in his mind of what he wanted his company to look and to be like. Then he asked himself how a successful company, such as the company pictured in his mind, can go about achieving its goal plans on a day-by-day basis. Finally, right from the very first day of starting IBM, Tom Watson began to act as he'd imagined he would.

Here's a simple three-step visualisation technique to try:

1. **Sit comfortably somewhere where you won't be disturbed, close your eyes, and take a few moments to focus on your breathing to relax yourself.**

2. **Think of an outcome that you really want. Create a picture in your mind. Begin to hear any sounds you might hear and any feelings that might be associated with achieving the goal.**

3. **Now imagine stepping into the picture as if you're looking at the movie you're creating through your own eyes. Turn up the volume on the sounds, intensify the colours, and really start to connect with the great feelings you're having as you experience this accomplishment right now.**

Take time to enjoy your movie for as long as you want. Anything you don't like, you can change, so each time you go into your visualisation you can tweak it until you have it picture perfect. Enjoy!

Setting an unrealistic goal, such as saying to yourself 'I will earn £250,000 by the end of this year' doesn't result in a miracle success story. You must break down your goal into manageable stages.

Say something like 'At the end of this year, I'll negotiate and get a salary increase from my boss; next year, I'll manage a project team from start to finish'. Include a reasonable amount of time to allow you to research your goal, work towards it, and set a deadline.

For more information on setting and achieving success and happiness in your life as a whole, check out _Life Coaching For Dummies_ (Wiley) by Jeni Mumford.

Finding What You Need to Live, Thrive, and Survive

Once upon a time all a person needed to survive was food, shelter, warmth, and company. In today's civilisation, people all but forget these basics, or take them for granted, as they strive for bigger houses, bigger toys, and bigger salaries.

As my mother once said to me, 'All these labour-saving devices your generation has now don't seem to have made your lives any easier.' She's right. People have become stuck on a treadmill of wanting more and more material objects while missing the contentment and happiness they seek.

A large part of gaining meaningful work/life balance is to find out how you really think: what is it you need and how do you plan to get what you need?

A slippery slope: Buying the stairway to happiness

Despite the fact that everywhere you turn, an advert promises that purchasing this or that wonderful product is going to bring joy and sunshine to your life, money can't buy happiness. Different degrees of wealth simply bring different types of worries. For example, some multi-millionaires can't enjoy their financial wealth because they worry that they'll lose it all. Other people in that situation find that making friends can be fraught with anxieties because they wonder if people are attracted to them because of their spending power, rather than for themselves. If you're feeling financial lack in your life, you might think that those are nice problems to have but trust me, we've met very many unhappy 'rich' people who feel impoverished in spirit. So why do people daydream of winning the lottery and buying their way to contentment?

Scores of psychological studies demonstrate the negative power of blindly pursuing material possessions, and the feelings and values that go with them. People who are more envious of others, who worry more about how many things they own, have stronger desires to acquire money and possessions, and place more importance on financial success, can find themselves becoming depressed and anxious. Desiring and using *less* can actually make your life simpler and happier.

Many people, however, thrive on accomplishing their material and success goals. The key is to be very honest with yourself about what these things give you and bring you in your life. The fancy sports car may be just what you want and give you great enjoyment and satisfaction – or it may be simply what you think you *ought* to want, only for it to turn out to be an empty pleasure.

Wanting or needing?

Affluenza is a popular term used by the British psychologist Oliver James to describe the over-consumption, debt, and stress that prosperous Western societies have developed into an unhealthy culture of overwork, jealousy, unhappiness, waste, and debt in their efforts to 'beat the Joneses'.

The dawn of the 21st century saw actual incomes, possessions, and economies reach much higher comparative levels than those of the past three generations. Yet people seem to be no happier than they were in the 1950s.

If anything, the culture of affluenza suggests that the mental and physical wellbeing of wealthy countries is declining, with major health issues, including psychological illnesses, drug use, obesity, and loneliness significantly increasing. The World Health Organization predicts that clinical depression will become the world's second-most prolific disease by 2020.

Research now reveals that having more and better 'things' doesn't increase happiness beyond a certain level, and may actually result in more unhappiness. For many people, achieving or exceeding their income goals doesn't make them feel happier. Instead, they raise their benchmarks for more financial success in a never-ending battle to furnish large homes, pay for upmarket cars, redecorate on an increasing basis, and accumulate more debt than ever before. Oliver James believes that the key to the affluenza cure is pursuing real needs over perceived wants.

One way to tell a real need from a perceived want is to ask yourself the following questions before you commit to a purchase:

- ✔ Is this item useful and will I feel the same way about its usefulness in a year, 5 years, or even 10 years (depending on the scale of the purchase)?
- ✔ How will this item enhance the quality of my life?
- ✔ Do I need this item now and why am I not prepared to wait to have it?

If your responses seem to include other people's opinions, you *may* be in danger of falling into the comparison trap. Similarly, if you find yourself saying things like 'I just *want* it', then take a close look at your motivation. Are you motivated by the spoilt child in you throwing a bit of a tantrum or by the mature higher self who is happy to give yourself a gift because you do deserve it? Listen to your wise inner voice and it will direct you!

Finding Your Soul Mate

What if you're so busy with the work part of your work/life that you never have time to date and really miss having that special someone in your life? Being single and happily so is wonderful, but if part of what you really want is a partner to share your life with, then you owe it to yourself to make sure that you create the best conditions to attract Mr or Ms Right.

Here are seven lucky tips to help you do just that, and which all provide a much more fun alternative than hanging out in bars – and fit right into your effective life balance strategy!

✔ **Do what makes you happy.** The very first golden rule is that you have to do something to make changes in your life – which means getting out there and adding in social activities to your schedule so that you can meet new folk. And that something that you do must be something that would make you happy in any case, regardless of meeting your soul mate. If you're having fun, challenging yourself, and being your best, you become naturally attractive to everyone around you. So what have you always fancied doing? Salsa? Rambling? Synchronised swimming? No matter how bizarre your choice, if you love doing it, it's worth it and you'll be putting yourself in the way of kindred spirits. Stick only to this golden rule, and you'll be fighting off suiters before you know it!

✔ **Make Internet dating work for you.** Yes, you've heard horror stories about Internet dating. And we bet you've also warmed to the odd tale of love at first sight when Internet buddies get together? If you're savvy and take heed of the safe dating guidelines offered by any reputable Internet dating site, you can have a great deal of fun, make loads of new friends, and perhaps find lasting love this way. It's also a really time-effective way of identifying hot prospects as you can e-chat to your heart's content till you're ready to meet someone in person!

✔ **Become a social networker.** The great news is that nowadays you can meet people as friends online rather than putting in legwork (literally!) going to clubs and societies. Social networking is exactly that – virtual communities where you can connect, be introduced to friends of friends and simply have fun. Less obvious than Internet dating but with so much more to offer, this may well be the best source of your new best friend as well as your life partner. You're spoilt for choice, what with Facebook and My Space, as well as professional networks like Linked-In. Don't just see these communities as being all about 'getting' – the more you give, by way of help, information, and by introducing others, the more happiness you're likely to feel because you're actually making a contribution. And you can soon be seen as the resourceful 'go to' person, which is never a bad thing for attracting great friends and potential romantic partners!

✔ **Take a class.** Combine learning with meeting new friends: if you choose your subject carefully, you maximise your chances of meeting a potential partner. Foreign languages are often good options as are cookery courses, which appeal to budding chefs of both genders. Remember the golden rule of choosing something you're interested in. Ladies – motorcycle maintenance may bore you rigid before very long, and for the men amongst you – don't even think about needlepoint unless it truly happens to be a passion!

✔ **Mix with other singletons.** A number of groups exist that are devoted to single people and which address the real need most people have of connecting with others whilst pursuing their favourite activities. One

superb organisation is called Spice (you can visit them online at www.
spiceuk.com) which organises activities, events, and holidays ranging
from skiing to needlepoint and rock climbing to meditation. Spice bases
all activities around what members say they want. Around 70 per cent of
people who join Spice are single, so it offers lots of potential for meeting
your next date. At the very least, you'll be surrounded with like-minded
folk who are up for having lots of fun and trying out new things.

✔ **Get involved.** Community projects and charity work can be a surprising
source of linking up like-minded souls. Fancy helping out to clear your
local river of rubbish? Or getting on the committee for a summer city
parade? Romance isn't guaranteed of course, but other singletons you
meet there are likely to share your values and your pride in your community too, and that's no bad thing to have in common.

✔ **Take the initiative!** Don't be faint-hearted. There are so many wonderful
people out there, one of whom may well turn out to be your true love, or
at the very least a brilliant new friend, that you'll kick yourself for being
backwards at coming forwards. Take a few calculated and controlled
risks. It may be that you 'waste' an hour getting to know someone over
coffee . . . or equally it may be the start of something beautiful. If fear of
rejection bothers you, remind yourself that regret of what might have
been can actually hurt more in the long run.

Finding Time for Your Partner

When you settled down with your partner, you no doubt believed that you
were not only in love but that you'd found your soul mate, your supporter,
your friend to the end, right? (Haven't found your soul mate yet? Then see the
preceding section.) Despite this, long working hours and the added responsibilities of keeping your domestic and social life ticking over smoothly may
make time spent with your partner rare, let alone of any quality.

The person you love most in the world is often the person who gets the least
amount of your attention. By attention, we mean unrushed time together.

Ask yourself this question: when your partner receives attention from you,
is it only to hear you complain about how much you hate your job, hate that
old bloke in the accounts department, how tired you are, how you just want
to slob on the couch, how you can't find the remote or don't want to answer
the phone. Is the only request you make of your partner to bring you a glass
of wine?

Making your partner your priority

Seven's a lucky number so here are seven ways (in order of importance) to make your partner feel like the most special person on the planet – well, on your planet.

- ✔ **Have breakfast together.** If you're both daytime workers, try having breakfast together. It may only be ten minutes and just ahead of being surrounded by school lunches, tired children, and the morning news. Setting the alarm ten minutes earlier and sitting together, talking quietly, can be quality time that's normally only associated with children.

- ✔ **Have coffee together.** Jill and Kent have three school-aged children and live too far away from their parents to arrange any short-term babysitting. They also have a mortgage, full sports and social lives, and have found that often they barely have time for more than a hello-and-goodbye relationship during the week. On Jill's one day off each week, in between shopping, washing, and cooking, she meets Kent at a cafe to have a coffee together. 'We literally savour the moment – good coffee, out of home, and no kids. It's a short time that we look forward to. We can often solve a problem in that time or talk about anything other than home and kids.'

- ✔ **Make a date at home.** Making a date to spend a night together (at home) is increasing in popularity as people who have mortgages, can't afford babysitting, or don't have a relative nearby are discovering. Tim tells me that on Friday nights he and his wife wait until the kids are fed and in bed before they have a 'picnic' dinner of smoked salmon, crackers and brie, fresh fruit, chocolates, and champagne together – all in the comfort of their own living room. 'We love it – we feel so decadent and we remember that our lives are all about us, and not about getting dressed up, or what restaurant we go to.'

- ✔ **Meet for lunch.** We've spoken to many people who find time to spend together during the work day. Joanne tells me that when Craig is in the vicinity (he travels around the city as part of his ongoing IT role), he phones ahead and meets her for lunch. 'It's a nice change from sitting at my desk with a sandwich and I get to see him in his work clothes and in work mode. It also feels like we're dating again.'

- ✔ **Say thank you.** Take one minute every day to find at least one reason to thank your partner, no matter how small. This daily effort shows your partner how much you appreciate him and reveals your respect and love. Pretty soon, he'll be thanking you, too.

- ✔ **Hold television-free evenings.** As people settle into long-term relationships, the urge grows to have a free evening together in front of the television. Instead, try a free evening together with the television turned off. Read, listen to music, talk. Don't do any chores, just be together. Even one hour together, without any other distractions, is time to have a decent conversation, a cuddle, or even hit the hay a little earlier to revitalise your sex life.

✔ **Use technology.** People complain about the unwanted chains that email, telephone calls, and mobile phones put on them, but communication technology can also work to your advantage. Typing a couple of sentences to your partner (keeping things clean of course) takes less than a minute and is an effective way of telling him how much you love him, how much you appreciated his cooking dinner last night, and so on. SMS can do the same.

Dealing with just the two of you

Chances are a date at home can work wonders for your sex life. However, if you need some help, refer to Chapter 4 about how to re-establish a connection that will make you happy. Other important items in a perfect-partner plan include equally dividing the household chores and finding time to get away from the city, the grindstone of work, domestic drudgery, and children every now and then.

Having equal housework loads

'Absence makes the heart grow fonder' but not when it comes to doing your fair share of housework. Household chores are very important because no partner ever wants to be forced to ask their significant other to help with the chores. This action implies that the responsibility for the chores belongs to one person, and that's not the case. You may not be surprised to find that arguments about household chores are second only to arguments about money in marriages. A useful way to address this lingering issue is for you and your partner to sit down and set your priorities for housework together. What do you feel are the most important chores? What skills do you both have (for example, my husband is an amazing cook whereas I (Katherine) hate cooking and would much prefer to tidy up afterwards).

What chores do each of you absolutely hate doing? What one partner hates, the other may be able to do in exchange for a job that he hates doing. You can also think about what chores you'd consider paying someone else to do, including cleaning, ironing, or lawnmowing. Hundreds of companies and franchises specialise in unpopular jobs, such as dog washing, gutter cleaning, gardening, and delivering groceries.

Taking twosome time-outs every year

Even the busiest couples can – when they grab their diaries, sit down together, and plan far enough ahead – find two weekends every year to go away. By going away, we mean without laptops, reports to read through, or children in tow. Two nights are better than one if you can manage the children's care arrangements, and two nights feel more like a mini holiday than a mere 12 hours away from home. Try to find a location less than an hour's drive from your house so that you don't waste too much of your precious time travelling. Arrange a late check-out from your accommodation if possible, so that you can enjoy the morning.

Use these times to practise being 'in the moment' with your partner. Focus on really listening and paying attention to them, maybe as you did when you were first getting to know each other. These times away are a great opportunity to block out everything else and experience exactly what is going on in the present moment as you appreciate the person you're choosing to share your life with.

Caring for your kids together

Not only do you yearn to spend time with your partner, but a recent US study shows that parents today spend around half the time with their children than their own parents spent with them. We suspect that the situation is similar here. To get more time back, try these simple steps:

- ✔ **Book a day off every month.** Even if you stay at home together, this special day off must exclude take-home work, answering the mobile phone, or doing any housework. Turn off the television and the computer, and don't accept any social invitations – this day is time just for the family. If you want to get out of the house, try a long drive with a picnic, a day at the beach, or a visit to a museum or wildlife park.

- ✔ **Find 15 minutes.** Every parent can find 15 minutes to spend with his or her children in the evenings after work. This family time can be cuddle time, taking a walk together, sitting in your child's room talking just to him or her alone, or looking through the day's school work.

- ✔ **Have a weekly family night.** Schedule one week night for every member of the family to be home in time for dinner. Take turns to cook dinner (or in teams) and then take turns to decide what the family does after dinner – play a board game, see a movie, go for a walk, watch a favourite television show – together.

✔ **Share dinner together.** A family meal gives everyone time to find out about each other's lives and also a time for parents to listen. Genuinely listening to your children during your evening meal assures them that you're interested in them and value their role in the family.

✔ **Tell them their strengths.** When tucking your kids into bed or getting them up for school, try telling your kids what you admire about them. Children love hearing about what you value and appreciate – as does your partner.

For more ideas along these lines, see Chapter 17.

Judging Your Job Situation

Company mergers, changes of government, restructures, and external audits can all serve as unpleasant reminders that the workplace and jobs are constantly changing. In fact, the only constant *is* that everything changes, so we'd all better get used to dealing with it and making it work for us!

Noting what you like about your job

When you worry about the future of your job, or feel as though you're under pressure to do too much work in too little time, the job starts to lose any enjoyment or worth. Using a two-column table (shown in Table 5-2), you can write down what you *do* like about your job to help clear some of the negative thoughts you may be experiencing about your role at work.

Table 5-2	My Job and Me
What I Like about My Job	*Why I Like My Job*
Good salary	Better than offered in job market; able to pay mortgage and bills
Interesting work	In an area I studied and enjoy; new projects come up regularly enough to keep me interested; boss gives me good opportunities to develop new skills
Friendly and productive team/colleagues	Good support staff; professional team; all easy to approach and work with; good senses of humour and camaraderie

(continued)

Table 5-2 *(continued)*

What I Like about My Job	Why I Like My Job
Decent hours	Flexitime; can work from home at busy times; can leave early for kids' sports days, and so on
Pleasant office surroundings and facilities	Good office space and equipment; prompt IT service; easy administrative processes; located near decent shops and park

Reading back through your list is an extremely effective method of seeing how many qualities you like about your work. Instead of the 'glass is always half empty' outlook, having a list of positives on paper can make you realise that your job has a bit more going for it than you first thought. This exercise makes it easier to think cohesively about improving your current or future job prospects with an unbiased eye.

Acknowledging what you dislike about your job

Now the time has come to look at what you dislike about your job and the reasons why, similar to the list shown in Table 5-3. Having the list in Table 5-3 and the list in Table 5-2 in front of you helps you to decide what aspects of your job you can live with, and what aspects of your job you need to change, whether immediately or further down the track.

Table 5-3	What I Don't Like about My Job
What I Don't Like about My Job	**Why I Don't Like My Job**
Salary	Believe I can earn more by looking for a new job elsewhere; financial commitments too heavy; big expenses coming up (school fees, new car)
Work no longer challenging	Been in same position for too long; need challenge and change of scenery
Uncooperative staff	Too much bureaucracy; delays in getting things done; no attention to detail; unable to motivate staff
Too much overtime	Overtime 'expected' instead of 'appreciated'; need to be seen to be an achiever; tiredness, stress
Low morale	Too many restructures; people leaving

Now you have two lists to read through and compare. Your likes and dislikes are going to start forming themselves as questions in your mind. Is the salary worth my staying in a job where the people are unfriendly? Should I risk leaving this comfortable and interesting job to find one with more money but more overtime?

People often tend to leave their current job and overlook the opportunity to fully examine the job to see if better ways of working can be achieved. Chapter 8 discusses how to find new working arrangements and how to negotiate them with your boss.

An effective way of assessing the value of your current job is to look at it from an outsider's point of view. Questions an objective onlooker is likely to raise (which in turn can be useful for you) include:

- Do you have any control over your job or decision-making?
- Do your colleagues enjoy their jobs?
- How can the job be done differently?
- Have previous people in your job moved upwards?
- What does your manager think of your work performance?
- What longer-term strategies can be put in place to make the job more satisfying?
- What opportunities does the job offer for training, career advancement, and challenges?

Ask yourself these key questions and you may find that by looking at your job differently, you may see solutions rather than problems:

- Can I improve my job performance?
- Can I take on any additional duties or responsibilities to make my job more interesting and satisfying?
- What new ideas can I try and discuss with my manager?
- What training can I take at work and outside work?

Answering these questions honestly can make you realise that the ways in which you take responsibility towards improving your current job are important to your future.

Part III
Size Isn't Everything: Small Changes That Work

'Your disguise doesn't fool me for an instant,
Mr Dinsthropp! You work from home, you're
35 years old & you're too lazy
to make your own lunch!'

In this part . . .

Getting the right work/life balance may be a big goal in your life but some of the best techniques involve doing lots of little, simple things to create your much-needed space. In this part, we look at the dragon of procrastination and show you easy ways to slay it. You can find great tips on managing your time more effectively and get a better appreciation of how you can create a little oasis of peace and calm in your busy working day.

Chapter 6

Finding Lost Time and Space

. . . .

. . . .

*N*o, this chapter isn't a sci-fi journey through the space/time continuum to find the perfect work/life balance. Instead, this chapter is a look at the two main culprits that lead to all that lost time and space: procrastination and clutter. Procrastination is the thief of time, and collecting clutter in your life and work is a sure-fire way to reduce the actual and mental space you need to focus on your priorities.

In this chapter, you discover how to recognise the signs of procrastination and apply the 'Do it now' principle to any tasks that take less than ten minutes. You also find out how to decrease your daily distractions, by controlling your phone calls and emails rather than letting them control you.

We look at how long jobs take, the advantages of batching similar work together, and the importance of delegation, which not only relieves you of work but provides valuable training for someone else. Finding 30 minutes on Friday afternoon to review your work and plan for the week ahead can free your mind to enjoy the weekend. Planning the week ahead is easy to do and easy to turn into a useful Friday task.

So with effective time management under your belt you'll also be able to make many simple changes to your working environment, creating more space and clarity to do your work. A messy desk and the wrong equipment causes inefficiency that can cost you hours of extra work. How many of you have a colleague who constantly walks over to ask to borrow your stapler because they can't find their own in the mess on their desk? A tidy desk would have saved your colleague, and you, five minutes each.

Dealing with the Long Hours: Overtime

People in the UK work some of the longest hours in the world, with the number of people working more than 50 hours each week rising significantly over the past 20 years. Much of this work is unpaid overtime, and overtime makes trying to balance a meaningful career with a personal life very difficult.

Very few people want to work hours of overtime, but feel trapped in an over-time culture. Parents may enjoy their work and enjoy being parents but they can't find ways to get away from the office when their day's work should be over. And single folk, intent on climbing the career ladder, sacrifice other important things in their lives, such as time with friends, family, hobbies, and interests, often because they feel that they have to be seen to put in the hours in order to be viewed as effective.

True effectiveness is just the opposite – working smarter, not longer, is the strategy that pays off.

One way to avoid overtime is to examine how much of the day's work you've put off till later because of that dreaded problem – procrastination. (See the upcoming section on this topic.)

Many people, hoping to avoid long hours, end up multi-tasking by juggling emails, phone calls, voicemail, MP3 players, SMS, laptop computers, and talk-ing on the mobile while driving through traffic to a meeting. These days, elec-tronic gadgets may be seen as the largest contributors to work overload.

Procrastination: Putting Off Until Tomorrow What You Can Do Today

Procrastination is when you intend to take an action but keep putting it off. In other words, you know that you've a task you must do, but you keep making excuses not to do it. You may start with the very best of intentions but, when emails and phone calls flood in demanding immediate response, the hours, days, weeks, and months can roll by without the original job being done.

Procrastination increases feelings of guilt because you haven't done the job, causing anxiety about what may happen if the job's not done, and creating negativity about the stress and additional workload that putting off the task causes you.

In addition, most people tend to overestimate the time a complex task is going to take when it's a job they dislike. When you dread doing a particular task, you may put off doing it, believing that later you may be more in the mood to complete it. This task then weighs on your conscience and, as the day moves on, the task looms larger on your list of jobs to do, creating even more worry about getting the job done. Are we reading your mind in procrastination mode about right?

Only you can tell whether you're a procrastinator. However, the following questions can help you decide:

- ✔ Do you do anything else to avoid a chore you dislike doing?

- ✔ Do you allow yourself to respond to every single email, chat to colleagues walking past your desk, jump up to fill your cup from the kettle boiling in the staff kitchen, and answer phone calls – even if the phone calls come through on someone else's phone?

- ✔ Do you find yourself justifying procrastination on the principle that 'I work best under eleventh hour pressure'? Even if you do always pull it off, you probably know that you'd have less negative stress if you beat the habit. And eleventh hour tactics sometimes lead to cutting corners and making errors.

- ✔ Do you spend ages planning out how you're going to do something and shuffling the papers around rather than just getting on with it?

Here's some irony for you: just as I (Katherine) was writing this section on procrastination (in a B&B overlooking a glorious cliff top and sea), the B&B owner's cute terrier, Candy, came sniffing at the door. I instantly stopped writing so I could rush outside to pat her ears and scratch her tummy. I could have kept writing my allotted number of words and waited until it was time for a morning tea break to seek her company.

When you look busier than you are

Procrastination can be given the status of 'need' for a job to be delayed because you're terribly busy. Many people have the impression that a person whose mobile is constantly ringing, whose briefcase is always full, and whose hands are always frantically tapping on her PDA must be important. This assumption is as untrue as the existence of the Super Woman.

Do it now in action

The following office example of procrastination may sound scarily familiar to you:

You arrive at your desk, sit down, look at the papers scattered all over the place and pick up one of them. 'Oh, this is from Roger.' You clear some space and start a 'To do' pile, placing Roger's on top. You pick up a second piece of paper, thinking, 'Oh yes, I have to call Beth back about that missing quote . . .' and place that paper on the 'To do' pile. The third item is a letter of complaint from a customer. 'Hmm, I need to answer this by the end of the week,' and this paper goes on top of the pile. A fourth item is a bit of a problem: 'I'll have to chat to the boss, next time she's around, about this one,' and on the pile goes the problem. The fifth piece of paper is placed on a new stack you probably call 'To do later' after you've decided that 'Yes, I need to take care of this but not urgently.'

What happens next is that you waste time shuffling through the papers, re-reading the papers, making 'do later' decisions and then re-reading them again when you get another moment to stop what you're doing and look at the papers that are waiting for you. No wonder you feel as though you're not achieving anything!

You're not alone. A few years ago, one of my roles was to help other colleagues clear out their desk spaces in order to set up some real work-and-time management strategies for them to use. My colleagues showed me their own piles of self-described 'To do', 'Do later' or 'Waiting on info' papers and they'd stand back with their hands spread as though to say, 'You can see how overloaded I am.' Instead of getting a sympathetic response from me, they'd be shocked when I asked, 'So, why haven't you cleared your desk yet?'

My colleagues' answers included, 'I haven't got around to it yet', 'I need to ask someone about it' or 'It may take too long'. I'd interrupt with, 'Well, show me. Don't put that phone call reminder on the pile, deal with it now.' Again, after a few 'Are you sure?' and 'But it may be boring for you to sit there and watch me' remarks, the colleague would make the phone call. I'd set my watch timer and reveal to them afterwards that the task had taken only two minutes. After working through at least three other tasks from their 'To do' pile, this colleague realised that applying the Do It Now principle was a way of quickly and effectively eliminating some stressful items from their desk.

People can appear to be excessively busy because they force themselves to respond to everything immediately. Some tasks can wait and others can be worked on before procrastination is used as an excuse because you're too busy to complete an important task.

In other words, appearing busy gives you the excuse to put off the job that you don't like because you can argue that, as you're busy now, you can attack the job later. The problem is that later, you're still busy doing that time period's immediate jobs and so the delayed job never gets done.

Doing it now – well, within ten minutes

Kerry Gleeson, in his book *The Personal Efficiency Program: How To Get Organized To Do More Work in Less Time* (Wiley) says people are as clever about doing jobs as they are about putting them off. Gleeson coined the term 'Do It Now,' which many other time management experts have universally adopted. *Do It Now* means you act on an item the first time you ever touch it or read it. This doesn't mean you must start working through an entire project, or make a decision that's not your responsibility to make, but rather to do the part of the work that you can do straight away.

Disciplining yourself to do a task within the next ten minutes rather than delaying the task seems like simple advice. But, as you know, changing habits can be difficult.

You can complete a surprising number of tasks in less than ten minutes. That's right – less than ten minutes. What takes far longer is the time to make up excuses for not doing the work, re-reading the work to assess when you can do it, and putting the work back in the 'To do' pile without completing it. You can complete one or more of the waiting tasks in that wasted ten minutes of shuffling papers.

Here's what you can do within ten minutes (if you don't do anything else at the same time):

- ✔ Delegate a task to a trusted colleague
- ✔ Draft a response to a letter
- ✔ File or dispose of papers that don't need action or reading
- ✔ Leave at least three informative phone messages
- ✔ Photocopy, post out, or fax an important document
- ✔ Respond to three urgent emails
- ✔ Return several phone calls

If you do these tasks one at a time, without worrying about the next task or without straying into reading non-essential emails, or setting up new piles of work, you're going to be amazed at how much work you've achieved.

Don't keep looking through your 'Pending' or 'Do later' piles of paper if you don't need to shuffle them. Picking up reminder papers and re-reading letters wastes time and adds to your stress. Ignore messages and emails that you don't need to deal with right now. Moving from one job to another, rather than spending a considerable time on one job, makes the day longer.

Not every job can be done now

So you're going to deal with your pile of jobs now rather than put them off. But what happens when you start to pick up a piece of paper on your desk that reminds you to phone a client, and the client doesn't answer your call? Follow some of these tips to get the job done:

- Find out if anyone else at the destination of your call can help you instead. Or have your assistant or a colleague follow up the call for you. If you need to make the call, find out when your client is in the office and schedule the call in your diary.

- Leave a message that passes the client on to your colleague who has the information the client needs. This means you don't have to take the call again.

- Look at the message to see if it contains information you can gather before returning the call to avoid your having to ring again.

- Leave a detailed message that gives all the info the person requires, so that you can avoid playing phone-tag.

Doing the worst jobs first

Next time you're in a cafe or restaurant, notice how many people apply the 'Worst first' rule to eating. It's not only children who dutifully eat their beans and carrots before they touch their chips; adults also laboriously chomp through the side salad before attacking their steak with chips and all the trimmings.

We're not advocating eating healthy food first in order to eat bad food, but the philosophy of doing the 'worst' tasks first can work for you. Selecting a task you enjoy the least, and doing that task first, achieves two positive results:

- The job is completed and you don't get that sinking feeling of dread that can be with you all day if you keep putting it off.
- The next jobs seem more pleasant to work on.

Reading about facing up to your less-favourite tasks first is fine in theory. But how do you actually make yourself do the more unpleasant jobs?

Try the following tips:

- **Clear your mind.** Many thoughts whirling around your brain have nothing to do with the actual task facing you. By working through and completing minor tasks that take less than ten minutes, not only can you get a lot of work done, but doing so removes a lot of your niggling worries about work you haven't yet tackled.

✔ **Do a job once.** Stop creating piles of paper that you plan on working through later. What looks like organisation and making priority piles is actually paper shuffling for no purpose – 'later' may never come. Be firm with yourself and do one task at a time. Don't look at the next piece of paper until the first one is completed and removed from the pile.

✔ **Schedule sensibly.** For true effectiveness, keep an eye on what jobs are both urgent and important. Be flexible enough to focus your attention on anything that could come under the label of 'busy-work' at appropriate times. Just because you receive your mail first thing in the morning doesn't mean you have to attend to it then if you have a critical deadline to meet. Routine is great, so work out if you have regular quieter times when you can plug in these tasks.

✔ **Do jobs while they're still easy.** Through painful experience, I (Katherine) know that tasks I don't want to face, however small, end up turning into larger, more destructive, and highly embarrassing problems later. When a task is a minor irritation, or you sense a small problem arising, deal with it *now* and the problem is solved. Merely hoping for problems or unwanted tasks to disappear can be far more dangerous. Unresolved problems have the potential for turning into crises.

✔ **Ignore distractions.** Many interruptions occur when people ask for an explanation from you about why the job you were supposed to do isn't done yet. No one likes wasting time chasing up work that's missed a deadline, and neither do you enjoy spending your time making excuses and having to respond to requests for project updates. When you do the job straight away, a significant amount of your interruptions disappear. (For more on this topic, see the next section.)

Reducing daily distractions

Ringing telephones, constantly arriving emails, and knocks on your door can be unwelcome interruptions that prevent you from focusing on the task in front of you. However, unless you live and work on a deserted island, you can't always stop others from assuming you're available to deal immediately with their needs. Despite that, you can avoid these interruptions to a certain extent:

✔ **Delegate.** If you have someone to assist you, take it in turns to take each other's phone calls during busy periods.

✔ **Get rid of backlogs.** Backlogged work creates more problems for you because this work doesn't go away and you have your current workload to complete as well. Schedule at least one hour a day to identify backlogs that must be completed. Decide which of this work takes priority and clear that first. Work out why you have a backlog and put steps in place to prevent the same issue becoming a backlog again. Little and often is the way to go here, and five minutes' attention a day on tiny, routine stuff like filing is usually more effective than blitzing for an hour a week.

✔ **Pat yourself on the back.** Guess what, you're getting the work done. You're not procrastinating – you're *actionating*! Yes, we accept that the word 'actionating' is not likely to make the *Oxford English Dictionary* in the near future. But hey, you deserve a positive verb. You're finishing your jobs within ten minutes and already your day is more productive. (For more on the ten-minute theory, see the section 'Doing it now – well, within ten minutes', earlier in this chapter.)

✔ **Schedule an hour per day to return phone calls.** Batching up telephone messages means that you can follow up queries or prepare information before you call. You can even try a voicemail message that tells your callers that you return calls at a certain time of the day, for example, between 2–3 p.m.

✔ **Schedule twice a day to check your emails.** Be strict with yourself, because answering emails is tempting (and time-consuming). Stick to your times, read work emails and leave personal or non-essential emails for your personal time. That way you quickly return to your work. You also build up the right expectations with colleagues who no longer take advantage of your good nature in responding immediately!

✔ **Schedule rest breaks at manageable times.** Work rest breaks into your diary so you can set times for completing specific tasks and then take a break, knowing that you've achieved something. This way you feel refreshed and ready to start on the next task.

✔ **Shut your door.** People generally respect team members who shut their doors (or post up a Do Not Disturb sign at their desk) to discourage interruptions. If not, start that culture in your workplace. Talk to your colleagues and establish team norms, such as 'When my door is closed, I don't wish to be interrupted unless in an emergency. I respect other people's needs to do so as well.'

✔ **Think about what you're about to do, not what you haven't done.** Constantly worrying about what you haven't achieved doesn't help you get your work done. Concentrating on the past wastes your time. Does dwelling on what hasn't been done get the job done? No. If you start your working days thinking about the past, you're already behind the starting line.

✔ **Turn off your electronic gadgets.** Switch off your mobile phone, pager, and PDA when you're attending a meeting or working on a specific project with a tight deadline. Electronic gadgets have message facilities, so you won't miss out on anything important.

✔ **Unsubscribe to outdated or useless email newsletters.** Email newsletters clog up your inbox and waste your time reading when you don't need them. Regularly review which mailing lists, newsletters, and updates you need.

✔ **Make a to-do list the night before.** This closes off the day nicely and enables your unconscious mind to start working on your tasks and solutions while you sleep! Having a ready-made to-do list also helps you to take advantage of the energy of the morning, getting straight into what you need to do.

Tidying Up Is Not Just a Job for Slow Days

Although people pay attention to their personal cleanliness by making sure that they shower and wear presentable clothes to work, many leave their desk spaces looking far messier than they'd consider acceptable at home. Many highly trained professionals can write informative articles, design engineering specifications, or stitch a wound, but have no idea how to organise the space in which they work. This observation is often swept aside with comments, such as, 'They don't pay me to do housekeeping.' A cluttered workspace makes it more difficult to do the work you're paid to do.

For example, imagine you decide to appoint an accountant to do your tax returns this year. If you walk into the accountant's office and see an overflowing rubbish bin, a stack of financial magazines balanced precariously on top of a haphazard bookshelf, and a distinct odour of old banana, are you going to feel confident that this accountant is organised and professional enough to deal with your finances?

Chefs are always taught to 'clean as you go': all food scraps, spills, and sticky messes have to be tidied up after a long shift in the kitchen. Art students, too, are taught to properly seal their paints and wash their paint brushes so that they're not damaged. Chefs and artists start with a clean environment each day. Arriving at work to a clean and tidy desk space, which contains your most important tools and the work you need to complete, makes sense.

In this section, we look at how to apply the chefs' clean-as-you-go method to desk spaces. Doing this is easier than you may think. Clearing up space during the day, and completely at the end of the week, prevents build-up of unwanted clutter that makes working effectively so much harder.

Having the messiest workspace doesn't mean you're the busiest worker

For many people, filing documents out of sight creates concern that they won't be able to find the documents when they need them. Some people also like having older files of completed projects on their desk to enhance the perception that they're very busy and important. What happens is the reverse. When I see 'historical hoarding', I assume the person isn't organised enough to archive the information, or worse – the person is putting up a wall to prevent new work challenges.

Discovering that out of sight is not out of mind

Many people worry that when they can't see papers on their desks, they forget to work on them. What happens instead is that the workspace gets filled up with what some people call 'visual noise' that makes people feel like giving up before they start. The end result is that what they think is current work is actually old and irrelevant information that makes locating bits of paper and file notes for their current work even harder.

During desk-cleaning exercises, I (Katherine) find that at least 75 per cent of paper found on desks isn't needed for that day's – or week's – work.

File away the out-of-date files on your desk or in your drawers. Allocate the freed spaces only for files that you're currently working on. Better still, get with the paperless office programme and apply good file management principles to your work on your computer. By keeping only your relevant files, you can locate information faster and increase your efficiency. Finding a draft document in a folder (paper or electronic) while you're on the phone talking to your client makes life a lot easier.

You can divide your working files into four categories:

✔ **General Information:** this file includes key telephone numbers, account codes, financial details, and regular procedures.

✔ **Matters to be discussed:** this file effectively contains any queries or issues that need permission or advice from someone else. If you answer to, or supervise more than one person, set up an individual file for each person.

✔ **Monthly functions:** you may need several of these files, depending on which monthly tasks and reports you're required to use on an ongoing basis.

✔ **Project files:** give project files their official names so that if you get 'hit by a bus', any of your colleagues can find them and instantly know what you were working on and at what stage you were.

As soon as you complete your projects, or the regular functions cease to be your responsibility, file them away. Reassure yourself that they're not destroyed. You can locate them when you need them – and your workspace is no longer cluttered.

Replenishing your toolbox

If you don't have the proper supplies on hand for doing your job, your tasks take longer as you waste time searching for or borrowing what you need.

When I (Katherine) started working for a busy director responsible for managing more than 100 staff , he asked to borrow my hole punch, struggled to find a pen to jot down notes during telephone meetings, and had only one tray to hold his handwritten phone messages and working files.

What he lacked was the basic stationery items required to do his job. He became one of the first 'victims' of my desk-clearing course. All of the stationery items he thought he didn't own were found amid the clutter. Excess boxes of pens, dozens of sticky note pads and far more items were returned to the central stationery cupboard. The broken staplers, blunt scissors and ancient rolls of no-longer-sticky tape were flung into the bin. The result was a clean workspace with a drawer full of essential equipment in good working order.

The fantastic four: Desktop trays to make your life easier

The following four trays on your desktop should keep your clutter, and your mind, organised and every paper filed where you know that you can find it:

- ✔ **In tray:** This tray is for brand new work, not for storing any problems, stuff you've handled several times or reading material. You take documents out of the in tray and do something with them immediately, even though you may just make a relevant phone call and file the document away. This tray spends most of the day empty.

- ✔ **Pending:** This tray is for current work that you're holding while you wait for information. Pending doesn't mean procrastination. The tray contains papers that you began dealing with but were unable to finish (for example, you're awaiting a return call, you were interrupted to do a more urgent task, or you require information from another colleague). This tray should be checked every day so nothing languishes for longer than two days.

- ✔ **Out tray:** Put your finished work here. Each time you leave your desk to go to the toilet or have a coffee, remember to take your completed work out of here and distribute it.

✔ **Reading:** This tray can be a hard one to control. I (Katherine) tend to find that a reading tray can soon become a Leaning Tower of Pisa, filled with documents I'd like to read but never do. This tray needs some brutal decisions. If you're given a document that's vital to read, put that document on top of the pile. Read through the table of contents and executive summary to decide whether this is a document you need to read through now or later. If the document is 'interesting, but not vital', put it at the bottom or see if someone else in your workplace may find it more useful to their work. If it's 'interesting but not relevant', then bin it – that bin under the desk is the handiest 'tray' of all.

Loosening the Chains of Email and Phone Calls

Mobile telephones and emails allow you to work virtually anywhere you like and still be in constant contact with your work colleagues and customers. What you need to watch is that phones and emails can demand your attention immediately and take your mind away from your core work.

You can take control of telephones and emails by deciding when you're going to respond to them. Treat phone messages and emails like faxes, posted mail, packages, and reading material so that *you* decide what needs to be dealt with first, rather than responding to which screams the loudest.

Easier emails

Receiving up to 150 emails a day is not unusual in a busy workplace. The way to deal with this many emails is to respond immediately and then delete them (if that's your company policy) or file the email message (if that's the way your company records emails). People often don't delete emails (or move them to appropriate subfolders) after they've read and answered them, which creates an unnecessarily cluttered inbox that becomes more stressful for you as it grows longer.

Effective ways to make managing emails easier include:

✔ **Creating email files.** Every email system includes facilities for filing away emails that you're not ready to delete yet. Click and drag pending emails out of your inbox into an appropriately named file.

✔ **Reading your emails only twice a day.** Don't read emails until you've time to respond to them. Schedule half an hour in your diary to read, respond, and delete emails first thing in the morning and, say, 3 p.m. in the afternoon.

✔ **Responding immediately and deleting.** Respond to emails that need less than ten minutes (which is most of them). Then delete the email from your inbox so you have one less task staring at you on screen.

✔ **Saving paper.** Electronic mail was introduced to save paper. Remember! Printing emails defeats the paper-saving purpose. Unless the email needs to go into a paper file, don't print it.

✔ **Turning off the automatic reminder notification.** This is the single most useful way to save time if your workplace permits you to do so. Turning off the automatic notifier means that you don't know what you have coming in until you've time to find out. It also stops tempting you to interrupt your work and stray into email checking.

Valuable voicemail

Voicemail is one electronic system that more than satisfies me, that is, when voicemail is used correctly. Perhaps we should tell you what *voicemail* – the ability for someone to leave a message on your phone at work for you to retrieve later – should not be used for:

✔ Avoiding calls that you should be taking.

✔ Deleting messages without listening to them first.

✔ Forgetting to check it twice daily.

✔ Having an out-of-date outgoing message on it (for example: 'I am available five days a week' if you're now working three days a week).

That's the negative stuff out of the way. On the positive side, voicemail can offer the following advantages to help your work day:

✔ Enable you to listen to all messages, write down the details and prioritise them in order of importance and urgency, get the information requested and return the call at a suitable time.

✔ Be set to automatically pick up your phone calls after the first, third, or fifth ring, if you're not following the 'avoiding calls' tip. If office rules permit, leave your phone on silent or the very lowest decibel ring so that you're not distracted from your work and wondering who's just called and why.

✔ Leave an outgoing message to your callers as to your availability. For example: 'I'm out of the office this week but can return your call on Monday the 27th.', or 'Please note that I can return your call at 2 p.m. today.' Messages enable your callers to find out when they can expect your call.

✔ Leave a message suggesting what information your callers should leave on your voicemail. This sounds so basic, but people don't always leave their full names, phone numbers, and reason for calling. Leaving a message on your voicemail safeguards against receiving useless messages, such as 'It's Ed. It's urgent you phone me back.' You don't know where Ed's from, what his concern is, or his number! As a better alternative, include something like this: 'Please leave me your full name, what company/organisation you're calling from, your contact number, and the reason for your call so that I can get back to you with the information you need.'

✔ Write down the date and time the call was received. Practical information can help you decide the priority of each call, especially if you've been out of the office for a few days (although we're hoping you had updated your outgoing message to advise your callers of that fact!).

Dealing with incoming phone calls

Not everyone can access voicemail (see the preceding section). At one organisation where I (Katherine) worked, voicemail was forbidden. The MD wanted everyone to answer the phone within three rings to ensure good customer service. This approach can be very effective when everyone in a team is knowledgeable about the same subject. However, when you're in a workplace with separate and specific projects, having to answer a call only to say, 'Sorry, I have no idea. I'll have to get Fred to call you back' is just wasting the caller's time, Fred's time, and your time, when ideally the call should have been taken by voicemail.

Nevertheless if voicemail isn't available to you, you can easily develop a team phone-share system in your workplace. Arranging to transfer your phone to someone for a couple of hours in the morning – and you doing the same for them in the afternoon – gives you both uninterrupted time to do your current work and deal with returning your calls later.

Returning calls

In addition to the hundreds of emails you may receive during the course of a day (see the section 'Easier emails' earlier in this chapter), you may get 20 telephone calls a day, each requiring your time and attention. (Of course, this figure is much higher for call-centre employees whose contracts require them to answer and deal with phone queries immediately.)

Taming the telephone at home

Justine says: 'When our home phone rings after a long day at work, I never want to answer it. Even though I know that the caller is probably someone I care about and normally would love to speak to, having another phone conversation is not what I want.

'My husband and I now leave our answering machine on between 5 p.m. and 8 p.m. because these are the hours that are most important to us and the time to spend with our kids. Telemarketers don't leave messages, so you often hear a click as they hang up. My parents and friends now know that leaving a message is better and we'll get back to them sometime soon.'

Batching telephone calls means that you allot a particular time each day to return any calls you've received. Batching your calls can:

✔ Help you decide which telephone calls have priority.

✔ Help you get the information required to return the call effectively.

✔ Save time without interrupting your current work.

Some people occasionally put off returning some calls because they know that the person they're calling likes to talk, and talk, and talk. With calls like this, honesty is the best policy. At the very start of the conversation, be clear that you're pressed for time, that you're tired after a long day, or that you're in the middle of cooking dinner. The important people in your life do then come to respect your needs, especially if you find other, better ways of maintaining a strong connection with them.

The Art of Delegation

Delegation is when you give tasks or duties to someone else as your representative. That is, you forward tasks to a colleague.

Far from being a public admission of not being able to cope, delegation is a very positive step. Good delegation can:

✔ Free your work time

✔ Provide on-the-job training opportunities for others

✔ Show a colleague that you value his or her work

✔ Show trust in a colleague's work and experience

Recognising and using effective delegation

A good delegator actively demonstrates the following elements in their day-to-day work:

- Ensuring that staff members fully understand the work required of them and the deadline for submission of the work.
- Finding the right person (with the right skills, experience, and availability) to do the job.
- Giving staff opportunities to develop new skills by providing them with more challenging tasks and responsibilities.
- Giving a staff member the task as soon as possible to allow enough time to complete the task effectively.
- Helping develop a timeline or project plan with the staff member (if needed).
- Keeping up to date with the progress and remaining available for queries and advice.
- Maintaining responsibility for ensuring that the task is done, but publicly crediting the person who did the work.
- Providing clear instructions to the person receiving the task and explaining why the task is important.

Organising achievable follow-up systems

Delegating tasks to others doesn't mean that delegators can then 'wash their hands' of the task. The delegator continues to take responsibility for ensuring the job is completed well and is on time.

Good delegators need to keep monitoring the tasks they have given to someone else to do without unnecessarily interfering with the task. The delegator also is available to the staff member when information or assistance is needed. This may seem like walking a fine line, but it isn't. After you decide on a date when the work is to be returned to you, make a note of that date in your diary. If the task is relatively simple to complete, then no monitoring is necessary. Tasks that take several days or weeks to complete need follow-up with the staff member at specified stages of the work.

Bad delegation equals a bad boss

I once worked for a department manager who sat on tasks, for which he hadn't the skills to tackle or was too busy to complete, sometimes for weeks. On the afternoon before a report was due, he'd call me into his office and ask me to 'drop everything' to complete the work. His instructions about the task were often very vague. This all-too-frequent ineffective delegation produced negative outcomes:

✔ An unsatisfactory result due to lack of information provided, unclear instruction, and not enough time to complete the job.

✔ A stressful workplace because of the crises points.

✔ Blame for the person the job was delegated to when the task was not completed satisfactorily because of lack of time.

Not surprisingly, he's no longer a senior manager.

Fortunately, your electronic diary can assist with delegation. I (Katherine) used to have problems finding an opportunity to talk to my director for advice. Now I use our software's 'invitation' feature on the electronic diary to see when he or she (and others we need to meet) is free. Then I can set up meetings for a time that's convenient for both of us. Remember though that modern mobile phones, often integrated with diaries, can be a blessing and a curse. On the one hand they help you to be more effective and on the other hand they can make getting away from work issues even more challenging. Build in the self discipline to monitor how you use these gadgets and make sure you break off from connection during times when you're focusing on quality personal space.

Ideally, you need to set your electronic diary to the one-week-at-a-glance viewing option. That way you can clearly see what's on your plate for the week without worrying about meetings or appointments that may be overlooked (out of sight, out of mind).

Your diary can do much more than merely record your upcoming meetings. With responsibilities and tasks that take more than ten minutes to complete, book a time to do them in your diary and stick to that time. Respect that booking as you would any meeting you've scheduled with your boss. For example, you have a monthly expenditure report due on the first Monday of every month. Schedule your diary to run the report by the Friday morning beforehand so that you've time to analyse the report and be prepared to present and/or discuss it on Monday.

Maintaining Your New Habits

You're saying 'No' to procrastination, doing a job immediately it arrives in your in tray, keeping a clean and organised workspace, delegating work where appropriate, and planning your week ahead. So how do you keep up these new habits when the realities of unplanned events, interruptions, and emails come flying at you on a Monday morning?

First, you look at your diary to see what lies ahead of you for the week. Stick to that schedule as much as you can – hopefully, you've scheduled two time periods each day to check your emails and batch your phone calls. Keep this up so you've more time to concentrate on other important tasks, as you've boxed emails and phone calls into specific times.

Block out the first hour (or two if you're determined) of each day for yourself. If you're an early bird, then you can think, plan, read, and get a few non-contact tasks (for example, writing a letter, working on a report) done before other colleagues arrive for work.

Of course, no one can fully plan their eight-hour day. With the best will in the world, you still need time off for the toilet, having a glass of water, a cup of coffee, lunch, conversations . . . let alone an urgent task.

Easy and effective weekly planning

I make sure not to schedule (or attend) any meetings after 3 p.m. on Fridays and – when I have the power to do so – set deadlines for Wednesdays or Thursdays to give breathing space for any unforeseen events. This means that my weekend can start without any work worries hanging over me.

Book half an hour in your diary on Friday afternoon so that you can:

- Add in rest and 'lag' times, to travel to and from meetings, take a mid-morning break, and lunch or mid-afternoon break – everyone needs to take a breather!

- Book in half an hour at 3 p.m. on Fridays for your weekly review and planning. By making this a regular weekly event you become better and better at properly planning your working time.

- Open your diary (electronic and/or paper) at the 'week-at-a-glance' view.

- Prioritise tasks and meetings, the most important at number one, the least important at number ten.

- Put in the regular meetings you've already committed to, then schedule in chunks of time for your tasks and meetings as per their priority order.

- Write down all of the tasks you need to do the following week.

You deserve an early start to your weekend

An engineer friend of mine always leaves his office at 4 p.m. on Fridays. He noticed a few years ago that when he arranged to leave early on a Friday to catch a plane for a holiday or to go away for the weekend, he was able to get through all the work in time to leave comfortably at 4 p.m.

'Why not do this every week?' he reasoned. 'I now know that on Fridays I have seven hours to do my tasks instead of the usual eight hours and I'm out the door at 4 p.m. whatever the weekend holds.'

For every appointment, task time, email reading or phone-call time booked out in your diary, put in 15 minutes of 'lag time' between each entry. This allows for any delays, urgent tasks, or simply recovery and thinking time before tackling the next job in your day.

If you're asked to complete a job that wasn't planned but is urgent, then this job makes a dent in your planned work. You may have to delay one of your other tasks to the next week. This is what we call covering yourself. If you're asked to do another task, take your diary in with you. Show the diary to your boss and say, 'Yes, I'm happy to help you, but let me show you what I've got on my plate today/this week so we can plan what can be done next week.' This means that your boss is aware of the tasks you're doing and you're not displaying a reluctance to be a helpful team member, and you're able to negotiate a different timeline for the new task, or for the task that it replaced.

Chapter 7

Being a Legend in Your Own Lunch Time

. . . .

In This Chapter

▶ Taking a break to refresh yourself

▶ Working out at lunch time

▶ Catching downtime in the office

▶ Eating delicious food

. . . .

The days of hour-long lunch breaks where everyone drops what they're doing and walks out of the office at the same time are long gone. However, experts are finding that all workers need to get away from their keyboards at lunch time in order to feel refreshed and more productive in the afternoons.

This chapter shows you how to start taking your lunch break (and regular, smaller breaks) without feeling guilty or that you're letting down the workers who don't stop for a break. We include useful ideas on activities you may like to try during your lunch time, after you eat and before you return to your desk.

Lunch breaks can also be used to do personal chores to save valuable time after work or at the weekends. This chapter gives you tips on how to shop for clothes, do your banking, and stock up on groceries in your lunch hour.

 Dinner time is time for a break. Dinner might also be a time to spend with loved ones, especially when you take the trouble to sit around the family table and discuss the day's events. If you live alone, it is a wonderful opportunity to celebrate the peace and tranquillity of your day and truly enjoy the experience of taking time to eat nourishing food. (Go to Chapter 10 for ideas on how to make dinner a special daily event to help you regain balance in your life.)

Breaking the 'No Lunch Break' Trap

The levels of obesity among UK adults and children are on the increase. However, that knowledge is usually not enough to motivate people to get out and exercise. You have genuine motives for wanting to exercise – to improve your health, increase your energy levels, keep your weight down, be part of a team, or just because it makes you feel good – but the time factor may prevent you from doing much about your exercise goals.

The need to exercise is one very powerful reason why you benefit from clawing back your lunch time. If you're like me, you have full-on work and home commitments that you struggle to juggle. Therefore, you may decide to sacrifice your lunch break to fit more into your day. You may also be telling yourself that if you spend lunch time at your desk, you won't have to work overtime, and maybe – just maybe – you can even leave a bit earlier than usual.

What actually happens is that eating an unhealthy, additive-packed sandwich over your computer while continuing to work, doesn't give you much more time and can actually reduce your productivity and disturb your work/life balance. Many experts agree that most people aren't able to be fully productive in the office for eight hours straight. Our eyes, brains, hands, and bodies need rest stops and an occasional change of scenery in order to work at their best. Ask yourself these questions: will you be more productive if you take five minutes to bolt down a sandwich and continue working on the report until you have a blinding headache? Or should you get up, do a few good stretches, go for a walk in the fresh air, have lunch outdoors, and come back to the report with a clear head and a refreshed body?

Instead of working through your lunch break, see the break as your own special chunk of time – to rest and do what you feel like doing, not what you think you have to do.

Escaping your office

If you find that you rarely get any 'alone time' at work, then definitely reclaim your lunch break. You've a right to step away from your work, eat your midday meal, and refresh yourself. Make an appointment with yourself – no job, home, or family responsibilities for the next 30 to 60 minutes.

TIP

Using your lunch break effectively

If you take your lunch to work (and avoid wasting time in takeaway shops) you can try:

✔ **Avoiding the lunch rush.** Schedule your lunch breaks earlier or later than the standard lunch hour to avoid the worst of the lunch crowds.

✔ **Donating blood.** Use your lunch hour potentially to save someone's life – after you've made your important donation you get to lie down and have a cup of tea and a biscuit (without guilt!).

✔ **Enjoying the local park.** Find a pleasant spot you enjoy to walk or sit in for half an hour.

✔ **Having a nap.** In some European countries, a two-hour siesta is still a tradition. We're not suggesting you slump at your desk for two hours, but if you have your own office, you may be able to catch a power nap at lunch time. Make sure you flag that to colleagues, of course – you don't want anyone to accuse you of snoozing on the job!

✔ **Learning something new.** Many local councils and inner-city university campuses hold lunch-time lectures and concert series. Read the local paper that covers the area you work in to find out what interesting events are on.

✔ **Leaving the car at work.** Whenever possible, choose activities within walking distance of your work so that you can get some exercise and avoid the hassle of driving and having to search for a park in a busy area.

✔ **Using the phone and the Internet.** Make a few calls – to your parents, or friends you haven't seen in a while. Use the Internet to shop, catch up on current events, or enjoy your favourite websites – subject, of course, to any policies that are in place at your company regarding accessing the Internet for private use.

✔ **Visiting the library.** Browsing and reading in libraries can be very relaxing. Choose a book and keep it to read at lunch times. Modern libraries offer DVDs of films as well; pick up something you can enjoy with family or friends without having to make an extra trip to the video shop. Go back every couple of weeks to return or renew borrowed materials.

✔ **Window shopping.** Check whether your work area has any interesting antique or art shops, or shops selling whatever takes your fancy.

TIP

Leaving your work place during your lunch break gives you a genuine escape as well as providing opportunities for exercise, errands, fresh air, stretching, thinking, and reading. Bring a simple and healthy lunch from home so that you don't have to waste precious time in queues at a takeaway shop or café.

Exploring your surroundings

Get out of your office. You heard: Get Out! We mean it in the nicest possible way, of course. When the time comes for your lunch, collect a good book and your walking shoes, and head outdoors. Find a spot on a secluded patch of lawn, under a shady tree, or bag a park bench and treat yourself to a chapter of a novel you've been wanting to read. Or don't sit down at all. Spend your break exploring your surroundings and getting some quick and easy exercise. If you work near a residential area, take a walk through the neighbourhood and collect ideas for your own house and garden.

Completing time-saving tasks

One really irritating aspect of working full-time is having to spend one week-night or the best part of Saturday doing the grocery shopping. You see hundreds of other tired and stressed working parents with shopping lists and unhappy kids in tow, trying to find that dream parking spot just outside the door of a shop that sells everything you need.

Lunch time at work can be the perfect time to carry out minor chores that would otherwise eat into your valuable weekend time. I usually ride my bike or take the bus to work and have fairly thoroughly explored the area surrounding my office to find out what services and shops are available.

Whether you're based in the city, or further afield in an out-of-town business park, you can explore the surrounding area to source shops and services to visit in your lunch break:

- ✔ **Bank:** Legend has it that people queue in banks at lunch time but this isn't often the case. Many people today bank online or via the ATM so if you need to visit the bank, you won't find the lines of customers who used to do their banking in their lunch breaks.

- ✔ **Hairdresser:** I (Katherine) don't consider myself a 'high maintenance' person so a simple haircut fits well into my lunch break. This again saves time because haircuts on busy Saturdays always take longer than during the week – and you have to juggle them with taking the kids to their weekend activities and doing the washing.

- ✔ **Mechanic/car servicing outlet:** If you have a reasonable car service station near your office, then book your car in for work to be done while you're working. Most open from 8 a.m. and offer same-day service. Nothing is worse than losing your car at the weekend when you need it for leisure activities.

✔ **Pharmacy:** Drop off prescriptions on the way to work so the filled order is ready for collection at lunch time. This avoids prescription queues on Saturday mornings.

✔ **Post office:** Post offices are no longer just for stamps. As well as paying bills over the counter, you can buy watch batteries, stationery, gifts for overseas friends, jewellery, children's presents, and books.

✔ **Supermarket/deli:** If you have only a small shop nearby that's a bit pricier than the larger stores, then buy just what you need that day. If you have a larger shop, then buy only what you can fit into your shopping bag or backpack. These degrees of shopping during the week don't cost too much more money and cut the weekend shopping back. This strategy can work really well if your workplace provides a nice big fridge for chilled items, but remember that others might have the same idea. You could consider investing in a cooler bag or stick to non-refrigerated items.

Sometimes, more time to spend with others is your goal. When your day is crammed with work, family, and home, your lunch break can be used to catch up with friends, and for a little romance – sounds better than a lacklustre, shop-bought salad at your desk, doesn't it?

TIP

Avoiding places you don't want to be at lunch time

You can find so many great places to visit in your lunch break, but other places offer situations that add stress rather than giving you a chance to relax. Please don't do any of these:

✔ **Eat at your desk.** Multi-tasking is messy and doesn't allow you to simply sit back, rest, and enjoy what you're eating. If you eat at your desk, you're multi-tasking because you have to deal with colleagues talking to you, the phone ringing for you, and – horrors – the boss demanding your presence. And you're probably going to over eat later in the day because you can't even remember having lunch.

✔ **Eat on the run.** My grandmother didn't approve of eating in the street so what would she think of eating on the run? It's about digestion – which can't work properly when you're stressed and hurrying somewhere while gobbling down a sandwich – and presentation – which can be very ugly, dropping food on your clothes as well as on the ground.

✔ **Enter fast-food places.** Yes, healthy fast-food options do exist, but why buy a tub of yoghurt or a salad (at twice the supermarket price) in a place that smells of hot chips. Stay away!

✔ **Visit the pub.** Alcohol is not a good idea for alertness or health and some work places have a clear no-alcohol policy. Add to that fried pub meals and you'll find that visiting the pub is even worse than eating at your keyboard.

Use your lunch break as an opportunity to get to know your workmates. By asking a new colleague or someone you want to get to know better to join you for lunch out of the office, you can increase morale and make a stronger connection. You may even discover you share similar hobbies, sense of humour, or interests that can lead to a friendship outside of work. Try developing your chats into a regular power-walking session.

You can even use lunch breaks to catch up with longstanding friends who you don't see often enough. Find out if any of your friends live or work close to your work place and arrange to meet them for lunch. You can offer to bring the sandwiches and they can bring the coffees or juices. If your parents or other relatives live close by, take your home-made lunch and make a quick visit. Making this a monthly routine can ensure that you don't lose touch.

Sometimes, the people you spend the least amount of time with are those you live with and see every day. You love each other dearly, but time at home can get too busy for you to talk about the subjects you need to discuss. If you work near each other, get together for lunch. Take a quick walk in a park, or meet for a cup of the best coffee in the area. Decide to talk about matters related to chores, kids, or housework. Or decide to talk just about yourselves. Live on the edge and try holding hands across the table, looking into each other's eyes as you talk. Hopefully you can re-ignite a tiny spark that may still be flickering after the kids are in bed.

If your partner or best friend works too far away to meet up with you in person, make lunch time a chance to pick up the phone. Eat your lunch and then head to a pleasant spot with your mobile phone to find out what's going on in your partner's day. If mobile phone bills scare you, use the office phone, if your employer doesn't mind you making personal calls in your lunch break. You can also send emails to your family and friends, updating your family's news.

Getting Physical in Your Lunch Break

Physical exercise is so good for you that many doctors are now agreeing that it can be just as effective as medication in alleviating depression. How you feel emotionally and physically plays a huge part in helping you to feel more balanced and to take the action that you need to take to make positive changes, so building in at least a little cardio on a regular basis makes a lot of sense.

Many people believe that you have to train like a marathon runner to get any real benefit from exercise. Not true. Just getting physical pumps lots of 'happy' chemicals around your system – you don't have to be Paula Radcliffe winning a gold medal to experience a runner's high! In fact, many studies show that moderate physical activity helps protect you against a wide range of diseases such as diabetes, stroke, colon cancer, and breast cancer. Medical experts have also found that moderate physical exercise reduces the risk of osteoporosis and can help in the treatment of depression.

This raises the question: what does moderately vigorous activity actually mean? Nothing too scary. Any activity that causes you to start breathing a little bit harder than usual and causes your heart to start beating faster than usual is moderate exercise. For example, if you can still talk normally (just), but you can't sing, you're exercising at about the right level of intensity.

Exerting yourself easily

Examples of suitable activities you can do at lunch time include:

- **Bike riding:** Get out in the fresh air if you have some nice wide open spaces near to your place of work.

- **Swimming:** Great for people who are overweight (or not) and who have a swimming pool nearby.

- **Walking:** Very easy to do and good for nearly everyone because you're doing a 'weight-bearing' exercise. Walking helps protect against osteoporosis in the legs, hips, and back.

- **Working out at the local gym:** Many gyms run lunch-time classes for busy workers. The classes last 30 minutes so you have time to shower, dress, and eat lunch afterwards. Check out if your employer has a deal with your local gym and save yourself some money too. Your work place may even provide shower rooms for employees to use. Lots of companies do now, and if yours doesn't you could make a case for it as part of your staff wellness policy. (See Chapter 8 for tips on getting buy-in from senior management on work/life balance initiatives.)

Regaining strength through resistance

As well as doing 30 minutes of moderately vigorous activity on most days of the week, taking on some resistance activity, such as lifting weights, and flexibility training (for example, stretching) is important. Resistance training helps to maintain your strength and muscular endurance, which is even more important for older people because their muscles lose strength with ageing. Resistance exercise is the only form of activity that slows down the rate of loss of strength. Exercises such as push-ups, sit-ups, and chin-ups are good examples – and they're free.

REAL-LIFE STORY

Making time for a run

My friend, Ian, is a very keen runner who's completed four marathons and plans to do more. He loves to run at least three lunch times each week.

Ian says, 'I used to feel bad about taking 40 minutes to run 5 miles and then another half hour to shower and eat lunch when everyone around me was still working and grabbing a bite to eat at their desks.

'Then I thought about how healthy and refreshed I feel and how I seem to be the most energetic and positive person by mid afternoon. At that time of day, my workmates are getting tired and starting to reach for the coffee and chocolate biscuits, which I reckon makes them feel worse. I now start work at 8 a.m. and leave at 5.30 p.m. so I can have my runner's lunch – and I'm proud of it.'

Organised and non-competitive exercise classes can be good for people who struggle to find the time and/or motivation to exercise. Examples include aquarobics (a good start for the unfit, the elderly, or beginners); karate; spinning (on bikes, not at wheels with wool in your hands); aerobics and circuit training. Pump and step classes can also provide an effective way to extend your social networks by organising a few of your workmates to attend a class with you.

In addition to your daily 30 minutes of exercise, try boosting your activity by heading back to your place of work using one of the following:

- ✔ Riding a bike if you have access to a safe route
- ✔ Using the stairs instead of the lift
- ✔ Walking short distances rather than driving

REMEMBER

Speak to an expert first

It's important to ask for professional advice from a personal trainer at your local gym about how you can safely and effectively include resistance training or weight training. You don't want to take on more than your body can handle and end up with injuries.

A suggested weekly training schedule may comprise four days of brisk walking, swimming, or bike riding for a total of 30 minutes each day, plus 10 minutes of resistance exercises on one day and 20 minutes of light weight training on another day.

Your personal trainer can organise a written routine for you to follow and the cost of one appointment is minimal.

Successfully Staying Inside

Don't let a rainy day stop you from having a lunch break. You have many opportunities to eat your lunch and then escape into the online world instead.

Close your office door or stick a note on your desk saying, Out to Lunch. Now you've a chance to catch up with your favourite bloggers or websites (making sure that they're 'work-friendly', according to your employer's policies). Do a little blogging yourself (have a look at Chapter 5 for more details on how and why blogging is good for you). If that's not an option at your work, take in a book or magazine (not work related) and venture off somewhere quiet to read.

Stretching your productivity

Taking regular breaks from sitting at your desk, especially if you're working on a computer, is very important. Some work places recognise the importance of stretching exercises and have software that pops up on screen to remind the user to take a break. For people who don't have access to such reminders, we suggest you try setting an alarm to go off every 20 minutes, stand up and do some stretching exercises. The break from work is refreshing and the exercises keep niggling shoulder pains away.

Saving time in cyberspace

The Internet is a wonderful invention for people who work at a computer and have little time. In the past ten years, I've (Katherine) embraced the Internet and I was proud to note that I bought all my Christmas presents last year via the World Wide Web, and they were wrapped and ready early.

Online shopping, banking, entertainment, and travel is a very easy way to do a variety of chores, without having to waste time travelling, browsing, or queuing for service.

Buying your groceries online

The good old Internet has lifted a huge load from my shoulders because I no longer have to waste Saturday mornings at the supermarket. I can order groceries online in my lunch break or at home in the evenings. I also find that the fresh fruit and vegetables my online grocer selects for me are far fresher and better in quality than fruit and vegetables that have been handled by dozens of other frazzled shoppers before my hands get to them.

Websites worthy of your lunch time

Let me share with you my favourite websites that I visit when the weather's too yucky to go outside and my brain needs a breather:

- **The BBC** (`www.bbc.co.uk`): Keeps you in touch with national and international news and links to TV and radio downloads if you've missed a favourite programme.

- **Gone to lunch** (`www.gone2lunch.com`): Actively encourages desk-bound workers to play online during their lunch breaks.

- **Internet Movie Database** (`www.imdb.com`): An incredibly detailed site on just about every movie ever made, with links to actors, directors, and, sometimes, their errors.

- **The Weather Channel** (`www.weather.co.uk`): Ever optimistic, even in the face of the evidence, we Brits need constant updates of the weather to plan our travel and leisure activities!

- **The Times newspaper** (`www.timesonline.co.uk`): For keeping abreast of the daily news and access to lifestyle articles.

- **Wikipedia** (`www.en.wikipedia.org/wiki`): Can tell you pretty well the meaning of anything. Just remember that anyone can contribute to Wikipedia so it may not always be accurate.

Most large retailers and supermarkets run online sites that enable you to view their products and place the items you want in a virtual 'shopping cart', where they're kept until you enter the virtual 'checkout'. At the 'checkout', you're asked to check your order and add or delete items as needed. The site then calculates the cost of your order including delivery charges – and asks you for your delivery address and credit card details.

Shopping online doesn't stop at clothes and groceries of course. After you explore the likes of Marks & Spencer (`www.marksandspencer.com`) and Next (`www.next.co.uk`) for the former and Tesco (`www.tesco.com`) and Morrisons (`www.morrisons.co.uk`) for the latter you can always hop across to the hundreds of other sites which help you source gifts and leisure items. For example, Amazon (`www.amazon.co.uk`) is a good stop for books and eBay (`www.ebay.co.uk`) can cater for just about anything if you really want to bid for a bargain. A huge amount of choice is available to you at the click of a mouse and the only challenge you may have is limiting your browsing time to ensure that you get all your work done!

Banking in the boardroom

Most UK banks allow you to avoid paperwork and lunch-time queues by offering a wide range of electronic banking services, including credit card payments, bill payments (telephone, gas, electricity, and council tax), cash withdrawals, account balances, account transfers, loan applications, and information on current interest rates.

A lot of busy workers have leapt into online banking with enthusiasm because you can do your banking when it suits you and you have immediate access to information about your accounts. To encourage the use of online banking, some financial institutions offer cheaper interest rates, or no-fee services, if you bank electronically. If you're 'techno savvy' like my husband (and unlike me) you may even be able to plan a budget by downloading information directly into a spreadsheet or financial planner.

Finding Fabulous Foods

Perhaps health experts now need to emphasise the importance of eating healthily at work. Everyone knows the importance of cooking and eating good quality, fresh foods at home. But finding time to make a healthy lunch to take to work can seem impossible.

Last-minute lunches from the vending machine, the cafeteria, or the deli down the street can seem your easiest option. Unfortunately, this usually means you're consuming foods – even in light or low-fat meal options – that lack vital nutrients and are often loaded with sugar. As a result, your energy levels and weight levels suffer the consequences.

Cutting your lunch

Making your lunch to take to work puts you in control so you're not limited to eating the leftover pastries from the breakfast meeting when you get hungry. Preparing your own lunch means finding five to ten minutes to put something healthy and edible together.

Try starting a new habit you can stick to. If you're not a morning person, pack your lunch before going to bed, or while you're making dinner. And if you're worried about leaving all that good food in the fridge in the morning rush, put your car keys inside your lunchbox – now you won't forget it.

Yummy lunching

Easy and nutritious lunch ideas you can consider are:

- **Bring along breakfast for lunch:** If you're too busy to whip up something decent for breakfast, grab some fruit and yoghurt and ensure that you have your missed-out meal for lunch. You could have a bowl of low-fat, high-fibre muesli or heat up porridge in the microwave. It may seem unusual but these foods are filling, nutritious, and can help you resist temptation in the afternoons.

- **Choose wholegrain over white:** This goes for rice as well as bread. When cooking rice for your evening meal, cook extra to take in for lunch the following day. Add chopped cooked vegetables (again, cook extra to put in your lunch rice) or salad ingredients for a filling lunch that can be eaten cold or heated up.

- **Lovable leftovers:** The nicest lunches are often the delicious-smelling and tasting curries, pastas, casseroles, and burgers, heated up from the night before. Just get into the habit of cooking extra to take to work for lunch, or to freeze for lunches later on.

- **Sandwiches:** Even famous chefs swear by the humble sandwich as the easiest way to make a satisfying meal. Don't feel limited to ham or cheese. Try taking a bread roll to work and add a small tin of flavoured tuna (lemon, ginger, and so on) with freshly sliced avocado. Take along some interesting cheese and salad ingredients and add them at the time of eating to avoid your roll getting soggy.

- **Satisfying salads:** Salad on its own is not likely to stop you feeling hungry for long. Bulk up your salad with nuts, low-fat cheese (goat's cheese is particularly good for flavour), capers, boiled egg, dried toast cut into pieces (for a low-fat version of croutons), chicken, smoked salmon, or tinned tuna.

- **Start up a lunch club:** Talk to your workmates – would they be interested in organising healthy lunches to share? You can set up a kitty (like a coffee club) and decide what healthy meals and ingredients to buy, or bring along something to share. Being good is easier if everyone around you is being good too.

- **Try tins of soup:** A can of healthy soup can make a great emergency back-up lunch when you're frantically busy. Look for low-salt, vegetable-based soups made with chicken, beans, or lentils for protein. Many healthy brands are low in fat and are loaded with vitamins and fibre. In addition, try good old baked beans – a cheap and easy source of fibre and vitamins.

Refer to Chapter 4 for information on super foods to give you more ideas on what to bring in to work.

Sensible snacking

We know, we know. You take to work fresh fruit, dried fruit, and nuts and then they sit in your desk drawers going mouldy as you push them aside and go for the chocolate bars instead. Some good advice to bear in mind is: 'Just *don't buy* the bad things. That way they won't be there to tempt you.'

Not walking down the confectionery aisle takes willpower. Amuse yourself instead at the deli counter and tell yourself that those snacks are much better for your health.

Healthy work snacks to try include:

- **Fruit:** Try buying a week's worth of fruit on Monday and storing it in a fruit bowl. The aim is to make sure the bowl is empty by Friday. This approach gives you an opportunity to walk to your local greengrocer and buy what's fresh and in season. Your workmates, too, can participate in the office fruit bowl experience. As long as you have a decent fruit knife available for coring and peeling, peeling fruit is as easy as opening a packet of crisps.

- **Houmous and pitta bread:** Okay, you have to put the houmous in the fridge, but the pitta bread can live in your drawer (if fresh) or slices can be kept in the freezer. You can buy many brands of low-fat houmous, tzatziki, and other vegetable-based dips that taste great.

- **Milk:** When was the last time you had a long glass of milk? Milk is very satisfying and can help keep the need to eat cakes and biscuits at bay. If milk doesn't appeal, try buying a carton of low-fat flavoured milk for a sweet treat that isn't too bad and goes a long way towards ensuring that you have your full calcium intake.

  Milk won't be such a good choice for you if you're lactose intolerant, which many people are these days. If this applies to you, try soya milk instead, which is a healthy alternative.

- **Peanut butter:** Spread peanut butter on wholegrain rice crackers to keep your stomach from growling.

- **Seeds and nuts:** You can buy sunflower and pumpkin seeds in bulk at supermarkets and health stores. Nuts of all kinds provide a great source of energy. Eat only a small handful of different nuts if you're watching your fat intake.

- **Yoghurt:** Yoghurt has more flavours, varieties, and sizes than we can list here. Find the flavour you enjoy and keep a supply in the office fridge (with your name on them).

Curbing caffeine

Apart from water, coffee and tea are the world's favourite drinks and ones that people turn to at work to keep them going. We also find that having a coffee or tea is a social activity. The time taken to make the drink in the work kitchen, hold a conversation with a workmate, wait a minute or two for your drink to cool and then drink it, contributes to you taking a mini break from the workload.

However, both coffee and many black teas contain the C-word: caffeine, which is also found in cola drinks, energy drinks, and chocolate. Health experts are asking you to use a bit of judgement in how much coffee or other caffeine-laden foods you take each day.

On the plus side, caffeine is believed to help prevent heart disease and some cancers. Caffeine also increases alertness and is considered to improve concentration. Your liver processes caffeine, which then passes into the bloodstream, entering the brain. In the brain it connects with dopamine receptors (they make you feel good) and adenosine receptors. Adenosine slows down nerve cells, causing drowsiness. When caffeine connects to the receptors, these nerve cells speed up, leading to feelings of restlessness and alertness. Sports supplements have caffeine included to fight against fatigue but they're banned in some sports. No wonder we reach for the caffeine when we hit a slump at work.

Although caffeine is not addictive, it's certainly habit-forming. Your body develops a tolerance towards the drug, which means you need more caffeine to produce the same results. Excessive caffeine intake (more than four or five cups of strong tea or coffee a day) can cause tremors, an elevated heart rate, frequent urination, nervousness, anxiety, stomach upsets, and insomnia. If you drink coffee before bed, you may find it harder to sleep. In addition, you may also only get deep sleep for shorter periods, making you feel less rested when you wake. Because caffeine acts as a diuretic, it can increase your rate of dehydration if you don't also drink water.

Withdrawal symptoms occur after a day or so without caffeine. The brain becomes very sensitive to adenosine, causing blood pressure to drop dramatically. The most familiar withdrawal symptom is the caffeine headache. Other symptoms can include irritability, nausea, and – ironically – drowsiness.

To work out how much caffeine is safe for you to drink, it helps to establish how much caffeine is in an average serving (see Table 7-1).

Table 7-1	Common Sources of Caffeine
One typical serving of . . .	*contains this much caffeine . . .*
Chocolate (30 g)	20–60 mg
Black tea (150 ml) – depending on type of leaves and how long you brew	30–100 mg
Cola (375 ml)	approx. 40 mg
Instant coffee (150 ml)	60–100 mg
Energy drink (250 ml)	80–100 mg
Espresso-made coffee (150 ml)	approx. 90 mg
Drip-percolated coffee (150 ml)	100–150 mg

Health experts recommend that adults have less than about four cups of strong drip-percolated coffee, or five to six cups of tea. Ideally, you're better drinking far less than that, and trying to avoid any caffeine drinks at all in the afternoons. Instead, train yourself to drink a green tea with less caffeine, which is a good source of water and full of those valuable little antioxidants. You may also find that after some experimentation you become even fonder of one of the many fruit or herbal teas on the market. Or be even kinder to your body and stick to water.

Part IV
Preparing to Work for Work/Life Balance

In this part . . .

Collecting examples of employers who adopt more flexible working practices that profit them and their employees is a great idea. In this part, we explain how you can find examples to compare with your own industry sector. Doing your homework before you talk to your boss puts you in a strong bargaining position to ask for more flexible working conditions. Here, we show you how to put together a compelling argument.

Do you have a boss who eats into your free time? In this part, we provide you with ideas on how to remain assertive and keep up your self-esteem. Finding a good mentor helps too.

And don't forget fun – yours and your family's. This part also covers how to get the most from your holidays and have time over to help your local community.

Chapter 8

Moving Your Manager towards Work/Life Balance

● ●

In This Chapter

▶ Understanding your boss

▶ Showing how work/life balance benefits everyone

▶ Explaining what you want

▶ Negotiating your way to success

▶ Handling opposition

▶ Accepting no for an answer

● ●

*Y*our boss may respect and appreciate the work you do and see that you want to balance your work and your personal life. However, people in management positions have their own goals to meet and these often affect the decisions they make. Putting it bluntly, your boss needs to think about matters other than just you.

Managers base their planning, decisions, and outputs on what best suits the entire team/department/company. They work out how your requested change in your working arrangements is going to affect productivity, staffing costs, performance, work outputs, and other staff.

This chapter shows you the importance of putting together a good business case that not only gets your boss to give you the go ahead for more flexible working arrangements, but also results in real benefits for the work place.

Managers Are People, Too

If you enjoy your job, the best way to get a better work/life balance is to ask your manager for more flexibility. This flexibility may involve one or more of these options:

- **Banking hours:** This is when you work overtime to be used up at a later date, such as for a school sports day, medical appointment, and so on. Banking hours can also be used to make up time when you need to leave work earlier than normal for an unplanned event, for example, caring for a sick child.

- **Compressing your working hours:** Some people choose to work ten hours, four days per week, in order to have one working day off each week.

- **Having flexible starting and finishing times:** For example, you may start at 7 a.m. and leave at 3 p.m., or start at 10 a.m. and work until 6 p.m.

- **Switching to reduced hours:** For various reasons, some people find they cannot continue to work full-time. Negotiating shorter working hours means the employee stays in the same job (job sharing is one solution to this) and the employer keeps the skilled and trained worker.

Nobody enjoys walking into the manager's office and asking for something that's not yet being offered. You may have a very good reason for requesting a change to your working hours or structure but you *must* make sure that you have fully researched what your manager – or your company – needs from *you*.

You know what you want – what does the boss want?

We're fairly confident that we know what you want from your work and your life:

- An enjoyable job and career progression
- Good training and development opportunities
- Good health

> ✔ More time with family and friends
>
> ✔ Affordable child care (if you have kids) or care for elderly parents
>
> ✔ More time for hobbies and interests
>
> ✔ Time to do some voluntary or community work, or otherwise contribute your skills and talents outside of your 'day job'

Are we mostly right? We also think that bosses want pretty much the same for themselves.

Check that your flexible working arrangement matches your needs

Before you march into the manager's office, ask yourself these important questions to be sure what you really need from your job:

✔ Do any staff already use flexible work options? What similarities are there between their situations and yours? What differences?

✔ Is your workload manageable? Can your work be divided into smaller chunks to allow for part-time work, job sharing, or home-based work?

✔ What are your most important work tasks? Can these tasks be done in fewer hours or outside of standard working hours?

✔ What staff meetings and seminars are compulsory for you to attend? Can you continue attending these meetings with your new arrangement?

Just as importantly, try the following questions about how changing your working arrangements can affect your personal life:

✔ Can you afford to take a salary cut, reduce your hours, or step down in terms of responsibility and challenges?

✔ Can you arrange appropriate child care under the new work conditions?

✔ Can you put your career plans on hold to achieve more flexibility?

✔ Have you taken pro-rata reductions into account? For example, you may have only 12 days annual leave instead of 20 if you work just three days a week.

What must your boss achieve?

Even more than your own job, managers' jobs are measured in terms of set outcomes and targets they must achieve. A great deal of their time is spent looking after the two layers of staff that surround them. A good manager tries to keep you and your colleagues interested, motivated, and working productively. A good manager also tries to protect your and your colleagues' jobs, responsibilities, and achievable workloads.

Managers want:

- ✔ Improved employee wellbeing, morale, and loyalty
- ✔ Increased employee productivity
- ✔ Reduced absenteeism
- ✔ Recognition and rewards by their managers for leadership and target achievement

For your flexible work-place arrangement request to be considered seriously, you *must* get managers' attention. This can be done by linking your proposal to the outcomes that they're interested in.

Motivating Your Boss to Care

Employers generally want to employ the best staff they can and no employer likes to lose valuable staff. Replacement costs accumulate through paying out a leaving staff member's entitlements, re-advertising the position, conducting a selection process, and training the new staff member. What is more difficult to calculate are the additional costs incurred through lost experience and corporate knowledge, having to re-establish good customer service relationships, and the general impact of staff turnover on other staff's morale and workload.

Many employers realise they now need flexible work places for these important reasons:

- ✔ **Ageing of the workforce:** As baby-boomers (the generation born following World War II) steadily reach retirement age, employers are accepting that their skills can be used beyond the age of 55. However, many people in the UK are opting to retire early, therefore companies need to offer more to attract this valuable sector of the workforce.

✔ **Fewer workers entering the workforce:** More people in the UK remain in full or part-time education for longer. Combine this with the fact that the baby-boomer generation is the single largest generation in the workforce, and it's easy to see that there's a much smaller working population available.

✔ **Instability:** Generation Y (those born after 1978) are more demanding on issues like corporate social responsibility and flexible working, and they shop around to find an employer of choice.

✔ **Child care needs:** The biggest trend in the labour market is amongst mothers with young children returning to work full- or part-time, a good proportion of whom are lone parents.

✔ **Non-traditional employees:** Retirees, people with caring commitments (for example, elderly parents), and people with disabilities have skills and experience of value to employers – when the employer can offer flexible work-place conditions.

Many flexible work options are on offer for employers to use to attract and to keep good staff. You can show your boss many advantages of using flexible work practices, including:

✔ Assisting and improving compliance with anti-discrimination and work-place relations laws.

✔ Being recognised as an employer of choice.

✔ Earning greater staff loyalty and higher return on training investment.

✔ Improving occupational health and safety records.

✔ Improving productivity.

✔ Maintaining a better match between peaks and troughs in workloads and staffing.

✔ Reducing absenteeism and staff turnover.

✔ Reducing stress levels and improving morale.

Show your boss this scary fact – the costs of losing good staff

The Chartered Institute of Personnel Development (CIPD) produce an annual benchmarking survey on recruitment, retention, and turnover in the UK. Their survey of 779 respondent organisations indicated that in 2007 the average (per head) cost of labour turnover was £5,800 and the resulting average cost of recruitment was £4,667. And for the most senior individuals, this total cost was actually more like £30,000!

Defining Your Demands

Thanks to the Internet, email, messaging systems, and working in a global economy that functions 24 hours a day, seven days a week, you're no longer bound to keep rigidly to working from 9 a.m. to 5 p.m., Monday to Friday.

Flexible working means adaptable or variable working-hours arrangements. Because the working hours are flexible, the arrangements can include many different versions, such as:

✔ Flexible leave arrangements

✔ Flexible rostering or scheduling

✔ Flexible start and finish times

✔ Job sharing

✔ Make-up time

✔ Nine-day fortnights/compressed working week

✔ Regular or occasional working from home

✔ Regular part-time work

✔ Rostered days off

Making a flexible-hours deal with the boss

According to the CIPD, part-time work is the main way in which many families attempt to balance their paid work and family lives. In their survey of 1,193 employees they found that 71 per cent of women and 38 per cent of men chose part-time working above other options available.

If your employer is a bit slow off the mark to adopt flexible work practices, you can use these statistics to argue for a change:

✔ Variable working hours (coming in/leaving late or early) – 52 per cent

✔ Job sharing – 34 per cent

✔ Working from home – 20 per cent

✔ Term-time only working – 26 per cent

REAL-LIFE STORY

Four days work and an extra day off

Penny and Ian work in the public sector, and both have chosen to work four longer days — of 10 hours — instead of five eight-hour days. 'It takes a bit of organisation because we have to plan who's dropping off and picking up the kids so that each of us can do our four long days.

'Before the kids started school, Ian took Mondays off with the kids and I took Fridays off so that we both had some time with them on our own. That way they needed be in child care only three days a week. Now that the kids are at school, Ian and I both have Fridays off together to do shopping, housework, and even have a lunch date before our weekend starts,' Penny said.

Downshifting: Finding flexible arrangements that suit you

The popular term *downshifting* is widely used, but with many definitions. To simplify the meaning of this word a little, we'll explain. Downshifting originally stemmed from the idea of *voluntary simplicity*, or simplifying the way you live. This simplification was (and still is) most commonly achieved by reducing your salary, minimising your purchases and use of material goods, and being more aware of environmental sustainability. Many people immediately picture the outcome of these actions as quitting their jobs in the city and heading towards country-cottage farms that provide their food, shelter, and a small income.

However, in terms of finding a work/life balance that's achievable (and presumably, a less dramatic move) for people with careers, families, mortgages, and an appreciation of some of life's labour savers, downshifting has two other meanings:

✔ Making the decision to change your lifestyle by taking a job that makes you less money but provides you with more fulfilment. This is achieved through the increased opportunity to spend time with family – by doing non-work activities and by negotiating flexible working arrangements. For more information on how you can do this for your own career and work/life balance, see Chapter 14.

✔ Taking a form of downshifting known as *voluntary demotion*, which describes when an employee, with the approval of her employer, elects to take a lower position than her current role. Many government positions have provisions for this choice but whether you can make the change depends on the needs of the department and of the employee. These demotions can be granted for many reasons:

Change of career direction

Changing from field work to office work (and vice versa)

Health/illness

Job relocation

Reducing commuting times

Reducing the stress and workload of a particular role

Reducing work hours

Undertaking more education

Upcoming retirement

To discuss downshifting, this book uses the first of the two definitions. We believe that this definition of downshifting provides a much clearer and more practical link to arranging the flexible working arrangement that suits you. You can apply these flexible working arrangements in a variety of ways:

✔ **Flexible start and finish times:** Employers can specify the core hours of the day when employees are required to be in the work place, and can give employees the flexibility to start early/late and finish early/late. This means that you're able to negotiate the most suitable start and finish times to suit your family responsibilities and also meet your work commitments.

REAL-LIFE STORY

Early-bird or night-owl hours

Kate's employer allowed staff to start work any time between 7 a.m. and 10 a.m. as long as they completed their eight hours of work each day. Kate was an early bird who chose to start at 7 a.m., following an arrangement for her husband to drop their children off at school in the mornings.

'This has been a godsend to us. I actually get more work done from 7 a.m. to 9 a.m. because no one else is about, no telephones ring to distract me, and I get to plan, draft reports, and respond to emails before the office starts filling up for the day.'

This arrangement also suits Kate down to the ground at the other end of the day, because it enables her to leave work earlier and to spend more time at home with the kids in the evening.

✔ **Shorter working hours:** Shorter working hours can mean two things. First, you can break the culture of working overtime and, instead, can go home at a reasonable time without damaging your career prospects.

Second, you can choose to reduce your working hours from full-time to part-time. Part-time work can range from four and a half days a week to only half a day, depending on your workload, budget, and career expectations.

✔ **Rostered or accrued days off:** Employees can work additional hours during the week in order to accrue sufficient hours to have a rostered day off once a fortnight or once a month. This arrangement doesn't change the total number of hours worked by an employee. Some employers allow employees to work additional hours during the week and have Friday afternoon off when the office is quiet.

✔ **Banking time:** Employees can accumulate extra hours worked to take time off in lieu of payment for a specific purpose, or at a time which is convenient to the employer and employee. For the additional hours worked, employees then get the equivalent time off on an hour-for-hour basis. If employees haven't banked enough hours to cover a particular absence, they can be required to make up the time within an agreed time frame. Accumulated hours can be banked for school holidays or for ad hoc or unexpected family matters, such as medical appointments, pupil-free days, and school or sporting events for children. Records need to be kept of additional hours worked. Employers may wish to consider placing a limit on the number of hours or days that can be accumulated, and a time limit for clearing the accumulated hours, otherwise workers may be at risk of working too many hours. This situation can cause problems when scheduling the leave that the employees require.

Breaking the 12-hours-a-day expectation

Changing the 8 a.m. to 8 p.m. expected work day was hard at first, according to Jon. 'My firm lives and dies on chargeable hours to our clients, and as a young, single guy, I loved the challenge and the long hours. However, after marrying, having a couple of babies and coping with the hours set by child care and school, I had to start saying no to more than eight hours of work a day, and sticking to it. At first I had to make a bit of a production about logging off and leaving the office at 5 p.m. and felt self conscious about being the first bloke to leave.

Eventually though, my work mates stopped inviting me to meetings after 4 p.m. and respected my commitment to leaving at a decent hour to spend time with my family. My boss saw that the quality of my work hadn't diminished. In fact, I started each day feeling fresher and more able to continue a high output because I was motivated to get in and get out within eight hours every day. Since then, other people in our firm have become new parents and I'm now not the only one who leaves at 5 p.m.'

✔ **Compressed working week:** The hours in a work cycle can be compressed into fewer, but longer, shifts, for example 10-hour shifts, giving employees the choice of working their ordinary working hours over four days rather than five days.

✔ **Term-time work:** This option gives an employee the choice to take leave without pay during the school holidays. It's an arrangement that particularly suits workers at kindergartens, schools, and universities, during the holiday periods. This leave is extra to their annual four weeks leave. Alternatively, they can purchase leave to cover the non-term time periods.

You can find better work/life balance by working at home

The Office of National Statistics (ONS) defines *teleworkers* as 'people who work mainly in their own home or mainly in different places using home as a base, who use both a telephone and a computer to carry out their work at home'.

Teleworking grew dramatically in the UK from the mid 1990s and by spring 2005 there were just under 2.4 million teleworkers in the UK, around 8 per cent of all people in employment. That's double the number of recorded teleworkers in 1997, when they were first measured as a group. Employers consider the benefits of teleworking to be:

✔ **Cost savings:** Employers who use teleworking hope to be able to reduce operating expenses, such as rent, maintenance, parking, and travel, often by implementing a 'hot desk' policy for when staff need to visit office premises.

✔ **Better use of technology:** Teleworking can make business more efficient. The spread of broadband and cheaper digital technology now means that work can be completed faster and more effectively – and where it's completed is less important, since video conferencing can replace many face-to-face meetings.

✔ **Effective employment:** When more workers need to be recruited to cover heavy workloads, teleworking provides opportunities for employment to non-traditional staff, such as disabled workers, rural-based workers, retired workers, and carers.

✔ **Increased productivity:** There's evidence that working from home improves productivity, as long as a sensible system of accountability is in place.

✔ **Reduced green issues:** Teleworking cuts down on travel, which should reduce pollution. As more and more companies buy into the concept of reducing our carbon footprint, teleworking is likely to be even higher on the agenda.

✔ **Work/life balance:** Perhaps most importantly, teleworking can provided a better work/life balance for workers by reducing the time spent travelling to and from work and by having the work environment (that is, in the home) closer to the employee's family and non-work commitments.

Win–win of working from home

Working as a telecommuter can be done full-time, part-time, or on an occasional basis by an employee. This is work done away from the traditional office environment, including working from home or via the Internet when the employee has to travel for work reasons.

By using the term telecommuting, we are separating the other 'working from home' employment system, which applies to people running their own businesses from home (commonly called *home-based business*). We discuss home-based work in Chapter 13.

Making an Offer the Boss Can't Refuse

Before you walk into your manager's office and ask for a more flexible working arrangement – for flexible working hours, unpaid school holiday leave, or working from home – you need to take the business's needs and goals into account and make sure that your arrangement won't impact negatively on the business.

Presenting a business case to your boss is an effective way of showing that you've thought your situation through seriously and ensured that your proposal can benefit your employer. Your boss needs to know that, under any flexible working arrangement, your job can be properly managed, that it has the capacity to provide you with flexible working options, and that it can be developed into guidelines for other staff to use.

Developing a compelling business case

For your purposes, a business case is not something you hide a newspaper and some soggy sandwiches in. A business case is a structured proposal for business change that is explained and justified in terms of costs and benefits. Here are some important pieces of information to include in your business case:

✔ **The impact on your customers:** Many customers like their preferred contact person available full-time. However, if two staff operate a job-share arrangement, the staff members can offer the customer earlier start times or later finishing times for contact on their particular day of working.

✔ **Identify the benefits:** You can introduce more work/life flexibility options to improve staff morale and wellbeing. For example, job sharing can create employment opportunities for workers not currently in the company. Job sharing can also prevent other full-time workers from leaving the company.

✔ **Identify what training employers can undertake:** Find out if any of the company's managers currently work flexible hours. Are they aware of what the company currently offers staff? Include suggestions to add work/life balance modules into manager training and inductions.

✔ **List HR policies already in place, and how they can be improved:** If the company has a flexible hours policy, find it and review it. Has it ever been used? Are staff members aware of it? Is it still relevant? An existing agreement may apply to maternity leave. Find out how many women return after maternity leave. If they don't return, find out why.

✔ **Show the savings:** Flexible working arrangements can save costs by reducing absenteeism, staff turnover, recruitment costs, and costs for training new staff.

✔ **State how your employer can monitor and evaluate the new workplace arrangements:** Explain that your employer can measure punctuality when core working hours are extended or reduced, can compare rates of absenteeism before and after the introduction of new flexibility options, measure rates of staff turnover and the reasons for leaving and staying (via staff exit interviews), and look for an increase in the number of applicants for newly advertised positions (because the business is now a preferred employer).

Using case studies to clinch the deal

Good case studies show a company or person identifying a problem, coming up with a solution, putting the solution into practice, and reaping the benefits. Case studies can also be used to encourage other employers to try new ways of working as well.

The Work Foundation provides a range of UK and European employer case studies to look through, and here's a significant success story to get you started:

British Telecom (BT) wanted to respond to challenging customer competition by providing the very best service, and recognised that technology alone was not the answer. Its commitment to its staff was seen as the biggest differentiator, enabling it to become an employer of choice and ensure the highest levels of motivation amongst its workforce.

BT therefore chose to harness communications technology to move from a fixed, site-based workforce to an 'e-BT' of employees to work flexibly or from home. In addition, it decided to deliver 70 per cent of its training online to employees at work or home. BT encourages managers to agree to flexible working practices and the focus in the company has shifted to outputs to allow this to be measured. BT's 'Achieving the Balance' Intranet site provides extensive support and information.

The following business benefits resulted from all these initiatives:

- **Improved retention:** Natural attrition was reduced to just 2.8 per cent per annum and 98 per cent of women returned to BT after maternity leave. Over the first two years, flexible working helped to retain 1,000 people.

- **Reduced absenteeism:** BT home workers averaged just 3 days a year sickness absence, a significant improvement on the norm for the whole of BT, and the industry as a whole, with absenteeism running at 20 per cent below the UK average.

- **Increased productivity:** Over 9,000 BT employees work from home with productivity gains of 15–31 per cent. Home-based operators handle 20 per cent more calls than site-based colleagues.

- **Happier customers:** Customer and employee feedback shows distinct improvements, with customer dissatisfaction down 22 per cent and home-based employees reporting themselves as 7 per cent happier than site-based colleagues.

- **Reduced costs:** The cost of supporting a home worker in Central London was calculated as less than £3,000, compared to the cost of supporting an office-based worker of around £18,000. On average, each home worker saves BT £6,000 a year and improved retention saves about £5m a year on recruitment and induction.

Finding case studies that interest you

Knowing that you're not the only one in your particular situation helps you find confidence and arguments to put your business case for more flexible working arrangements. Here are some websites where you can check out the cases of people who may have similar situations to your own:

- **Employers for Work Life Balance:** www.employersforwork-life balance.org.uk.

- **The Chartered Institute of Personnel Development:** www.cipd.co.uk.

- **The Trades Union Congress:** www.tuc.org.uk.

Dealing with Objections Positively

Your boss has a lot on his/her plate and needs to consider your request as part of a much bigger staff picture. If the boss has large responsibilities and you need to supervise more of the work, the boss is less likely to want change and your proposal can be seen as a negative for the business.

All good negotiators in business and in life – both cases apply to you in this instance – are able to anticipate what the other party (your boss) is likely to raise as a reason or concern for not approving or buying your proposal. Examples of questions that an employer may raise include:

- ✔ Have you proved to me that you can be trusted to work with little or no supervision?

- ✔ How do I measure your work output and performance other than whether you're at your desk in the office?

- ✔ If I grant you flexible working arrangements, won't I then have to do the same thing for everyone else?

- ✔ If this flexible working option is approved, can you still get the work done?

- ✔ Can you do the work to the same level of quality, and get it done on time?

- ✔ Is this arrangement going to affect the level of customer service you provide?

- ✔ Can you be contactable when I need you?

Providing answers and finding help

Try to put yourself in your boss's shoes when you think of a likely objection to your flexible working arrangements and then think of ways to a solution. Be a step ahead of your manager and show you're anticipating queries and developing strategies to resolve the problems raised.

Continuing customer service

Most jobs these days rely on providing a high level of customer service. Sometimes customer service is the deciding factor that brings repeat business or new work. Having a strategy to deal with customer service in your new arrangements shows your boss that you appreciate that the team – and your job – values customers and that you're part of a highly effective team working to continue this standard.

Recommend that your customers should be advised of any new working arrangements to ensure that they feel as though their business is valued and their needs are still being met. This advice not only shows professional courtesy but can also make you a key contact person who can communicate with them by phone or email as well as in person. In addition, mention trialling a buddy system where each staff member trains another to deal with their clients effectively. This system not only covers part-time or flexible hours of work but other absences, such as sickness or holiday leave.

Dealing with the 'more work for me' dilemma

To ensure that your boss feels listened to, agree with his or her concern that your new arrangements may create more work for your boss. You can also clarify this situation by pointing out that adopting new working arrangements may create more work at the start, but less later. Studies have shown that when employers trust their workers to get on with the job with minimal supervision, the result is greater motivation, loyalty, and productivity. Time-saving methods that your manager may consider include changing team meeting times and changing staff communications so that staff working part-time or from home can fit in with them.

Managers can also involve their staff in helping to come up with ways to make the arrangements work, such as giving their employees an increased say in rostering times, email etiquette (only emailing when necessary and combining multiple emails in one), bunching up queries (to save lots of interruptions), and running shorter and more effective team meetings.

Fumbling with flexible performance assessments

Managers become concerned with how they're going to assess a staff member's performance in a flexible working arrangement. This concern is valid because very few bosses are trained in how to incorporate flexible working into their teams or how to manage staff who work flexibly. Some ideas for your boss to consider include setting a meeting with you to discuss and set the following measures:

- ✔ Agree on the best times to hold one-to-one meetings and the best times to communicate with each other via phone or email.

- ✔ Agree on what staff meetings you must attend (after considering the hours you're at the work place), any training and development you may still need, and any other organisation or team-wide responsibilities you have. Be realistic about what you can contribute if you're reducing your hours.

- ✔ Discuss what the most important aspects of your position are and come up with solid measures of your performance, such as projects completed, customer satisfaction, and achievement of team goals.

Unlocking the floodgates

How many times have you heard the phrase, 'Oh, if I do it for you, I'll have to do it for everyone else'. Avoid rolling your eyes if your boss utters these words. Instead, listen and acknowledge your boss's concern as a valid one. An effective way to keep your manager on side is to say something like, 'Not necessarily, because you still have the authority to assess each application on its merits, including the responsibilities of the particular job, the skills of the worker, and the needs of the team.'

You can also mention that the Chartered Institute of Personnel Development (CIPD) has useful tips on how to assess, approve, and review flexible working arrangements and where to go to seek help and advice. Furthermore, if other staff members seek a flexible working arrangement and your boss can manage this, the worst that can happen is that the manager ends up with a motivated workforce of employees determined to see the new arrangements succeed!

Test driving

If your manager is still unsure about the idea of how your flexible working arrangement can succeed in practice, suggest a trial period. Ideally the trial period should be for a set period of three to six months, with some performance targets set before starting. Recommend to your manager that during this period you can schedule regular fortnightly reviews to address any issues and to discuss your workload, how you're communicating with other staff and customers, and what your most productive times are.

At the end of the agreed trial period, you and your boss can review the flexible working arrangement, address any changes you both need to improve the arrangement, and decide whether the arrangement is to continue. Whatever the outcome, suggest to your boss that the decision be put in writing and signed by each of you. You can revisit the arrangement at a later date and your experience can help you develop a more suitable alternative.

Keeping your cool at crunch time

As if summoning up the courage to ask for what you want isn't hard enough, you also need to practise how you're going to manage your emotions during the negotiation process.

Getting angry or showing frustration and disappointment aren't usually ways to impress someone or get what you want. Your boss is likely to consider your business case more favourably if you make an appointment with your boss and sit down to calmly discuss the issue.

Some quick tips to consider if you think that you may become a bit emotional during the meeting:

- **Involve your manager:** Thank your boss for taking time out to meet with you and for being prepared to discuss a solution that suits both of you. This way you come across as professional and mature and leave behind a good impression.

- **Know what sets you off:** If you worry about forgetting key points, write them down and read directly from them so that your boss can see that you're serious and have done your homework. If you think that you may get teary, give the business case to your boss in writing beforehand so that your case has been read and digested, which helps you to avoid going on the defensive as soon as you sit down.

  Think you may become angry? Take some deep breaths, read slowly from the list of points you wish to discuss, and dare to pause and take a breath every now and then. Presenting your case calmly is more likely to be successful than rushing through your opening statements and demanding a 'yes' immediately.

- **Listen, listen, listen:** When your manager wants to ask you a question or throw in a comment, listen to what's said. Active listening shows that you're not easily distracted or just waiting for the boss to stop talking so that you can jump in again.

- **Offer choices:** Providing more than one solution shows your manager that you're considering a range of options and can discuss how and why they work. This way you reveal that you're taking your boss's needs into consideration.

- **Take notes:** Concentrating on listening and taking notes of what's said has worked for me on many occasions. If you're at a job interview, or in a meeting that you're nervous about, having a pad and pen handy to jot down some notes does three things:

  Helps you to understand properly what the other person is saying.

  Enables you to write down the other person's point without judging it or immediately arguing about it.

  Gives you a second or two to collect your thoughts and think about the best way to respond.

Coping with 'No'

Heaven forbid that your boss should say no to your request for flexible working arrangements. Remember if this happens, all is not lost. Here are some other avenues to investigate:

- ✔ **Ask your boss to put the reasons for the decision in writing.** Having a written statement that clearly explains the reason for your rejection gives you something to read through in a quiet place and time where you can think about the reasons when you're not in the meeting.

- ✔ **Request a review of the situation and set a date.** By asking your boss to review the decision in six months' time, you can have an opportunity to re-work your business case. This review becomes your second chance to find ways to present your proposal. Do more research, understand your manager's views, consider other flexible options, and make sure that you're presenting enough different reasons to be convincing.

- ✔ **Seek advice from your HR representative.** Your employer may have staff policies that can set guidelines for flexible working arrangements or give you information on the processes you need to go through to set up an arrangement. Furthermore, your HR manager may know of other staff who successfully used flexible working arrangements in other parts of your company and who you can contact.

- ✔ **Seek advice from your trade union.** The Trades Union Congress (TUC), at www.tuc.org.uk, is a great organisation to contact if you believe that you've been treated unfairly at work. The TUC can help you find the union that's relevant to your industry, and offers a number of Know Your Rights leaflets as well as a helpline that provides free and confidential advice.

Chapter 9

Maintaining Your New Working Life

In This Chapter

▶ Showing you can balance work and life

▶ Improving your work/life balance even more

▶ Keeping your boss under control

▶ Testing the success of your work/life balance

*I*n order to maintain a realistic level of work/life balance, you have to juggle a lot of situations. You need to look after your physical health (refer to Chapter 4), improve your time management and prioritisation skills (refer to Chapter 6), take decent breaks (refer to Chapter 7) and find the flexible working arrangement that best suits you, your family, and the organisation you work for (refer to Chapter 8). Having all those challenges on your plate may make you feel like going straight back to bed and staying there. You can't because you have even more work to do . . .

By *work*, we mean making sure that your new arrangements don't become forgotten or 'eaten into' by managers and workmates or crushed by unforgiving workloads. On the other hand, you don't have to be unyielding and rigid when genuinely unforeseen and crucial deadlines come up and you're able to make the appropriate arrangements for child care, after-school care, or care for your elderly relatives.

This chapter discusses how to improve and gain skills in assertiveness, get access to good advice, help write guidelines for other staff members, and develop a determination to get the lowdown on other good employers to find out what they're doing successfully. Add to these challenges the ability to negotiate with a manager who may not be as supportive as your previous manager, and stir in a willingness to review and evaluate the progress of your flexible working option. It may sound daunting, but by following the guidance in this chapter you can make it easy, and the rewards will be well worth it.

Setting an Example

Guilt can all-too-frequently invade your time at work, whispering into your ear that 'You can't leave at 3 p.m. today because you haven't finished your report for the boss yet' or 'You're letting everyone down because the rest of the team can't move to the next stage of the project without your input'. And try this one: 'Come on, you're the only person who can do this'.

And if your own guilt doesn't keep you at work, ignoring your flexible working arrangement, then well-meaning colleagues or the boss can set up meetings that fall on your non-working day and expect you to shift your week around to accommodate them.

It's important that you make rules about your working arrangements and stick with them. For example, make clear to your team that you can be contacted at A and B times, but definitely not at X and Y times. If you're working from home, you won't be at your computer after 7 p.m. or at weekends. That doesn't mean you can't work additional or different hours if the work need is genuine and you can arrange your schedule. But by sticking to your rules most of the time, your team soon knows when to arrange a meeting if they want you there, or when the best time is to contact you. Most email programs have an automatic message and signature system that can include this information for you.

Easy steps to ensure that your guilt or your colleagues' lack of consideration doesn't fritter away your flexibility are:

- **Be active:** Participate in committees, working parties, or meetings on specific projects, and even organisation-wide committees on flexible working and how the changes can benefit other colleagues. You may find that colleagues who appear to misunderstand or resent your arrangement may in fact want to establish one as well. Smile, listen to them, and see if you can show them how.

- **Be organised:** Be thorough in delivering file notes, hand-over reports and regular emails about your progress on various tasks and projects. Arrange back-up support for your absences in advance and advise your colleagues of the arrangements and who to contact and for what. By keeping them updated, you reduce misunderstandings and keep them aware of how you work and what you're doing for the team/business plan.

- **Be reliable:** Stick to your side of the arrangement and complete your tasks when they're due, or let your manager know as soon as possible if you have a problem. Don't ever let your boss feel that he or she doesn't know what's going on in your work day.

✔ **Make yourself accessible:** Broadband, the Internet, email, SMS, mobile phones, and even the good old telephone exist for you to communicate with your boss (and other people).

✔ **Publicise your availability:** Communicate. Be sure to let your colleagues know what you're doing and when. Make sure that they know when you are – and are not – available. And stick to the rules, without sounding rude or unhelpful.

✔ **Show flexibility:** Fill in for a colleague in an emergency or attend occasional out-of-hours meetings. These helpful tasks go a long way to revealing that you're still a team player who can be relied on during emergencies. Flexibility can, and should, cut both ways!

Keeping Your Hard-Won Working Arrangements

So how do you assertively maintain your flexible working arrangement? Being assertive is honestly expressing your feelings, opinions, or needs. That means being able to stand up for your rights and not let another person take advantage of you. Assertive also means being able to say what you want in a clear fashion in a way that shows you have confidence in yourself and your point of view.

You were probably taught by your family and teachers at school that concentrating on the needs of others and not your own needs is good manners. The truth is that everyone benefits when you assert your own needs while also considering those of others.

Your self-esteem affects assertiveness in two very significant ways. If you have a low opinion about yourself, you can find difficulty mustering up the confidence to speak for yourself. Alternatively, anxiety may make you become aggressive at inappropriate times. You can appear irritable or angry and scare off other people when really you're the one who feels scared and lacking in confidence.

I (Katherine) once worked with a senior manager who used to regularly announce that she 'didn't suffer fools gladly'. Her aggressive behaviour sent the message to the staff members that she considered us all fools. The staff members used to surmise that she was frustrated because she had been overlooked for a more executive role and wanted to take out her frustrations on the people around her. With the benefit of hindsight, I now see that she may have been scared to show her disappointment to us.

We're sure you know that you need to be more assertive at times and have even given other people advice on being more assertive. However, when it comes to your own situation, being assertive can be a challenge. People who know how to assert themselves – or stand up for their rights – in a respectful manner are often the most successful in retaining a good work arrangement and the support of their managers. People associate assertiveness with positive self-esteem.

Being assertive doesn't mean being aggressive. Assertive behaviour doesn't involve blaming, threatening, or demanding. Aggression includes threats, sarcasm, name-calling, and gossip tactics – none of which help gain the respect of colleagues or the boss and aggression certainly won't win the battle.

On the other hand, people avoid being assertive because they're afraid of upsetting others and of not being liked. This urge goes way beyond the school yard. Nevertheless, not asserting yourself can make you feel you've been taken advantage of and reduces your self-esteem even more.

By not asking for a new project or a salary increase, because you generally find it difficult to ask for anything, you not only feel bad about yourself, but you're showing you're not in control of your career.

You may even try telling yourself that if your employer valued you, then your boss would notice how good you are at your job or offer you new projects and a pay rise without you having to ask for it. Sadly, if you don't ask, you don't get. The consequences of not being assertive can mean that you continue to doubt your abilities and feel even more like a powerless victim of your employer.

Ask yourself the following questions to find out how assertive you really are:

- ✔ Are you able to say 'no' when you don't want to do something?
- ✔ Do you ask for help when you need it or question matters when you're confused?
- ✔ Do you express anger and annoyance appropriately?
- ✔ Do you offer your opinion when you disagree with others?
- ✔ Do you look people in the eye when you're talking to them?
- ✔ Do you speak up in meetings regularly?
- ✔ Do you speak with a generally confident manner, communicating a genuine interest in your subject and confidence in your opinion?

Increasing your assertiveness at work

Non-assertive behaviour can damage your career prospects because you allow other people not to take you or your skills seriously. During staff meetings for example, if you constantly allow yourself to be interrupted, your manager may interpret this behaviour as a reflection of your abilities, regardless of how competent you actually are. Ways to increase your assertiveness and be heard include the following:

✔ **Be aware it's all about you.** Use 'I' language, the most useful for expressing negative feelings. 'I' language helps you to focus your anger constructively and to be clear about your feelings. For example: 'When you do (say the other person's behaviour), the effects on me are (say the results of that behaviour on you) and I feel (describe the emotion you feel). Avoid saying 'you are . . .'.

✔ **Don't apologise for speaking up.** You may find yourself starting a sentence by saying, 'I'm sorry, but . . .'. What your boss or colleagues may perceive you saying is something rather different, such as, 'I'm sorry for having an opinion, but please let me share it with you anyway,' which removes the assertiveness from your statement.

✔ **Don't permit unnecessary interruptions.** Remind yourself that your turn to speak is now. Hold up your hand and politely say to anyone who interrupts, 'Excuse me, I haven't finished.'

✔ **Keeping your voice down low.** A common way people unconsciously communicate powerlessness is by letting their tone of voice rise at the end of the sentence as though asking a question instead of making a statement. This intonation makes the speaker sound unsure and not very credible. Do you raise your voice like this? To add power to your statement, try making a conscious effort to drop your tone at the end of the sentence,

keep your voice level, and maintain eye contact. Practise at home in front of the mirror.

✔ **Listen to the speaker.** Let people know you heard what they said in response to your statement or opinion. Ask questions for clarification.

✔ **Practise your 'I' statements on family or friends.** Ask people you can trust for honest feedback. Start with less stressful situations, such as why you don't want your spouse to leave the wet sponge in the cupboard under the sink. Don't be discouraged if you behave non-assertively in your first tries. Instead, see your practice sessions as a chance to figure out where you went off course and how to improve your handling of the situation next time.

✔ **Stop being submissive.** Avoid behaviour such as dropping your eyes in response to another person's gaze. It makes you look too meek and mild and your opinion won't be heard or valued.

✔ **Say 'No'.** When saying 'No', be decisive. Explain why you're refusing but don't be overly apologetic (refer to Chapter 3 for more information on saying 'No' without guilt).

If you've secured flexible working arrangements and you're now able to attend virtual meetings via conference calls while you work from home, you can still apply many of the above points. In addition, to help you avoid falling into the conference call communication black hole of not knowing how or when to speak up, you can initiate with your manager an agreement about how to run the calls. This means that whoever hosts the call makes sure to invite responses from all attendees. Getting this arrangement in place enables you to build your profile as someone who comes up with great ideas and gives you the confidence that you'll always get your turn to speak.

Finding Mentors to Stay at the Top of Your Game

A *mentor* is usually a more experienced employee, willing to spend time sharing professional and personal skills and experiences with a more junior employee. A mentor–employee work-place partnership is based on encouragement, relevant advice, mutual trust, respect, and a willingness from both parties to learn and share.

Mentoring can be a very effective support tool for you to ensure that you're not alone in your efforts to maintain a fulfilling job – and career path – while also staying in contention for future promotions. Mentors have often already been in your situation and can be the best weapon in your fight for better work/life balance. An experienced co-worker knows the employer's policies and special cases and can provide examples of other employees who set up a good flexible working arrangement.

A mentor enables you to confidentially discuss any work issues of concern and provides you with encouragement, constructive comments, trust, and advice. A mentor provides you with contacts that help you in other areas of expertise, such as finding the right Human Resources (HR) professional to help you, or showing you how to move sideways to increase your skill level. Establishing a mentor partnership also provides you with valuable support in times of job change or organisational restructure.

The benefits for you, the less-experienced employee (or *mentee*), include

- ✔ A smoother progression through promotion and management levels.
- ✔ A supportive and confidential forum where your achievements and disappointments can be discussed.
- ✔ Improved understanding of each of your roles within the organisation.
- ✔ Increased self-confidence.
- ✔ Increased skills and knowledge.
- ✔ Increased understanding of the culture and unwritten rules of the organisation.

Simple ways to find a good mentor

Look for someone just a few years ahead of you because they'll remember what you're going through. Key steps to finding the right mentor include:

✔ **Asking good questions.** Potential mentors are most interested in mentees who ask questions that show they're ambitious and skilled. Intelligent questions demonstrate that you understand the mentor's expertise and you intend using their advice effectively. Mentors want to look after a winner, not someone who needs constant hand-holding and doesn't have goals. Ask questions such as 'What further skills can help me get to be a project leader?' and 'How did you go about getting your skills on the job?' Avoid questions like 'Can you get me a job working with the head of the finance department?'

✔ **Being a good listener.** You drive the conversation and then when you're asked a question – listen. If a mentor needs to know more, the mentor can ask. Don't find yourself talking more than the mentor or the mentor ends up wondering why you asked for help in the first place.

✔ **Identifying a potential mentor.** This person can be any age, but the most effective mentor is someone approximately five years ahead of you in your career. A mentor at this stage knows how to navigate successfully through the company from the position you're in because the mentor can remember being where you are now. Choose someone you admire and someone with good communication skills.

✔ **Keeping your eyes open.** One mentor may not be enough. People often need a few mentors because no mentor lasts forever and each has a different field of expertise. Peter, a high-level government executive director, said, 'Two of my best mentors were very different from each other. One helped me to fit in with the organisational culture so that I could meet other more senior managers and become more familiar with the future directions of the department. The other mentor helped me to keep my focus when balancing my work and life, so that my becoming an available parent was possible rather than difficult.'

✔ **Showing that you're serious.** You can demonstrate that you value your mentor's advice by carrying out that advice, showing the results, and then going back to review and discuss the situation. If your mentor suggests you participate in a particular project, then volunteer to be part of it. Do a good job and report back to your mentor adding that you're grateful for the advice because you were able to learn a lot and perform well.

When you approach your potential mentor, you can explain that studies have shown that having mentors helps employees benefit from:

- Challenging discussions from mentees with different perspectives (and knowledge of other aspects of the organisation) who aren't already part of the management.
- Enhanced knowledge of other areas of the organisation.
- Opportunities to reflect upon the mentor's career and current role.
- Renewed enthusiasm for the mentor's role as an experienced employee.
- Satisfaction for the mentor for contributing to your development.

As for your organisation, encouraging skilled and senior staff to mentor others can result in opportunities for improved communication between different teams, managers with improved people management skills, and reduced recruitment and selection costs.

Dealing with a Dreadful Boss

As you know, a good boss is someone who can effectively run a company or team and is able to communicate with, and understand, their employees. If your boss consults you on business decisions, shows appreciation for your hard work, and responds with rewards, you most likely enjoy working for him.

Unfortunately, you're not always going to be lucky enough to have the perfect boss. Although you may be able to find ways to work around – or in spite of – him. Bad bosses have a huge impact on your working life and, in turn, your work/life balance.

Many national and international workers compensation jurisdictions have found that a difficult working relationship between employer and employee can have a negative impact on your work performance and lead to physical and mental stress. This situation damages or hinders the effectiveness of any flexible working arrangements you may have made with that boss or an earlier boss.

Examples of difficult behaviour shown by some bosses include lack of communication, reluctance to consider any ideas or opinions of their staff, verbal bullying, outmoded thinking, and rudeness. All is not lost however. You can improve your working relationship with your boss.

Taking your problem to a higher power

Everyone deserves the right to a stress-free working life and to be treated fairly at work. If this isn't happening for you, in the very short term, keep calm. If your boss simply has terrible people skills, don't take his behaviour personally. Assert yourself in a reasonable manner. Don't yell back, or take abuse silently. Explain politely that you don't appreciate being spoken to in such a way.

If things don't improve, try these tips in this order:

- **Speak to a trusted colleague.** Have your colleagues noticed that the boss treats you poorly or are you overreacting? Find out how and why your colleague gets along well with your boss. How does the colleague treat the boss differently from the way you treat the boss? Be careful to avoid spreading negativity, though. You're seeking someone's impartial opinion to check that you're not being over-sensitive, so don't let it turn into a mission to get sympathy.

- **Seek advice from your HR professional.** When you have clarity about your situation and feel that you do have a case to make, speak to someone within your Human Resources (HR) department. HR staff are trained professionals in helping to resolve work-place issues and if the situation warrants it they can bring in specialist mediation services to get an agreement on a way forward.

- **Take your case higher.** If your boss's behaviour is aggressive or abusive, or if all attempts by you to build a reasonable relationship fail, talk about your situation to your boss's supervisor.

- **Contact your trade union representative.** Don't think that the old-fashioned stereotype of the jobsworth shop steward applies these days (if it ever did outside of sitcoms!). Your union representative is ideally placed to help you understand your rights and to help you negotiate a fair outcome. Union reps are able to draw on their own and other reps' experiences of resolving similar issues.

- **Seek training from a skilled -psychologist.** You can develop skills to make you more assertive when talking to your boss, and also to make you more resilient to criticism and not gaining your objectives. Some psychologists specialise in work-place relations.

What not to do with a bad boss

Behaving as badly as you believe your boss behaves may be tempting but it's not professional or helpful to your career. Behaviours to watch, when managing a difficult boss, include:

✔ **Avoiding interaction as much as possible.** Trying to avoid your manager in the office kitchen, remaining silent in meetings, and communicating only via email won't improve the relationship.

✔ **Increasing the number of sickies (absenteeism).** Employers see frequent sickies as weakness and lack of interest by you, rather than as the outcome of the management style. You may miss out on projects or promotions.

✔ **Leaving the position or organisation.** Resigning can be the easiest way out of some unpleasant work situations. However, resigning can merely serve to clear the way for someone else to end up in the same miserable situation that you escaped.

✔ **Mirroring the manager's behaviour.** This may include rudeness, verbal insults, or back-stabbing behaviour. You can end up like two children endlessly yelling and arguing with no resolution, only increasing anger and worsening behaviour.

✔ **Remaining silent and meekly obeying.** The manager may like your timidity but you can find yourself seething, dreading coming in to work, or becoming depressed.

How to meet on common ground

If you and your manager disagree on issues relating to your access to work/life flexibility policies, the workload involved, types of work you're required to do, or even how to run the work place, various methods can be introduced to encourage communication between you, including:

✔ **Aiming to solve the disagreement.** You don't have to win every single argument you have with your boss. Instead, you can ask for your boss's opinions on an issue. Really listen, take notes, ask open-ended questions, and find the positive comments.

✔ **Being calm and reasonable.** Your boss doesn't have to feel the same way about an issue as you do and isn't going to continue discussing an issue with you if you lose your cool.

✔ **Complimenting them.** Yes, you can compliment your boss on any suggestions that you think are workable. You can always find some common ground – no matter how minor – that you already agree on, so tell the boss when you agree with a comment.

✔ **Recommending instead of demanding.** Suggest your ideas rather than insisting on your way or no way. Explain how your ideas can benefit the organisation.

✔ **Researching.** Your boss may be more interested if you can show that you've thoroughly researched your ideas and can present them professionally, discussing both the possible benefits and the drawbacks.

WORLD WIDE WEB

Finding your work entitlements

If you've tried everything within your power to establish a fair working arrangement and are still struggling to get it under way or secure the support of your manager and colleagues, there are several avenues you can seek help from:

✔ www.acas.org.uk: The Advisory, Conciliation and Arbitration Service (ACAS) offers free, confidential, and impartial advice on all employment rights issues.

✔ www.lra.org.uk: In Northern Ireland you can get the same kind of advice offered by ACAS from The Labour Relations Agency (LRA).

✔ www.citizensadvice.org.uk: Your local Citizens Advice Bureau (CAB) can also provide free and impartial advice.

✔ www.tuc.org.uk: And if you're a member of a trade union they can support and represent you if things get tricky.

Establishing Excellent Work/Life Balance Policies

A very effective way to ensure that your own flexible working arrangement continues is to help your HR department or manager write a policy on work/life balance. You may be surprised at how enthusiastically your offer of help is accepted. A lot of work places like the idea of introducing work/life balance or *wellbeing* policies but don't know where to start.

Most effective work/life policies currently in place around the world contain at least some advantages to both employers and employees. Through discussions with your in-house experts (HR officers, your boss, other managers, and key staff members) and by searching out what other employers are doing, you can offer recommendations you think best match your work place.

Flexible working options

Everyone wants flexible working options available if and when needed. Employees also want their bosses to have guidelines to help consider employee requests fairly and promptly. We've done some of the hard work and sought out tried and tested options adopted by many employers, which have been shown to work. Some options that may suit your work place include:

✔ **Compressed work week:** Working a full-time week in four days.

✔ **Flexi-time:** Starting and finishing at variable times.

- **Job sharing:** Two people split one job.
- **Part-time working:** Working less than standard full-time hours.
- **Telecommuting:** Working from home on a regular or as-needs basis.
- **Term-time working:** Working only during school terms.

For more information on these options, refer to Chapter 2.

Personal work/life balance

Development plans let managers and companies review work/life balance policies on a regular basis. Planning ahead for the busiest working times or recruitment drives, or accommodating the changing needs of staff (for example, people moving from full-time to part-time work) can be done using:

- An open-door approach to problems, as well as groups for managers to establish good rapport with their staff to ensure meeting their business and personal needs.
- Individual development plans and regular appraisals.
- Mentoring by experienced colleagues or by external trainers.

In addition to standard amounts of annual leave, sick leave, and maternity leave, employers are increasingly adopting more flexible leave options to attract and retain their valued staff, and listing the options in their work/life balance policies. These new options can include:

- **Additional purchased holiday leave.** This leave is commonly known as 48/52 where an employee gains four weeks of extra leave and spreads the salary impact of this leave without pay over each salary period for the year.
- **Career breaks or sabbaticals.** Employers can make these options available at any stage of employment but usually offer them to staff who've served for at least a couple of years. They normally negotiate arrangements individually with employees about returning to work or maintaining their skill levels while enjoying the break.

  Employers are recognising the value of giving their staff longer breaks from work, especially for employees approaching retirement age, or for travel and study needs. Employers can see that providing leave without pay enables people to take a longer break and return refreshed instead of burning out and leaving altogether. (See Chapter 13 for more on this topic.)

✔ **Paid paternity leave.** New fathers need time from work to adjust to the demands of a new baby. This can be anything from a week to six months, depending on the employer, industry, country, and whether the employer offers a father leave that's paid, part-paid, or unpaid.

✔ **Study leave.** For many years, employers readily offered study leave (especially during exam times) to staff studying in a field that directly benefited their work. Nowadays, more employers offer study leave opportunities to staff members studying in unrelated areas as a means of rewarding the employees for their work, their loyalty, and their need to have greater work/life balance. (See Chapter 12 for more on this topic.)

Carer support

Employers can help with family care responsibilities, especially when some workers provide care to elderly parents or relatives, as well as for their children. Here are some ways to do that:

✔ **Child-care providers.** Provide information on where child-care centres, family day care, and other child-care providers are located close to the work place or en route to work from the employee's home.

✔ **Partnerships with local child-care centres.** Larger employers sometimes partner with child-care centres to offer subsidised child care or preferential places to employees.

✔ **Salary sacrifice.** Some employers make this offer to help the worker with child care by providing vouchers towards the cost in return for an appropriate reduction in salary. This might seem a roundabout way – after all, if your salary is higher, wouldn't you be able to afford the child care without the vouchers? In fact, arrangements like this normally have some tax advantages, so the benefit might well be worth more than the cash that you sacrifice.

Asking the experts

Most employers in reasonably large organisations have a Human Resources (HR) expert (or department). HR professionals are there to help employees. Most UK employers with more than 100 employees have some guidelines – however vague or outdated – that cover the types of leave available to workers. In addition, HR professionals actively seek more information and training on work/life balance issues and are open to reviewing and re-drafting policies.

So how do employers get their workers to take an interest in the new work/
life balance policies you may have helped HR produce? Here are some ways:

- ✔ **Create opportunities for open discussion.** You can establish a specific Intranet discussion group on the work/life balance policy and call for suggestions, problem solving, and the gathering of case studies from other employers. Invite the contributors to add comments anonymously. Most office network packages have this option.

- ✔ **Include the policies in training.** Make sure that your work-place work/ life balance policy is a mandatory part of in-house management and training courses and is included in induction courses for new staff.

- ✔ **Make the policies available.** Add copies of the new work-place policies to recruitment materials, new staff manuals, and the HR section of the staff online information portal.

- ✔ **Provide rewards.** Staff and managers who work together to achieve a happier work place through appropriately adopting the new policies can be rewarded via a salary increase, a staff lunch paid for by the company, a 'bring your spouse/child/dog to work day' chosen by the staff member, gift vouchers, and time off to attend a course or conference. The ideas are endless.

- ✔ **Publicise success stories.** In work places with more than 50 employees, word-of-mouth stories about how Peter's compressed hours led to improved customer service, or why Melinda is working at 7 a.m. are likely to miss a few people who may be genuinely interested. Publicising the policies and details of the staff members who are benefiting from the policies can be easily done via a weekly staff email or a staff-only Intranet site.

Measuring Success

Becoming familiar with the ways in which your manager and/or HR profes-sional monitors staff levels in order to determine how successful their work/life balance policies have been can be very useful to you. Noticeable improve-ments in staff retention, reduction in recruitment and training costs or outputs can help you – and other work/life balance champions and HR pro-fessionals – emphasise the importance of work/life balance policies to senior management. You may even be asked to help run a working group or commit-tee to review the results and work out ways to improve your organisation's uptake of flexible working options, publicise the policy, or think of ways to improve it.

One of the simplest ways to help draft a work/life balance policy is to ask the staff. Staff surveys are readily available in easy-to-adapt templates on the Internet and can provide some good insights into what employees need if they're to stay with the organisation and remain productive.

An established method of determining if your work place is making improvements in retaining good staff and reducing staff turnover is to monitor the numbers. Most work places have computerised HR-management systems capable of tracking employees by age, gender, position within the organisation, full- or part-time status, and rates of sick leave taken – amongst other things.

Here are some questions that can be asked of staff statistics to help you determine work/life balance policies:

- Do women who take maternity leave return afterwards? If not, why not? If yes, how many work full-time and how many work part-time?

- How do overall staff turnover, maternity leave, sick leave, and workers' compensation claims compare with other employers in your industry?

- What are the key causes of absence from work?

- What are the key causes of work-place injury (physical and psychological)? What areas of the organisation create the most claims? How do the numbers of claims compare with the past few years?

- What are the rates of absenteeism this year compared to the previous year?

- What are the reasons for staff turnover? Does the organisation conduct exit interviews or provide exit surveys?

- What is the level of staff turnover? What was it like twelve months earlier? What was it like two years earlier?

Employees can run a work place

Gavin joined a large institution last year after spending the majority of his working life at an executive recruiting firm. After familiarising himself with the institution's human resources policies, he was shocked to discover that they had never conducted a focus group or run a staff survey in the organisation's 20-plus year history. So Gavin approached his new employer and suggested a staff survey that promised to make work practices better for the employer, the employees, and himself.

'After running a focus group with key staff representatives, we drafted a confidential survey that went out to nearly 2,000 people. We had a response rate of more than 50 per cent and received a lot of very valuable information – not just from the tick-a-box answers but in the comments fields. People were just so relieved to have been asked to contribute ideas to our work/life balance and some even put down their contact details.'

Gavin contacted the employees and put together a working group given the responsibility of drafting and implementing a work/life balance policy. 'One of our executive directors is also on this committee to ensure that we have senior level representation. Twelve months later, the policy has been launched and all managers are required to have the work/life balance policy as a permanent agenda item for their monthly meetings. Uptake on the policy has been significant.'

Chapter 10

Putting the Life into Your Work/Life Balance

*W*hen you think of work/life balance you can fall into the trap of making sure that you meet your commitments at work and have enough time for home – only to fall into a heap when you walk through the front door.

This chapter discusses what areas of your home life are important to ensure that you have genuine work/life balance that's right for you. Simple activities like eating meals together around the table can bring your family closer together. Taking advantage of the assistance from grandparents and good child-care providers also eases the burden of responsibilities. Taking regular holidays also contributes to restoring a work/life balance that is important to your health and wellbeing. (No job is so important that you're required to work 365 days a year to get it done.)

Another significant factor in your work and life is being able to contribute to your community. Communities need help and you can offer yours. This chapter provides you with ideas of how you can contribute, including asking for days off, sponsored by your employer, or giving up a couple of precious hours to create something on your computer for a community project.

Doing Time for the Family

The concept of quality time (how well you spend your time with your significant others rather than how much time you spend) is something you've heard and read about for years. Trying to get all the members of your household in the same place at the same time can be difficult. However, when you rush between work, school, sports, and social commitments, and feel as though you're holding down a second job (with housework, cooking, pet care, helping with homework, and sticking to bedtime routines), it's no wonder you collapse when you arrive home from the office.

If you're a busy, single professional you'll often find it just as challenging fitting in a social life and managing all your domestic responsibilities. Just slumping on the sofa in front of the TV in the little leisure time you have left can often seem the easiest and most attractive prospect at the end of your working day.

Getting back to basics, such as eating dinner together, involving grandparents and other relatives with the children, and turning off the television to talk to each other, are some strategies you can try in order to find unstructured time with family that enables you all to stop rushing around and instead, spend some real time together.

For singletons, planning ahead so that you make the effort to enjoy your life outside of work can really pay off. Think of it like the feeling you get when you've been working out for 20 minutes or so and are beginning to enjoy it, even though you had to drag yourself to the gym. A little foresight and effort at the right time can increase your energy and help you get more out of life.

And if your pets are your main immediate family, don't ever feel silly about making time to connect with them too – research shows that stroking a pet has a directly positive effect on the happy chemicals in our bodies and actually reduces stress!

Families that work well

Families no longer consist of just Mum, Dad, and the kids. Families these days have many variations. Whatever the structure of your family, the people in it form the most important part of your personal life. They affect everything you do, including your working life. Studies show that healthy families make time for talking and listening, show affection and encouragement, accept differences, share chores and decisions, keep in touch, and make time to be together:

✔ **Make time for talking and listening.** Talking with your kids is as important as paying the mortgage and making sure that the house is relatively clean. By talking, we don't mean nagging. Think back to how you felt as a child. The people you connected with best were most likely the ones who listened to what you had to say. Listen to your child without finishing their sentences or lecturing them. Check that you're understanding them by repeating what you just heard but in different words and encourage their conversation by adding, 'Really!' or 'Mmm, hmm, and then what?' Again, try to remember what it feels like when you want to talk and have someone just listen.

✔ **Show affection, encouragement and appreciation.** Kids feel good when encouraged and appreciated, the same as you do. Tell your child what you love and like about him or her and show your affection through hugs, thoughtfulness, and kindness.

Most people find it easier to criticise than praise, a role that's very easy to slip into as a parent: 'How many times have I told you to . . . oh sorry, you've already done it.' Have you found yourself making that silly comment and then having to backtrack? You think about what you say to adults. Think about what you say to kids as well, before you say it. Pause for a few seconds and think about the positive words you can tell your child about their behaviour, how nice they look, how well they're doing at school, and so on.

✔ **Set little rituals for larger reasons.** The little family rituals that you do every day can help provide a sense of security and comfort to you all. You may have special little routines for breakfast together, with specific roles for each family member. For example, 8-year-old Lauren feeds the dog, Dad gets the breakfast cereals out, Mum makes the coffee and 5-year-old Millie opens the curtains in the kitchen and family rooms. Rituals can help in saying goodbye on school and work days and they can also help ease you back into the home zone after a day at work. Lauren says, 'I love it when Dad comes to pick me up from after-school care because we walk home holding hands and I can tell him about the things I did that day.'

Opportunities arise for special family-time rituals at weekends. The authors of this book do this in different ways. In Katherine's house, her husband cooks breakfast on Sunday mornings, helped by her daughter, Carly. The three of them take their time to enjoy the meal, sitting at their kitchen bench chatting together, still in their pyjamas. Jeni, who lives the city life in the company of her two daft cats, likes to meet up for breakfast in her favourite café with a close friend and they natter about their week as they people-watch and drink hot chocolate. It's our time to relax and not have to rush off to school, work, or activities. Time to just 'be'.

TIP

Coming up with great family activity

Thinking up activities to do together isn't difficult. If you have some time to put aside for your family, ask your loved ones how they would like to spend the time. In addition, try some of the activities given below:

✔ **Be active.** Not only are you setting a good example when your loved ones see you power walk, play golf, hike, or go jogging, you're helping your family members (especially your children, if you have them) develop a love for exercise, fresh air, and more playing time with the family.

✔ **Find a shared hobby or project.** Choose a fun activity that appeals to you and your child's interests that you each look forward to doing and talking about afterwards. Simple activities, such as cooking, painting, or going for walks in the countryside, give you a chance to show a side of your character other than just work.

✔ **Help with homework.** This is a great way to show your child that you're interested in her school work and want to spend time helping (not doing it all) and encouraging her.

✔ **Play games.** Turn off the television and computer and show your kids how to play board games. The games that you used to play as a kid can still provide hours of laughs, competition, and conversation.

✔ **Plan family outings.** Get out of the house and go for a drive with a picnic lunch in the back of the car. Visiting your local park, zoo, or beach can be a time to just enjoy being alive without any other distractions. City treats like art galleries and museums are far from stuffy these days and often have interactive exhibitions that are a lot of fun for all ages (especially the big kid inside you!). Taking the time to plan and enjoy

outings like these shows your children how much you value your time with them.

✔ **Read together.** Reading to your kids develops an interest in books, languages, and discovering their world and it increases their attention spans. Parents reading to their children has long been acknowledged as one of the most important activities you can do together. If the child is very small, the experience can be enhanced by asking questions about the story and by looking at the pictures together.

✔ Start a family calendar. Have a large calendar near the telephone or on the fridge with key work commitments and family events marked on it. Encourage the whole family to contribute to this schedule and refer to it first before accepting any further invitations. With work schedules becoming increasingly hectic, family time can end up becoming a low priority if times aren't properly planned. A schedule keeps your family time free from interruptions or cancellations.

Whatever you're arranging to do, remember to:

✔ **Accept each other's differences:** no one should feel like the odd one out in a family, regardless of that person's love of reality television, punk bands, or Goth gear. Successful families appreciate and value the differences in each family member, knowing that everyone is special. Valuing one another's differences allows each member of the family to feel happy about his or her role and personal interests, and to respect others' interests as well.

✔ **Share the load:** show children how to do specific jobs around the house. By doing so they contribute to the family and see the value in helping others. The younger the child, the more supervision is required from you, but give children chances to do tasks by themselves and genuinely praise them for their efforts. Use your powers of grown-up control wisely – preferably through humour and encouragement, rather than put-downs and threats. Doing jobs together also shows them the value of team work and that you're practising what you preach.

My mum and I (Katherine) used to do the dishes after dinner and despite it being a chore, we had some of our best conversations together during that time.

That all family members benefit from this approach goes without saying, so remember to include partners too! Think about the work schedules you both have and plan out a fair arrangement that takes everything into account.

Ditching dinner in front of the television

Are you guilty of eating your evening meal in front of the television and not at the dining table? Many UK families still do. When the majority of your working time is eaten up (pun definitely intended) with work, slumping in front of the television with a plate full of food can seem like the easiest option.

Eating in this way concerns some dieticians, who believe that turning on the television can make you grope automatically for a snack that's usually not particularly healthy, and continue snacking when you're not feeling particularly hungry. Also, evening meals in front of the television are often takeaways (the much maligned timesavers). Being focused on the screen means that attention to details, such as complementing the meal with some vegetables, salad, or fruit, is forgotten.

Dietary concerns aside, eating family meals together around the table, with the television turned off, provides the opportunity to promote and encourage better eating habits at the main time of the day when the family gets to be in the same place at the same time. If you're living alone, it can be tempting to settle for collapsing in a heap onto the sofa after a long hard day and find yourself reaching for the easiest snack that you can consume while still leaving one hand free for the TV remote. Setting the table, and preparing fresh food for a healthy and delicious evening meal can seem like far too much work after all that business work. But you regain a greater sense of balance by giving yourself the gift of taking care of yourself. Simple foods, freshly prepared, don't usually take much more time than convenience options. The ritual of food preparation can actually become a way of unwinding and separating yourself from the business part of your day. Your digestion thanks you for sitting up at a table to eat and you feel generally more centred and cared for. You're worth it, you know!

Does eating at the table work for your family?

Here are three versions of advantages when the family eats together at the table:

✔ Richard says, 'We always eat at the table during the week and usually kick off our conversations with the usual, "So what was the best part of your day?" question. Even the grumpy 15-year-old hangs around for the conversation (even though he rarely contributes), as well as eating every morsel of food placed in front of him.'

✔ John says, 'When is there a better time to talk to your kids and your wife, to find out what's happening in each other's lives? We eat healthier, balanced meals, the kids do better at school because they don't feel neglected, and I know that our kids have better table manners than most of their friends.'

✔ Rachel says, 'It's not only eating together around the table that's important in my home. It's also the growing or buying of the food and getting the kids to help. Having our own little vegetable garden means that the kids find out about the seasons, how much better food tastes when grown naturally, and how they helped contribute to our meal. Another good outcome is that the kids like vegetables, such as broccoli, cabbage, and beans, because they've helped grow them.'

Balancing babies

Whether it's your first child or your fifth, returning to work after taking time off for parental leave can sorely test your strength, as well as any efforts at establishing some work/life balance. When you return to work in the first months or years of your child's life, you can make life easier for yourself and for your child with some simple changes.

Arranging flexible work times with your boss is essential. Explain that you need to cover yourself for unexpected difficulties with options such as later starting times. Starting later helps you to hang around a bit longer with your child while getting familiar with the new carer and child-care surroundings.

You have to face the fact that difficulties always crop up. Work and child care introduce major changes to the life you've known, and situations such as sickness and accidents inevitably arise. You need to be ready to deal with these as best you can when you're at work.

Arranging a carer for your child can happen smoothly. Key steps include:

✔ **Choosing the kind of care your child needs.** What kind of personality and temperament does your child have? If your child is sensitive and gentle, then a one-to-one or small intimate care situation is best. If your child is outgoing and energetic, then a larger group provides opportunities for social interaction and development, especially for 2–3-year-olds.

✔ **Considering your child-care options well ahead of time.** Visit different types of care and get the feel of the places and the people and how they may suit you and your baby. If you're looking at a child-care centre, inquire about waiting lists and application forms to be completed. Ask your friends for recommendations.

✔ **Developing reliable habits.** Set specific rituals for the mornings you drop off your child and the evenings when you get back together. Try to spend at least ten minutes together when you get home to reconnect through cuddling and playing, before starting with the dinner and bath.

✔ **Involving yourself in your child's care.** Have a good discussion with your child's carer before you go back to work so the carer knows your child's likes and dislikes. Build a relationship with your child's carer that means you can openly discuss any concerns or successes experienced during child care.

✔ **Providing information.** For a younger baby, make sure that the care is as similar as possible to what the baby's used to at home. Let the carer know what your baby likes to eat, how he or she likes to be held, the words you say when comforting, your favourite songs, and which toys are favourites. Make sure that the carer lets your child have their favourite cuddly toy when you've left for work.

✔ **Talking about child care.** For toddlers and older children, you can prepare for the change not only by talking about child care but also by acting it out with dolls, teddies, and toys. Emphasise that at the end of the time apart, you're coming back together and returning to the familiar and secure home.

✔ **Visiting the child-care centre.** Visit the centre you're using as many times as you can before you start work. Visiting regularly is an effective way to introduce your child to the arrangement. You can stay with them for the first couple of times and then leave for increasingly longer periods. Even if he or she is sad, make sure that you let your child know each time you're leaving so he or she can trust you not to sneak out.

Despite all of your well planned return-to-work preparations, you're going to experience lots of conflicting emotions. Although you may be looking forward to chatting with adults, having extra money, or resuming your career, you may also be worrying about your child's safety, whether the child's fretting for you, or about the stages of the child's development you're now missing out on. These emotions are understandable for parents returning to work after months or years spent minding babies.

However, with a manageable routine, you're going to have as much time with the child as possible outside working hours. If your child is restless at bedtime and can't go to sleep without you being near, make it a time for you both to get some rest. Don't stress yourself out about uncompleted household chores – they're still going to be there waiting for you after you adjust to work and child care.

You can practise leaving your work stress where it belongs too, so that you can have real quality time with your child. A friend of mine has a lovely symbolic habit of imagining that she hangs up her little bag of work niggles on a tree just outside her front gate, ready and waiting for her when she sets off again the following morning. Not only does she find this puts her in a good frame of mind to be peaceful, happy, and relaxed with her child, she quite often discovers that the metaphorical bag feels lighter the following morning. Sometimes she even feels that this 'bag' somehow contains a magical solution that she wouldn't normally have come up with through worrying and fretting on and off for the whole evening.

Groovy grandparents

Your parents – your children's grandparents – can play a hugely important role in your children's lives and help you achieve some work/life balance. The traditional image of a grandmother is of a grey-haired old lady in spectacles, knitting. These days, many grandparents are young at heart and fit, and are likely to live an active life for many years.

Grandparenting gives your parents the opportunity to spend time with their grandchildren that they may not have been able to do with you because they were working. Also, grandparents provide you with very welcome child care and parental support.

Your parents aren't required to have their roles and responsibilities for your children set in stone in the way your roles are. Talk to your parents about what you'd like them to do with you and your children. Issues to cover can include:

✔ Asking them what involvement they'd like in their grandchildren's lives. This can lead to discussing whether they're happy to babysit. However, don't assume your parents are going to replace paid child-care arrangements. They've already done their share of child-rearing and may only wish to take on the kids occasionally. Grandparents have their own social lives, clubs, and holidays and you need to be prepared for some re-scheduling or cancelling of previously arranged babysitting dates.

✔ Agreeing convenient times for phone calls, and when not to ring (for example, at meal and bath times).

✔ Listening carefully to your parents' views on bringing up children. If the rules have changed – and they do for every generation – explain your ideas and listen to theirs. Grandparents may not behave with the children exactly the way you do but they mean no harm, so you may have to accept their different ways.

✔ Allowing your parents to say when caring for the children is too much for them and when they need some time to themselves. Looking after more than one child at a time can be very tiring. People need to feel free to say 'No' sometimes without the world ending.

Helping your parents mind your children

If you're fortunate enough to have your children's grandparents nearby and they're willing to watch your kids, then make the process as easy as possible for them. (After all, you want them to extend the offer again!) You can make it a lot easier for your parents to look after your kids by providing:

✔ **Assistance in childproofing.** Your parents' house may no longer be safe for curious toddlers. If your children are very young, it pays to double-check that your parents have put special things (such as ornaments, glass tabletops, and pot plants) and poisons such as medicines and washing liquids, safely out of reach.

✔ **Books.** All children love stories. In addition to finding your own childhood favourite books, you can keep up an ever-changing and affordable supply by visiting library sales, garage sales, and second-hand book shops. Stories don't have to be printed either. Encourage your parents to tell your

kids stories about the 'olden days' (that is, before the change of millennium).

✔ **Freedom to allow your parents to have their own set of rules.** Grandparents are allowed to spoil their grandchildren – it's in their job description! They may be stricter in other areas such as the limits set for the amount of TV, DVD, and computer in their home.

✔ **Invitations to your children's activities.** School concerts, sports days, and so on are ideal activities for grandparents. Showing your parents that you value their involvement in more areas than just providing baby-sitting also shows your children that their grandparents are proud of your children's achievements.

✔ **Toys and games that are different from what they have at home.** See if your parents still have some of the old board games, toys, and books that you loved when you were a child. Or even some of the toys and play equipment that they loved when they were children.

Having Happy Holidays

Take a second to think how often you've thought, or heard others saying, 'Oh no, I can't take time off work now, I've far too much to do,' If you had a pound for every time you'd heard other saying it, or thought it yourself, you'd would not only be rich, but hopefully on a relaxing first-class holiday.

In fact, those types of comments are like the proverbial red flags frantically waving in front of your face, trying to get your attention. Work/life balance is calling you. Get over yourself and your own sense of importance! No one is irreplaceable and the work place can survive without you. If you're one of these people, remember that you owe it to yourself, your family, friends, and your workmates to take a decent break and recharge your batteries. If you don't take a break, you may find yourself not only suffering physically, mentally, and emotionally, but also causing others around you to suffer from your unrealistic expectations and your rapidly declining work quality, not to mention how the family copes with your increasing exhaustion and irritable moods when you finally drag yourself home every night. Friendships suffer as well as you miss call after call from important people and feel too exhausted each night to get back to them and keep your connection alive.

Go on, get out!

Researchers say that good holidays have benefits that extend longer than time spent away from work. Workers who take holidays also tend to develop and stick to new habits, such as exercise and improved diet. And being on holiday can help re-establish relationships with your family and friends.

Here are some tips for a fruitful holiday:

- ✔ **Get over yourself:** Facing facts is your biggest challenge. Telling yourself that you think that your work place can't cope without you at work is arrogant. You owe it to your health and your loved ones to take a break. Most importantly, you deserve one.

- ✔ **Leave your work gadgets at work:** No email, laptop, or mobile phone on holidays, thank you. Maintaining your contacts with work – or telecommuting by stealth – only increases your state of tension as you continually scan your emails for bad news or complications.

- ✔ **Listen to your body:** Stay tuned to your body's warning signs. Fatigue, difficulty falling asleep and waking up, irritability, low concentration span, neck, headaches or backaches are all physical signals telling you that you need a break.

- ✔ **Reminisce:** Think about the best holiday you had. What was so good about it? What did it do to refresh you? How can you plan a holiday to repeat that experience? Reminiscing makes you want to have another holiday like the best one.

Surviving the summer holidays

When the long summer holidays are almost here, the children get more and more excited. Parents, however, react very differently. Trying to stretch out your entire annual leave entitlement into the kids' allotment of summer holiday is, for most people, mathematically impossible.

If you can't take annual leave during school holidays, sorting through the options can be stressful, with contacting friends to share care with on specific days, wrangling with ex-partners over where the kids are to spend their time, and being pressured to spend on expensive entertainment to keep kids from getting bored. No wonder holidays feel too much like hard work by the time July comes around.

Admitting that the long summer holidays are challenging is perfectly okay. You're not alone with these dilemmas and you don't need to feel additional guilt over not being able to spend the entire duration of your child's school holidays each year at home, entertaining your children 12 hours a day. Nor should you feel like a third-rate parent for not being able to afford to take them to EuroDisney for a fortnight or on expensive days out shopping or paying entry fees to theme parks.

Finance-friendly fun for kids

Not every event in the school holidays needs to cost you a fortune. Here are some activities to consider when trying to keep kids happy and your eye on the budget:

- **Find art galleries and museums:** These often have children's days, or visiting exhibitions that are of particular interest. These visits encourage your children's creative or scientific interests as well as you discovering new areas together.

- **Find out about local events:** Check your local newspaper, mail drops, your local council, and tourist information centres for what's happening in your area.

- **Get the kids to design a game that you can make the next day:** Give the children ideas to keep the game simple, such as making paper planes to race, mobiles to create and hang outside, and dens from empty boxes. It's amazing what you can do with toilet rolls and sticky tape.

- **Keep it simple:** If the weather is good, go to the local pool for a swim. When it's sunny but not too hot, do something easy like a picnic. You can visit a nearby playground or play in your garden.

- **Make a list of your favourite childhood games:** Chalk drawings on a blackboard, jigsaws, skipping, hopscotch, marbles, home-made play dough, or cooking. Old favourites like these won't cost much and your kids can enjoy finding out what you used to play when you were young.

- **Staying at home is okay:** Your children can use their imagination and independence by playing in the garden or in their bedrooms.

- **Visiting your local library:** Kids can find books, DVDs, and computer games to enjoy and borrow. In addition, many libraries hold special holiday events, such as storytelling and art and crafts sessions during the school holidays. See if you can find some books on keeping kids occupied on holiday rainy days.

Here are a few tips that can help you not only survive, but somehow enjoy the holidays, whether you're at home, away on holidays, or working:

✔ **Being bored is not all bad:** Allow your kids to feel bored. When you hear them complain, feel free to say the same thing that your parents said to you: 'Go and find something to do.' Kids need to fire up their imaginations and have opportunities to think up their own ideas to keep themselves occupied. And you then have the opportunity to read a book or do some gardening while they're busy.

✔ **Encourage hobbies and interests:** Check out the children's summer courses and day programmes available in your area. Most libraries, community centres, schools, and sports centres run activities designed to encourage kids to try new activities.

✔ **Get the whole family to decide on activities:** Kids love the chance to be part of the decision-making process. It may be a drive to the beach, deciding what restaurant to visit for dinner, or choosing the park for a picnic. Children come up with some interesting ideas: you'll find that among the suggestions to visit the North Pole or eat your body weight's worth in red frogs, they decide on an adventure playground, visiting grandparents, cooking, and so on.

✔ **Lazing around is okay:** Like you, kids need some unstructured time to just hang around watching television, play on the computer, or listen to music. It's their holiday and they need to rest and refresh themselves as well.

✔ **Leave info and rules:** If you have to leave your older children alone at home while you're at work, give them clear instructions (written and obvious) about what to do if a problem arises. Leave a list of phone numbers of people they can contact or go to in case they can't reach you.

✔ **Plan ahead and get your diary out:** Look for what child-care options are available in your area ahead of time. See whether other parents attached to your child's class may be interested in scheduling in some days where you can take turns in looking after each other's kids for a day or two. Better still, if you can mix the time with some days of your own annual leave, plus swap days with other parents, and book in some vacation care, you may find that, with your careful planning, the holidays are under control.

✔ **Remember that it's your holiday too, even if you're at work:** If your kids are being looked after by a friend, your parents, or at a structured and safe holiday event, relax – this is partly your holiday too. Don't feel guilty if you pack the kids off for the day and you stay home alone or if you get a babysitter so that you and your partner can have a night out. Kids need a break from you and a change of scenery too.

✔ **Reintroduce routines in the last week of school holidays:** You need to get back to normal bedtimes before school resumes. Your kids are used to later nights and sleep-in mornings on holiday, so by reintroducing normal bedtime before term starts, you'll find that getting up in the morning won't be such a struggle for them when they go back to school.

Travelling with children

Travelling with children is what my brother describes as 'rewarding, not relaxing', but you can plan beforehand to reduce the strain of grizzling kids when you still have miles to go before reaching your longed-for destination.

If your children are old enough, ask them for their help and ideas to plan the itinerary for the trip so they can get excited about it. Complicated trips require lots of travelling. Jam-packed itineraries or too many visits to adult-oriented attractions, such as museums, can be difficult on children and stressful for parents. Keeping your trip as simple as you can reduces the number of problems because children have short attention spans and get tired very quickly.

Some tips to make family holidays a little easier include:

✔ Asking your travel agent for suggestions.

✔ Giving older children your camera or their own disposable one so they can take their own pictures. Encourage them to write a diary entry every evening to record their holiday adventures.

✔ Hiring bulky baby items, such as a pram, cot, and high chair when you arrive at your destination, to save you dragging along your own.

✔ Making use of the kids' club or babysitting facilities at your hotel from time to time so you can have some time alone.

✔ Selecting appropriate accommodation, such as self-contained apartments with a separate bedroom and breakfast provisions, or caravan and camping sites that provide lots of facilities.

✔ When visiting tourist or historical attractions with older children, try negotiating specific adult and kid times, such as doing something the grown-ups want in the morning and something child-friendly in the afternoons (which can also be winding down time and a good opportunity to go for a walk or sit by the pool).

Coping with Christmas chaos

If you're like me, Christmas can feel a fair bit less about celebration and goodwill to your fellow men and more like credit card debt, never-ending shopping, fighting for car parking, and feeling more burned out than the over-cooked turkey lunch. Don't despair. With a bit of planning and organisation, you can survive Christmas and even enjoy the sights, sounds, and silliness of the festive season:

✔ **Delegate duties.** Many individuals are guilty of thinking that the shopping, cooking, cleaning, entertaining of house guests, responding to invitations, writing cards, and so on is entirely up to them. Not so.

Ask your family to help and hold a meeting to delegate tasks that are appropriate to age and skill (for example, if your other hald cooks like a chef, you could put up the decorations and load the dishwasher afterwards). Arrange for any Christmas events you're hosting to be bring-a-dish catering and get your creative kids to gift-wrap the presents. Kids like to be a part of organising Christmas and they then get to appreciate how much work – and fun – Christmas preparations can be.

✔ **Double up your duties.** Buy presents online during your lunch hours and have coffee with a friend you won't be able to catch up with at the weekend. Forgive yourself for buying the pudding from the supermarket and cook a chicken breast roll instead of spending hours wrestling a turkey into the oven. Set up the tree as a family after dinner one night and together decide what news and photos you're going to contribute to your Christmas email.

✔ **Make some time for you.** Scheduling time out for yourself is one of the best gifts you can give to everyone so that you don't end up turning into a red-eyed and frantic Christmas crackpot. When everyone else is busy fighting over the last limited-release, must-have computer console, go for a long walk, settle somewhere quiet with a good book, or take yourself off to see a movie.

✔ **Save paper and postage.** Instead of being forced to write 100 Christmas cards to family and friends over the country, make a donation to a preferred charity and email everyone explaining what you've done. Use your family email to wish your friends all the best for the season. You may start a trend so that they too no longer feel the obligation to send out cards that clutter up mantelpieces and fall over every time the door opens.

✔ **Save your holiday spirit by staying in.** Make sure that you have at least two nights of the weeks leading up to Christmas and New Year to sit home and relax with your friends and loved ones. Sharing a favourite family dinner, renting some DVDs, or having a board-game night are easy ways to share some simple socialising time.

✔ **Use your diary for decision-making.** You have four invitations for the same night but you're allowed to choose between them. Don't make the mistake of thinking you can make an appearance at all four functions. As you do at work, do at home – prioritise the events that are most impor-tant to you and make sure that you also have enough free time to do your preparations for Christmas and simply take a break. Say 'No'. Many people have too many commitments over Christmas and would, in fact, prefer to accept your offer of organising a get-together in January or February instead.

How to meet your own needs during a family holiday

You've finished the most important parts of your job and left enough emails, notes, and back-up information to keep the office ticking along in your absence. The house is locked securely and you're ready to get into the car with your family and get away. But you're forgetting one important fact: what are you getting from your holiday? Here are some answers:

✔ **Empty diary.** You may want to see and do everything you can to get the most out of your location, accommodation, activities, and the money the holiday is costing you. Stop! Take it easy. Dashing around like an over-caffeinated roadrunner is the best way to make sure that you come back from your holiday feeling just as burned out as when you left.

✔ **Manageable holiday budget.** Remind yourself that impulse buys cancel any relaxing effects of your holiday if you're faced with whopping credit card bills when you get home.

✔ **Flexible and realistic attitude.** Accept that parts of your holiday are going to work out better than you expected, while other parts aren't going to be as wonderful as you dreamed. That's normal. Take a deep breath, make sure that everyone in your holiday party is safe and then relax.

✔ **Willingness to spoil yourself.** Scheduling periods of utter nothing is wonderful. Set aside a few hours a day to stop, read the paper, put your feet up, or nap like a 3-year-old.

Working for the Weekends

Your weekends are precious. You work all week while dreaming about the weekend and how much fun you're going to have. Yet often weekends can end up just as time pressed and stressful as the week, leaving you feeling resentful, tired, and dreading work even more. If you work shifts you may not always get a 'weekend' so it's important to create one for yourself – a couple of days on a frequent basis when you can leave work at the actual or metaphorical office and concentrate on other aspects of your whole life.

Making plans for your weekend can help you to achieve what you want to do without getting side-tracked by chores. If you're planning for the traditional weekend, jot your plans down on Monday night and allot some time to do a few major chores during the week, such as a couple of loads of washing on Wednesday night and ordering your groceries online during Thursday lunch time. Planning means that when Saturday morning rolls around you won't have the grocery shopping and washing hanging over your head in between the sports and birthday party taxi runs. Some other useful tips to enjoy weekends, whenever they occur for you, include:

✔ **Breathing fresh air:** This is wonderful, although the weather can be a problem. When the weather's fine, go for a walk, jog, visit the local park, or ride a bike with your kids. Something as simple as getting fresh air and exercise can make you feel refreshed. And getting out in nature is as good as meditation for calming that chattering mind!

✔ **Finding a new hobby:** A new hobby can help you avoid getting stuck into a routine of housework and chores. Your hobby can give you a treat to look forward to, whether with your family, with a club, or by yourself as part of your planned time out.

✔ **Fixing up the niggly chores:** We know that your weekend is about fun and relaxation but weekends are also handy for doing small jobs that have been bugging you for a while. Simple maintenance jobs, such as oiling squeaking doors, taking your old clothes to a charity bin, or sorting out your recycling can go a long way to reducing the visual stress factor when they're left undone. Even sitting down one evening and working through your unpaid bills, tax statements, and so on, lifts a weight from your shoulders and you feel you're achieving something worthwhile during your two days off work. The trick is to develop a different mindset and find ways to turn these little victories into a game.

✔ **Getting out of the rut:** Being in a rut takes a lot away from the idea of rest and relaxation. When life's busy, you can find yourself doing the same old things every weekend. In fact, the two precious weekend days away from work can be juggled far more freely than your work days. Try inviting a friend or group of friends over for a meal (even if it's just a takeaway) or go and visit somewhere you've never been but always wondered about. The washing and lawns are still going to be there on Sunday.

✔ **Meeting up with your friends:** Make the effort! You're busy all week on the phone at work and even though you love spending time with your friends, the thought of getting on the phone again and trying to organise a catch-up seems like too much hard work. Arrange to meet up for a coffee after the Saturday morning footy game or even a fully fledged dinner party. Other alternatives can be to get up earlier on Sunday morning and do a walk together or see a movie together straight from work on Friday night. Whatever the event, you can get a lot of enjoyment out of socialising with your friends.

Contributing to Your World

An extremely satisfying way to gain some work/life balance outside of your own home is to share your strength, skills, and experiences for the benefit of schools, not-for-profit organisations, or specific projects in your community. Volunteering your help can benefit you in a variety of ways, namely through giving back some of your benefits to less fortunate people in society, staying active, making friendships, being with other people, and gaining a clearer sense of your role and value in your community. You could gain a greater sense of personal fulfilment and even reduce your stress levels from feeling like you're making a greater contribution outside of your home. That doesn't sound too bad, does it?

 Volunteers don't get paid for their involvement and you may sometimes have to cover some out-of-pocket expenses, such as travel, meals, or stationery. Volunteering should never be forced on you or make you feel obligated, and nor does it replace paid workers (or threaten their job security). Look through your local paper and contact your council or community centre to find out what's out there for you to do.

Making time for volunteering

So here you are, reading a book on work/life balance, and we're suggesting you try to carve out even more time from your frantic schedule to volunteer?! Well, we agree, volunteering isn't for everyone, and maybe it isn't something you choose to do as a permanent part of your life. Even so, and quite apart from the benefits we mentioned above, some volunteers find that their time of service leads to wonderful new careers that actually suit their lives better than their former choices. And although it may seem ironic, the more we talk to people who volunteer, the more they seem to agree that giving up a bit of their 'free' time just makes them feel so great that they seem to have more energy and resources for everything else in their lives. The trick is to find volunteer work that really engages your heart and soul and then make sure that you only commit the time you can really afford to give.

A sample of organisations that need your help

The list of worthy organisations that can use volunteer help is never ending. Here are some great websites to get you started on your volunteer adventure:

- **do-it.org.uk** (www.do-it.org.uk): Launched in 2001, this was the first, and remains the main, national database of volunteering opportunities in the UK. Local Volunteer Centres post opportunities – part-time, full-time, temporary, and permanent – and you can search on this website to find a Centre local to you if you want more personal contact from their advisers. Registration as a volunteer is free.

- **Timebank** (www.timebank.org.uk): Similar in operation to do-it.org.uk, Timebank acts as a recruitment agency, matching volunteers to organisations and institutions. It was created by the founders of Comic Relief in 2000 and continues to run innovative marketing campaigns to attract volunteers to a huge range of worthy causes. More than 220,000 people in the UK have been attracted into volunteering through a Timebank campaign and you can register for free on their site so that they can match you to relevant opportunities as they arise.

- **Community Service Volunteers** (www.csv.org.uk): Part of the same stable as Voluntary Service Overseas (VSO) this organisation (CSV) has been running since 1962 and attracts people aged 16–35 into community projects. CSV focuses mainly on full-time volunteering for a period of time so you need to think about how that fits with your current work commitments. Remember, however, that these days, employers in the UK are much more open to the idea of supporting sabbatical leave for all sorts of mutual benefit!

- **The Mentoring and Befriending Foundation** (www.mandbf.org.uk): Runs projects that include working with refugees, unemployed people, older people, disaffected young people, offenders and ex-offenders, care leavers, disabled people, homeless people, pupils and students, and lone parents. Mentoring tends to focus on helping the individual to set and achieve goals, whilst befriending tends to develop more informal social relationships, perhaps over a long period of time.

- **The Prince's Trust** (www.princes-trust.org.uk): Helps young people 'overcome barriers and get their lives working'. If you fancy making a difference to the lives of disadvantaged young people, and especially if you have good commercial experience, you can volunteer to act as a mentor to a young person setting up in business who would otherwise never source the skills and support to do it.

- **The Samaritans** (www.lifeline.org.au): Lifeline receives more than 450,000 calls a year from distressed, lonely, and isolated people needing counselling and support. Lifeline needs telephone volunteers, people willing to work in their second-hand shops, administrative help in head office, and fundraisers.

- **Make a Wish** (www.makeawish.org.au): Grants 'magical wishes' to children and young people suffering life-threatening illnesses. Make-A-Wish was founded in the UK in 1986 and since then has granted over 4,700 wishes ranging from being a princess or a policeman for a day to a special holiday. You can support the organisation in lots of ways as a volunteer or as a fundraiser.

✔ **National Blood Service** (www.blood.co.uk): Collects vital blood donations from voluntary donors. If you want to give your blood rather than time, you can do so in your lunch hour at mobile units, or seek out a city-based centre. Whichever you choose, it's a nice opportunity for a lie down and a cup of tea afterwards to go with the feel-good factor!

✔ **Oxfam** (www.oxfam.org.au): Provides help to communities in 27 countries to help end the struggle against poverty and injustice. Oxfam is seeking volunteers in event coordination, training, media/writing, web development, cross-cultural communication, customer service, and counselling. And of course you can volunteer a couple of hours at the weekend if you like, to serve in the shops. If you're addicted to bargains yourself then volunteering in charity shops like Oxfam can be a great win/win!

✔ **Realbuzz.com** (www.realbuzz.com): Caters for the energetic You! Ever wanted to run a marathon? Well, Realbuzz.com gives you plenty of inspiration and signposts you to the main charities that you can support as you get fit and go for your goal. It needn't be the full 26 miles – you can do plenty of shorter charity races. Another positive double whammy!

Corporate volunteering work

As charitable organisations receive less and less financial support from governments, increasingly the corporate sector fills the funding gap by sponsoring or funding projects. These companies aren't silly: they benefit from their community contributions by gaining positive exposure, which can lead to increased business networks, the narrowing of the divide between big business and the local community, and enhancing their recruitment levels. They can also benefit by granting sabbatical leave to employees who then return to their roles with renewed vigour and a fresh perspective.

Cycling sets a new standard for conferences

The good news is that parents now find it easier to make additional roles, such as volunteering for community jobs, more public in the work place.

Greg, a Human Resources professional for a large government department, uses an automatic email response and posts a note on his door that states he leaves the office at 3 p.m. on Tuesdays to help coach his son's football team. 'I've been to a couple of urgent meetings wearing my cycling gear, ready to ride over to the school,' he says. 'That gives my work team the signal to keep the meeting short and decisive.'

Part V
The Bigger Picture: Getting What You Want Long Term

'So this is your first office-cleaning commission
since you changed jobs, Mr Wisdish?'

In this part . . .

In this part, we look at how getting a little bit addicted to learning can help your work/life balance. Signing up for an adult education course, embracing vocational qualifications, or even studying for a university degree can all help you in the longer term to secure the most flexible career options for you.

New skills and qualifications can lead you to a completely different career. Changing jobs requires an updated and succinct CV, good writing skills for a covering letter, the ability to perform during an interview, and the know-how of successful networking. This part shows you different ways to change career direction, including changing jobs within the organisation in which you currently work, changing companies, buying a franchise, working from home, running a small business, and taking time off from paid work.

Chapter 11

Casting Your Net Wider

. . . .

In This Chapter

▶ Finding a new job

▶ Writing a winning CV and covering letter

▶ Surviving job interviews

. . . .

*Y*ou may be feeling as though you've achieved all you can in your current job and see no future career development if you stay with your present employer. But more exciting job prospects await you. Believe me!

This chapter shows you how to expand your list of valuable contacts and support systems by networking. Yes, we know that word has horrible 1980s connotations of shoulder-padded careerists trampling over each other while striving to get to the top, but these days you can find many more efficient ways to improve your job situation.

The first stage in your new job hunt is to write up or revamp your curriculum vitae (CV), keeping it simple and concise. This can be harder than you think, and so we give you tips on how you can achieve the art of simplicity and show off your skills at the same time. Writing a killer covering letter is also discussed in this chapter, as are the all-important interview survival tips and tricks, including how to make sure that your potential employer embraces and encourages work/life balance strategies for workers.

Changing Jobs and Employers

If you're unhappy in your current role or feel that no future career path is open to you with your current employer, you need to ask this question: can moving to a new job clear up your current unhappiness and give you more work/life balance?

Living the high life in London

Sophie, an IT expert, admits that she can be influenced by higher salary and prestige positions such as company size or recognition factor when attracted by positions offered in her profession. So much so that she forgets that the reason she sought a new job was to set an achievable career path.

'Not for the first time I find myself in a job that's just as bad as the one I left in Manchester. The money is better but the high cost of living in London cancels out that advantage and I'm working much longer hours than I was at home.'

Recruitment agencies report that electronic applications for jobs are more common than in the past, a convenience, some say, that leads people to being more encouraged to jump ship rather than to resolve their concerns with the current job. If a new role is only a click away, the danger is that you may also be less likely to think through the consequences of changing jobs and whether the new role is really better for you than the one you want to leave.

Before applying for that newer, shinier, better-sounding job, take the time to write down which aspects about your current position you don't like. Apart from the salary, the clashes with your boss, or being worn out by a heavy workload, are you doing your bit to communicate clearly? Is your employer aware of the existence of work/life balance policy and its importance in the process of keeping good workers? If so, is your employer just 'talking the talk' and not putting work/life balance policy into practice? After listing what you don't like about your current job, write down a list of the factors that may entice you to leave.

Work/life balance – and having the opportunity to implement the employer's policy as a flexible working arrangement that suits you – has a huge impact on whether you're going to enjoy, or end up hating, a job. Your motivation, loyalty, and energy levels reduce considerably if you don't feel valued enough by the employer to ask and receive an adaptable working arrangement. If that's your situation, chances are that your future career isn't going to be with that employer.

Why work/life balance features should be considered in your job hunt

Although newspaper employment sections and websites offer useful articles on job search techniques, including how to write your CV, covering letters, and how to conduct yourself during interviews, they supply relatively little information about actually finding a job that offers improved work/life balance.

Increasingly though, employers are becoming aware of the importance of these issues in their recruitment practices. A Chartered Institute of Personnel Development (CIPD) survey in 2004 looked specifically at the problems facing UK employers in recruitment and retention. 85 per cent of respondents reported recruitment difficulties. They mostly attributed these difficulties to the challenge of finding individuals with the right specialist skills, and the incidence of recruitment freezes and redundancies as the economy has begun to tighten highlights this problem even more.

The CIPD survey indicated that the most common approach to resolving this challenge was to recruit people who had the potential to grow but didn't have all the specialist skills required. Good news for candidates who may feel anxious that they're not ticking all the boxes on recruitment ads. Even more encouragingly, the introduction of new flexible working guidelines by the Government in 2003 led to an increasing number of organisations (17 per cent of those surveyed) offering better arrangements to existing staff and new recruits.

There's still plenty of headway to make on flexible working but it seems that UK employers are beginning to embrace it as a key strategy to recruit and retain their most valuable resource – you!

Networking Your Way to Success

Like it or loathe it, networking is the single most effective way to source your exciting brand new career opportunity. The reason for this is that you're selling *you* first and foremost – your unique qualities, skills, abilities, and even that quirky sense of humour of yours. So much of what makes you special is really hard to convey in a CV, or even at an interview. When you network, people get to see the real you, and you give yourself the best chance of making a great and unexpected connection that can lead to the best job of your life.

What's out there for you?

You can eagerly read through the newspaper employment sections at the weekend – but don't restrict your search to the papers. Online employment sites not only advertise positions vacant but also allow you to post your CV for it to be emailed immediately to relevant positions vacant, according to the industry you're seeking, position description, location, and seniority levels that you nominate. Some of the more popular online sites include:

✔ **Public and Not for Profit vacancies** (www.jobsgopublic.com): The main site for finding local, regional, and national vacancies if you're a public sector worker or have not-for-profit charity expertise.

✔ **General vacancies** (www.jobcentreplus.gov.uk): The days when the Job Centre only serviced people coming 'off the dole' have long gone; this website opens up a world of vacancies across the board, as well as signposting you to help and support for re-training.

✔ **Hays** (www.hays.com): Amongst the recruitment consultancies, Hays is the largest publicly listed recruitment group in the UK, providing specialist support to professional jobseekers in securing permanent, temporary, and interim positions.

✔ **Manpower** (www.manpower.com): Originating from the US, Manpower is another global leader in employment services, offering through their website vacancies, listings, and career advice.

✔ **Monster** (www.monster.co.uk): You can go-it-alone and post your CV, gaining access to many thousands of vacancies. Monster offer lots of helpful career advice and tips too.

✔ **Fish4jobs** (www.fish4.co.uk): Makes job-searching as simple as looking for a new car, a new home, or a holiday. Like Monster, this website helps you get yourself out there and identify hundreds of potential vacancies that may be right for you.

So put aside any reservations you have. Networking is simply about getting out and about and meeting people who can help you and who you may be able to help in return. What's so scary about that?

Studies show that only one third of all new jobs are posted in the classified advertisements, in the newspapers, or on the Internet. Two-thirds of positions are filled by word of mouth. In reality, networking isn't about job seeking as much as establishing a working relationship with people who share the same interests as you in the professional arena. When you decide to look out for a role beyond your current employer, your contacts can help you.

Networking can be done anytime, anywhere – sitting next to someone at a training day, on a bus ride home, or in a social setting. You never know when and with whom you may strike up an important conversation. These informal conversations can help you build up a picture of which employers offer the kind of work/life balance arrangements that best suit you.

Spreading the word

Without realising it, you may already have many important connections among the people in your life – perhaps through your work, location, a related industry, or your family or community. A simple but effective way to start networking – and keep your eyes open for a new job opportunity – is to tell everyone you know (and trust) what you're seeking. The news spreads and your friends let you know when they come across a job that you may want to investigate further.

Brimming with business cards

Keep your CV up to date and always have business cards with your contact information handy. Feel a bit silly at the idea of carrying business cards around with you all the time? Well, don't! Even if your current job isn't one where you normally require business cards, this practice is more about you and your personal brand. These days, simple cards can be printed up in a variety of low-cost ways – you can even do them yourself on your home PC – and having a business card is a time-tested method of creating a good impression and helping people get in touch with you. You can think of it as paying homage to the old-fashioned practice of leaving calling cards, if you want to be all Jane Austen about it!

Where appropriate, you can follow up by sending a brief email telling your contacts how much you enjoyed meeting them or running into them, and attach your CV or brief profile to the email. This practice is polite and helps make it more likely for you to linger in their memory banks than the 300 other business cards that live in their top drawer.

 As an alternative to a business card, why not experiment with a postcard-size image and perhaps an inspiring or funny quote to go along with it? That way you can write on the back and personalise it. Again, this is a great way of standing out from the crowd and displaying your personality.

Asking questions and actually listening to the answers

Ask your contacts questions about their backgrounds and in particular how they ended up with a particular company. People love to tell their story and this approach really helps you establish a rapport with your new contact. Letting them do most of the talking also allows you to really listen and gives you a few moments to collect your own thoughts. Ask contacts how they manage to achieve balanced work and lifestyles. Their answers give you personalised information about work/life balance because it involves the actual situation of the person with whom you're networking.

Relating to your customers

You don't have to have the confidence of Donald Trump to network successfully. Ian, a photo-copier sales supervisor (and a karate sensei, or teacher), doesn't consider himself your every-day salesman because he feels he belongs in the introvert personality group.

Despite this, Ian is successful in his job because he can develop relationships with customers rather than hyper-selling them products. Ian always meets or exceeds his sales targets.

'I just tell the truth. I listen to what they want, and I try to help them. They trust me.'

Christine recalls, 'I struck up a conversation with a top-level recruitment manager at a mediation course and we started talking about the joys of having a toddler and doing the day-care run. We exchanged cards and I thought no more about it until several months later when the woman rang to see if I'd be interested in applying for a role in her department.'

Volunteering to help others

Whenever possible, take on volunteer jobs that allow you to gain visibility and develop relationships by showing off your skills. If you're handy with finances, be the treasurer of your child's sports club or a not-for-profit organisation you care about. If you're an organised person, help with office duties for a busy but underfunded community group. Working as a volunteer helps you to be noticed by others without your having to actively network.

I (Katherine) am always surprised at how small the world can be – a CEO of a private hospital I used to negotiate business with was the man running the next stall to mine at a local community fete. We chatted and I found that in future work situations our relationship was much friendlier. The same can be true if you take on paid, temporary roles. For instance, a former colleague of mine, who avoided networking like the plague, accepted a secondment to another government department for six months. During that time, she met many different representatives from community groups – one of whom offered her a job as his group's finance officer. For more information on volunteering, refer to Chapter 10.

Taming the telephone

You may find the idea of making cold calls to potential contacts and employers very intimidating. Keep in mind that the people you're reaching are only human just like you, and they have their own fears and anxieties. You never know when you're going to get through to just the right person and make that person's day because he's been searching high and low for someone just like you to join his team. Cold calling is a skill like any other and you can learn it easily. Here are some tips from the experts to help you:

✔ Create a plan and stick to it. Set goals and be focused about achieving them. For example, make a plan for one telephone call a day. You can telephone a company you're interested in during your lunch hour if you can do so discreetly and appropriately. Ask for the name and title of the relevant HR or line manager so that you know specifically who to address in your letter of application. Then revamp your CV to highlight the most relevant skills and qualifications that are likely to most interest the recruiter. Also, make sure that you include a covering letter explaining why you're contacting the company and what you think you can offer.

✔ Know what you want to say when calling. Before you call, jot down a script or some bullet points to help you remember the most important subjects to discuss. Be sure to speak to the right person. Don't launch into a big speech only to hear, 'Please hold while I put you through to the HR department.' When you're put through to the right person, consult your script to make sure that you raise all the points you want to discuss. It really is worth spending some quality time simply researching your list of potential contacts and keeping that activity separate to the times when you're aiming to get through to a decision-maker. Research can be a great way to 'warm up' your cold calling, as you're simply getting in touch with switchboard operators to confirm who specifically is the right person for you to approach.

✔ Perform at your peak time. If you're a morning person you may prefer to get your challenging phone calls over and done with early in the day. However, if you know that you're energetic and more courageous after lunch, save your calls until then and focus on something else in the morning.

✔ Practise, practise, and practise. If you dread meeting new people, try practising what you want to say with your partner or a trusted friend. Ask about their interests, job, and background and then explain yours. Role playing these scenarios makes you more confident about what to say when you're in the real interview situation.

Hanging in there

Networking can feel like hard work. The best networking produces contacts that can benefit you in the longer term, so don't become discouraged when you're not immediately swamped with party invitations and job offers. The right job may take time to emerge. What you can do is make sure that you're one of the first people that a company executive, recruiter, or an interesting speaker at a seminar remembers when he's looking to fill a job in his organisation. In the meantime, concentrate on new ways and places to network. It really is a numbers game and it pays to remember both aspects of that – so keep your numbers of contacts high and aim to have fun in the game!

Pinpointing your passions

Many people panic about the thought of having to telephone or make conversation with strangers at conferences and other industry events. You can overcome this fear by focusing on an aspect of the other person's field of work that genuinely interests you. It's easier to start and maintain a conversation with someone when you're passionate about the subject matter. Discussing something you're passionate about with someone who you know shares your passion is your reason for approaching that person.

Retaining referees

Contacting referees and letting them know when you're applying for a new job, especially if you're short-listed for an interview, is polite. Some referees who aren't given this courtesy can be annoyed and sound irritated when they suddenly receive a call from your potential employer without notice. This call gives you an opportunity to brief your referee about the job you're being interviewed for and to refresh the referee's memory of who you are and what you achieved when working with them.

Many recruiters don't like calling a mobile phone number because they can't verify who the person at the other end is, and common though email is for everyone these days, it has the same potential drawbacks. Provide the general company switchboard numbers so that the recruiter can double-check the referee's name, title, and email address if they wish before making contact.

The what-not-to-do list

Like everything worth doing in life, networking can be taken too far. The result is you burn your bridges and destroy any future chance of being remembered or helped. Some common pitfalls to avoid include:

Applying relentlessness instead of skilfulness. You may know of someone who keeps applying for any and every position at a company where they desperately want to work. Unnecessary bombarding of an employer for positions that aren't always suitable to an applicant's skills and experiences can result in that person's applications being automatically thrown into the wastepaper basket as a waste of the boss's reading time. Job hunters of this type reek of desperation rather than qualification.

Being the unwanted guest. Eager job seekers sometimes take networking and assertiveness too far, showing up in the reception area of desirable employers or recruiting firms and asking to see the HR manager. This action won't win you points because it's arrogant and impolite. Make an appointment for a more appropriate time.

Being too personal. Communications such as 'I got married three months ago and have just returned from our fantastic tour of Europe and was wondering if you have any job vacancies going?' are bad news. Keep your email and covering letters professional and remove any unnecessary personal information that makes you look immature, and as though you can't get to the point.

Boss-bashing. No one wants to hear an applicant bad-mouth a former boss. This action suggests the same disloyalty can happen to the new employer. Even if your criticism is genuine, blaming and insulting someone who's not there to defend himself is wrong. Remember too how small the world is – for all you know, your despised former boss may be the brother-in-law of the MD you're hoping is going to employ you.

Telling untruths. Don't start networking or expressing interest in jobs unless you can be honest about everything. Even merely hinting that your own job may end in the foreseeable future when you've already been made redundant and are now twiddling your thumbs at home is not being honest. An untruthful applicant doesn't present as a trustworthy worker.

Whingeing about work/life balance. Yes, we know that this may be the key reason you're out networking and looking for a different job in the first place, but bear in mind that griping to other people doesn't win you much beyond polite sympathy and a desire to get away from you to someone else more interesting. Instead of whingeing, try discussing the subject of employment in a more general way. Ask: 'Do you find that more people are working flexible hours, for example, from home after the kids have gone to bed or earlier in the mornings so they can pick up their kids from school?'

Crafting Clever CVs

Your *curriculum vitae* (CV) is an outline of your educational and professional history that you provide during a job application. Writing a CV can seem a bit intimidating if you haven't done one for a while, but don't feel too exhausted just yet – you can find great ways to make yours stand out from the crowd and display your considerable talents to best effect!

HR professionals and recruiters don't want to sift through 25 pages detailing your primary school achievements or squint at size 8 hot-pink wingdings. A two-page CV is fine if you've been in the work force for only a few years. Three to five pages is the ideal number for anyone with an established employment history. Think 'short attention span' whenever you're crafting your CV!

Layout

Keep the layout of your CV simple – and we mean really simple. Times New Roman (12 pt) or Arial (11 pt) are two of the easiest types to read so it's kind to choose these or similar fonts to save your reader eye strain. Using bold for headings is all you need to make details stand out – any more embroidery and your CV looks too busy.

Fancy fonts can also be very distracting and detract from the content of your CV. Avoid using table formats because they can appear overcrowded and difficult to read. Instead, use tabs to separate job titles from dates and duties.

REAL-LIFE STORY

When a CV is too good to be true

We can't emphasise enough how important honesty is in a CV. A senior department manager and I (Katherine) once tried to find a project-manager with specific skills in statistical analysis and project writing. After attending a group-selection process, run by the recruitment agency, we selected five people to interview. Colin particularly favoured 23-year-old Rachel, liking her confidence and her employment history. The referees she nominated gave glowing reports of her prowess. And yet something didn't sit right with me. I had an inkling that she had exaggerated her skills and experience, considering her young age.

As luck would have it, Colin and I knew someone at Rachel's company (James), who was not included in her list of referees. When we contacted him to see if he knew of her achievements, the response was decidedly negative. According to James, Rachel was impetuous, immature, and didn't obey instructions. The organisation's HR department later discovered that she hadn't completed the final year of her science degree. 'We're glad to see the back of her. That's why her referees are so dazzling,' James said. Colin and I learned to check anything on a CV that appears to be too good to be true.

Contact details

Add your full name, address, phone number, and mobile and email details at the top of the first page of your CV. Also, put your name, mobile phone, and email address as a header or footer on each page of the CV in case the pages become separated. Never use a shared email address or one that may be hilarious in online chat rooms but not so professional for job hunting.

A friend of mine eventually changed her private email address from BigButt to GeoSci + surname when she was applying for a job in geo-sciences. Starting with your name or an abbreviated version is the simplest method. To get with the times, don't bother putting your marital status or birth date on your CV: neither is relevant to the position you're applying for.

Strengths

List your key strengths as bullet points to make your CV simpler for recruiters to scan through. Keep your points brief but thorough. Putting 'outstanding communicator' or 'strong team member' is pointless because these descriptions are too vague. Instead, write something like, 'Excellent written and verbal communication skills attained through tertiary study and in leadership roles in sales department' or 'Productive member of the team responsible for winning the tender to construct our city's new police headquarters'. In other words, offer the recruiter information they can envisage and understand as an example of your strengths.

Employment history

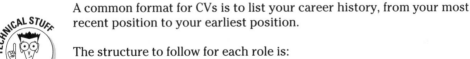

A common format for CVs is to list your career history, from your most recent position to your earliest position.

The structure to follow for each role is:

- ✔ **Job title, employer, dates:** What you did, for whom, and when.
- ✔ **Description of employer:** only include a description when you've worked for an overseas company that's not generally known in the UK. Global firms, such as Coca-Cola, Procter & Gamble and Microsoft need no such descriptions. Alternatively, if you're working (or have worked) for a UK company whose name doesn't identify the industry, then use a description.

✔ **Responsibilities:** People make the mistake of believing that the more responsibilities listed, the better. Include only the key positions where you were responsible for achievements. Don't list every single task you performed. We've seen CVs where people listed: 'Attended monthly sales meetings'. Which skill is involved in that task? Instead, write, for example, 'Chairing the monthly sales meeting' because that is a responsibility and implies specific skills and abilities.

✔ **Achievements:** Achievements show your initiative, creativity and ability to work hard for results and give a clear indication of what additional benefits there may be in employing you over someone else. For the purposes of your CV, achievements mean those tasks that you did at work (or in the wider community) that you were not required to do, or were over and above your expected performance. Examples include staff awards, community recognition, or specific projects and suggestions that you developed, which resulted in an increase in business or savings.

Listing achievements on your CV gives you a chance to indicate your interest and participation in work/life balance initiatives. For example, if you chaired a steering committee that was given the responsibility to research and implement a job-share policy in your former job, put that on your list.

✔ **Education and training:** Start with your highest qualification first. The education and training section can cover university, NVQs, industry courses, in-house courses, and any other professional training. Here, too, you can include any courses that involve recognising the importance of flexibility at work, such as 'Managing change', 'HR principles for managers and supervisors', 'Motivating staff', and so on. Unless you left school within the past five years, you can leave your secondary school history off your CV.

✔ **Professional memberships:** Include only those memberships relevant to your career, and add any positions you hold (or have held), sub committees you belong to, or any significant events (for example 'Awarded 2007 Annual Work/Life Balance Society scholarship').

✔ **Hobbies and interests:** This section isn't compulsory and you're best to err on the side of caution if one of your favourite pastimes happens to be nude stage diving or auditioning for reality television shows. Better to leave this section out if you're applying for a position in a conservative industry or charity.

✔ **Referees:** As a general rule, referees are included at the end of your CV. Referees' names, position titles, and company details should be included with contact details, or you can add 'Contact phone numbers available on request'. Getting a phone call to find out your referees' details gives you an indication of whether you're short-listed for the job and you can then contact your referees to discuss their description of you and your work.

Many different ways exist of structuring your CV. Alternative ways of presenting your information can be more appropriate if you've spent only a short time working on a recent job, for example. Take a look at *CVs For Dummies* by Steve Shipside and Joyce Lain Kennedy (Wiley) for more information on this topic.

Cracking the Covering Letter

In your haste to get your job application posted off to win you that dream job, you quickly type out a covering note and staple it to the front of your CV. Beware! Your recruiter may not even bother to turn the page over and look at your details. Check your letter for spelling and typos, that it addresses the job specifically, and gets the name and title of the recruiter correct. No employer likes getting a formulaic letter that's obviously been sent to a hundred others because that says you couldn't be bothered to tailor your application to that employer's needs.

As a former English teacher and veteran of more than my share of recruitment drives, I (Katherine) can vouch for the strength of a great cover letter. During one recruitment project I received 60 letters from applicants for an administrative position and only read through 15 of the attached CVs. Despite our newspaper advertisement specifying my name and job title, several letters were addressed to 'Dear Sir or Madam' and 'To Whom it May Concern'. No points were awarded to those not smart enough to read the advertisement correctly.

Of the 15 applications short-listed, only five covering letters specifically discussed how the applicants met the selection criteria, despite the advertisement clearly stating that applicants had to address each point specifically in the application. Luckily for me, out of the five applicants, we found Tracey, who has since moved up in the ranks in a very short span of years with that organisation.

And don't think that email gets you out of writing the covering letter! Your introductory comments are even more important when it comes to the electronic version because so many people scan and delete anything that looks like junk or time-wasting email. Be sure to apply the same principles of tailoring your application email so that your potential new employer does actually want to click on the attachment.

Make your covering letter a cracker by:

- ✔ **Feeling passionate.** Writing a stilted, clichéd covering letter is likely to have your CV put on the reject pile. Tell the potential employer why this job opportunity makes you feel enthusiastic, what you can bring to the role, and how working for the organisation can motivate you. What recruiter doesn't want to hear the organisation described as an exciting employer of choice?

- ✔ **Getting a fresh set of eyes.** Ask an experienced colleague or trusted friend to review your letters for any typos, gaps, and possible improvements. You'll be amazed what someone else can find that you can't see because you wrote it.

- ✔ **Referring to the job for which you're applying.** Explain why you're the best person for the job. For example, write 'I see this position as an ideal opportunity to extend my developing skills in project management and in technical writing.'

- ✔ **Slipping in a suggestion.** For example, show you may even be able to improve the employer's work place. A powerful way to intrigue a potential employer is to show that you know enough about the organisation and the position to see room for improvement. For example, 'As the leading supplier of belly-button fluff collectors, I can see additional ways you can expand your business through sponsoring relevant Internet sites, such as . . .'.

- ✔ **Taking your time.** Make sure that you discuss every aspect of the job advertised and why you're the best person for the job – this takes a lot of effort. Taking the time to research the organisation, the role applied for, and presenting your best writing can take a few hours and lots of revisions. The covering letter is your chance to tell the employer more about yourself than just what's listed in your CV, and show your communication skills at the same time.

To make sure that you don't fall into the trap of exaggerating your achievements, ask your partner, a friend, or someone who has worked with you to play devil's advocate. Give them free rein to challenge your covering letter details as to why you're the best person for the job. Ask them to question you further about your achievements and whether you can discuss them in more detail.

The referees you include in your application *must* be able to support your claims. You may get away with asking your best mate in the call centre to be your boss, but you always run the risk of the recruiter contacting someone else they know who works there. Instead, email your referees your covering letter and CV and give a few bullet points on what key qualities and skills you plan to emphasise in your interview. Conclude your note to the referee with, 'Here are the details I intend to give during the interview. I'm hoping that you're able to support these.'

Only promote skills, accomplishments, and successes that you can prove. Being honest and admitting that you don't have the knowledge or skills in a particular area may, in fact, be a sign of integrity. Immediately follow up this admission by describing a desirable attribute. For example, you can say: 'No, I'm not familiar with that accounting package, but I was responsible for familiarising myself with MYOB and training 30 other staff members in the small-business package with only a month to develop the in-house training manual.'

Bypassing the Boss for Good Referees

Finding good referees may sometimes seem a daunting task. You may be unhappy in your current position, have been frustrated in trying to set up a more flexible working arrangement, or don't have a positive working relationship with your boss. If you have acted with integrity (and we know that you have!) then a current boss should always give a fair recommendation to a future employer. But in these circumstances, maybe the reference isn't exactly going to be the glowing praise that you'd like. Also, there are times when you simply can't use a current employer as a referee because you want to keep your job search hidden from your immediate boss and workmates.

Tips for finding great referees for your CV include:

- **Asking a colleague to be a referee.** By colleague we don't mean Darryl from IT, who's hilarious company at lunch time. Choose someone who knows your work and how you contribute to your team, and make it clear that they're commenting from this perspective. You're aiming to inform, not mislead.

  When Natalie had problems with her manager and started to scan the employment websites, she spoke to Jane, a manager who was on the same organisational change-strategy committee as Natalie during a recent restructure. 'Jane had seen my research and written reports, and experienced how I interacted with others in our team. She can also comment on my ability to contribute ideas in meetings and work with minimal supervision to get things done.'

✔ **Asking your previous boss to be your referee.** The value of having a former employer as a referee can't be underestimated. If you can offer several contacts from your recent career history that also helps to build up a picture of someone who's a good bet. Avoiding your current employer and then only citing one positive sponsor can beg a few questions, so help your prospective employer to feel reassured that you have a good long track record of exemplary employment.

When Hamish resigned from his ministerial liaison role after feeling burned out and not getting the support he needed from his manager, he didn't feel comfortable asking her to be his referee. He instead used the former manager as a referee and found a job in a larger, more publicly focused agency. As Hamish's situation shows, trying to keep in touch with former managers and supervisors is important. That way when you're job searching, you can keep them updated on your situation and ask whether they'll agree to be a referee for you.

✔ **Seeking out important customers.** You can be creative with your referees by reaching further into your network to valued customers with whom you've worked in the past. These supporters can provide different viewpoints from those of employers and can also be a way of publicising your achievements to your new employer. If you introduced a customer who now spends more than £1 million a year at your former company, or you managed to solve a long-standing problem to a customer's satisfaction, then that customer is going to be a great referee for you. It really pays to stay in touch with these important contacts in your life as you never know when, or how quickly, you may need to call on that person's goodwill.

Interviewing Like a Winner

If you're lucky, your covering letter and CV results in an invitation for you to attend an interview. Regardless of whether this interview is your first for years, or whether you attend interviews regularly, you may feel nervous about attending. It's good to feel that way, and shows that you care about making a good impression. Being prepared helps you turn those nerves into excitement!

Getting the scoop on the company

Most interviewers and potential managers ask you what you know about the organisation you're applying to join. Many applicants fail interviews because they haven't bothered to find out anything about the organisation. To get ahead of the game, try:

✔ **Visiting the company's website.** The organisation's website has all the material it wants the public to know. Here you can find specialist documents, including introductory information, press releases, reports and publications, and careers sections.

✔ **Analysing annual reports.** When the latest annual report isn't available via the company's website, try Companies House (`www.companies house.gov.uk`) All UK companies are obliged to file their accounts here, although in the case of a start-up company, there can be long delays. If you still can't get hold of one, ring the employer directly and ask for a copy. The employer is going to be impressed at your level of preparation and the report itself can be a wonderful source of information about staffing, finances, special projects, and key performance targets.

✔ **Asking the recruitment consultant.** When an employment agency does the recruitment, ask the recruiter for an opinion on whether the employer offers flexible working arrangements and if the employer is amenable to discussing an alternative working arrangement. The recruitment consultant is the liaison point between you and the employer and can tell you if your work/life balance issues are likely to be viewed as a positive ('Yes, the company supports flexible working policies and needs an experienced person to help them put more into place.') or a negative ('No, the advertisement is specifically for a full-time arrangement with some overtime as required.'). Recruitment consultants are skilled negotiators and it is clearly in their interests to get you the best possible deal, so help them to do that by being clear in what you want, and open to appropriate accommodations.

✔ **Searching the World Wide Web.** Your search engine can probably bring up links that refer to news bulletins, articles, or other websites associated with the organisation. Throwing in a line at the interview, such as 'Yes, I read the article in *The Financial Times* the other day about how your new product has . . .' won't do you any harm , rather the reverse.

✔ **Seeking other opinions.** When you know someone who works for the organisation – even in a completely different department – ask about the organisation as an employer. What support does the company really give to work/life balance policies? Has your friend used any flexible working options available or seen colleagues use them? What have been the benefits? What are the work-place issues to look out for in the organisation?

Preparing for the actual interview

Practise your interview technique with a friend or family member; it's a very useful way to get your answers concise and considered. Your mock interviewer can let you know when you're rushing through your answers too quickly or if he finds the content of your answers too vague or difficult to follow. Ask your companion to rehearse with you over and over again until you finally feel your answers flowing and your confidence increasing.

Here are a few tips to help you prepare for the best possible interview:

- ✔ **Provide examples:** Interviewers often like to use a questioning technique known as *behavioural interviewing*. Such questions ask you to provide an example from your work or personal experience that states your case in the belief that your past performance is a good indicator of how you're going to perform in the new job. These types of questions usually start with questions such as, 'Can you tell me about a time when you . . .?' or 'Give me an example of . . .' Prepare yourself by thinking about lots of specific examples of when you displayed your skills, particularly in the way they relate to the ones that this new role demands.

- ✔ **Name names:** Find out the names and titles of each person who'll be conducting the interview with you. If such details escape you in the thrill of the news that you actually have an interview, call the recruitment consultant back or ask to be put through to the organisation's HR department. Knowing these details and referring to interviewers by name can go a long way to easing nerves and impressing the interviewers. You can personalise your answers by saying, 'Well, Dennis, I believe that the best way to begin is by . . .' and close the interview by saying, 'Thanks for your time, Mary.' (Watch this one – sometimes over-using people's names can come over as a bit condescending or studied, but the occasional use does show respect.)

- ✔ **Feel good:** On the morning of the interview, go for a walk or spend some time doing exercises that you particularly enjoy. The natural high arising from a good workout boosts your circulation and improves your ability to breathe deeply and relax. (It may be best to avoid anything too strenuous and risk an injury that may keep you from attending the interview of course!) When travelling to the interview, adopt a straight posture as you walk into the building, and smile. After all, what do you have to lose?

If *you* smile, the receptionist smiles back at you and may even strike up a conversation (we've managed to get a few good snippets of information this way). When you're in the interview, you'll feel surprisingly good about yourself. If your stomach is still lurching uncomfortably, remind yourself that being nervous is perfectly natural and okay. Better to be nervous and focused than too confident and arrogant.

- ✔ **Look good:** Take extra care with your appearance. If you don't want your colleagues to know that you're going for an interview, try to dress up more on the days before the interview to avoid the dreaded comment, 'Looking good today – going for an interview?' that often is meant to be flattering but can be embarrassing to fend off. Make sure that your clothes are clean, ironed, and don't have any loose threads or stains visible. Even if you're applying for a position at a funky firm, try to avoid selecting anything that screams out 'I'm groovy too', such as loud ties, brightly patterned dresses, or too much jewellery and make-up.

Selling your strengths and transforming your weaknesses

The interview question: 'Tell me about your strengths and weaknesses?' is the one to dread – and the one to prepare beforehand. A friend of mine once chuckled and responded with: 'You don't really expect me to tell you my weaknesses?' She got away with her quick retort and was offered the job but such a situation can leave you sweating and giving away something that may be used as the reason for not offering you the job.

Professional recruiters ask this question because they want to see if the applicant is aware of their limitations and where they think that they need to improve their work performance. Additionally, recruiters want to find out what you think you're best at achieving. After the interview, the recruiter then checks with your referees to confirm you have the skills that you claimed to have in the interview.

Don't try to be clever here and come up with a weakness that is really a strength – such as 'I'm so hardworking that I sometimes forget to take lunch.' That isn't going to impress your interviewer or help your case for work/life balance. Instead, realise that you can turn this question around by focusing on exactly how you're addressing your development areas. Being authentic and self aware is a very attractive quality in a potential recruit, so be open about your skill areas that need more attention and demonstrate how you compensate for any potential problems that may arise. Keep your focus on your strengths to show how you balance it all out, and, where you have a genuine skill gap, be enthusiastic about the opportunities there may be for you to benefit from the training that's on offer at your prospective new company.

Also, pay attention to your hands and nails, making sure that they're clean and don't have chipped polish, and ensure that your hair doesn't need constant pushing back out of your eyes. We're on the nitpicky bandwagon now: other distractions to avoid include wearing aftershave or perfume that's overpowering, choosing over-sized jewellery, or having a loose hairstyle that forces you to flick back your head to get the fringe out of your eyes. There you are – all our pet hates covered! But you get the point – focus on a clean, simple, elegant, and professional look and if you're not sure exactly what that should be – canvass the opinions of wise friends and mentors!

Passing the interview test

Knowing the dos and don'ts of how to behave in an interview can help you survive the interview process as the winner rather than a loser. Try these handy tips:

✔ **Show that you've done your homework.** Have a couple of questions ready in case you're invited to interview the interviewers. Tailor these questions to show an interest in the organisation and include a question about who you'll be reporting to and how your new team is structured. This is also the best time to raise the issue of work/life balance – find out what policies the organisation has in place and what arrangements staff members currently make.

✔ **Don't interrupt any of the interviewers.** Listen carefully and rephrase their question back to them if you feel as though you've misunderstood (this strategy also buys you a few seconds of thinking time).

✔ **Don't say anything negative about your current employer or past employers.** Instead, focus on what those experiences taught you.

✔ **Hold something.** If you're particularly nervous in interviews, it helps to have something in your hands. For example, if you feel nervous in an interview, or afraid that you may forget to discuss your most significant achievements, you could take in your own copy of your CV (in a folder) to use if you need a reminder. This is a distinct way of showing your employer that you're keen to include all of your achievements. Another bonus is that holding the folder can give your shaking hands something to grip so that they remain still.

✔ **Keep your answers to the point and fairly brief.** The interviewer asks you when more information is needed from you. And refrain from giving just 'Yes' or 'No' responses.

✔ **Maintain eye contact.** When more than one person is conducting the interview, speak to all of them, even if you have to tell yourself, 'Look at Denise, smile, answer her question, and meet Dennis's eye as though inviting his next question'. Not making eye contact appears as though you lack confidence in your abilities or aren't being truthful.

✔ **Never raise the issue of salary at the first interview.** This delicate topic is raised by the employer at the stage when the job is being offered. At that stage you have the opportunity to negotiate and you don't have to accept the salary package on the spot. Any salary package needs to be carefully studied and thought through, so politely ask if you may take it away and study its details.

Entertaining Job Offers

The question that comes straight after the much-desired statement, 'We'd like to offer you the job' is the one many people don't feel equipped to handle. That question is, 'So what are your expectations for this role?'

This is the time to tell yourself, *carpe diem* – seize the day. This is the time to put your work/life expectations on the table and point out clearly and conclusively that you're interested in the best working conditions that can produce the best productivity and promote the ideal personal and family standards.

Here are some of the factors that can be part of your negotiation conversation:

✔ Access to local child care or child-care provision on site.

✔ Application of work/life balance policies, including family-friendly provisions.

✔ Availability of professional training and development opportunities.

✔ Availability of study support (financial assistance and/or additional leave).

✔ Establishment of flexible working options, such as part-time work, compressed hours, negotiable starting and finishing times, or purchase of additional annual leave (refer to Chapter 8 for more information on this option).

✔ Freedom to work from home when required.

✔ Provision of a laptop, mobile phone, and Internet access from home.

✔ Recognition of prior service, being able to carry over your accrued long-service leave to your new employer

Negotiating your salary

The other question that comes straight after the much-desired 'We'd like to offer you the job' statement is a question that's just as difficult. You need to be quietly assertive and tactful when you're asked, 'So what are your salary expectations for this role?'

At this stage of the game, the employer has selected you. You're wanted for the role and you want to negotiate. A little. Don't get over confident and make threats you don't want to carry out. Don't say, 'I'm out of here if I don't get £200,000 and a BMW full of chocolate'. No one is irreplaceable.

When you're selected for a job, don't be afraid to ask for what you believe is a fair salary. If you've done your research to find out what the going market rate is, you're in a strong bargaining position.

Research your industry for current market rates well before you go to a job interview. A website recommended by HR professionals is the annual Hays Salary Survey (`www.hays.com.salary-guides.aspx`), which gives you and your employer some well-researched, impartial evidence of current market levels for your position.

In addition, take the opportunity to think beyond the pound signs and discuss what other options may be available to you. You can start your list with:

- Administrative support for the role
- Business class travel and club membership
- Car parking (very important in inner-city areas)
- Expenses for conferences
- Having the employer pay for your moving expenses
- Office size and location
- Performance bonuses (not just size but guaranteed minimum amount)
- Salary and conditions review (a minimum guaranteed salary increase)
- Superannuation and salary-sacrifice arrangements
- Securing additional leave days in lieu of certain other benefits

How you state your case is up to you. Try to anticipate the employer's reaction to what you say. Rehearse your requests beforehand, remain calm when you're speaking, and be prepared to hear 'No' to some things, but hopefully not all. If you don't ask, you won't get!

When you don't get an offer

This may sound difficult, but when you come second, you have every right to ask why. Not in a complaining or hostile tone, but so that you get feedback on how you can improve your next job application, as well as discovering what the interviewer considers are your strengths. If you're nervous about telephoning, phone the receptionist and ask for the interviewer's email. Write a brief email, asking for some honest feedback, for example, 'Can you tell me in which areas I need to improve?', or 'Does my interview performance let me down?', or 'Did I lack enthusiasm for the role or downplay my skills?' Don't let your natural disappointment get in the way of obtaining really valuable feedback which can provide just the insight you need to secure the job of your dreams next time around.

Chapter 12

Studying for Success

In This Chapter

▶ Identifying practical study options

▶ Getting a handle on vocational qualifications

▶ Exploring the possibilities for mature students

The term *lifelong learning* is everywhere these days and refers to the need to regularly review your abilities and undertake whatever additional learning is necessary to keep your skills up to date. You can no longer afford to do one course at the start of your career and have that small amount of study carry you through the rest of your working days. With rapid changes in technology, communication, global marketing, and industry and job definitions, evaluating your skills and capacity to continue to perform well in your job is essential. Put bluntly, if you want a rewarding career – or even to just enjoy your job without feeling as though you're barely keeping your head above water – start studying to revise your skills and keep your knowledge base up to date.

Study doesn't mean that you have to go to university and lock yourself into years of intense study. Instead, more and more workers are undertaking short courses that provide a general overview of the area they're interested in to keep up with changes to their working lives and technologies. This chapter shows you what types of study are available and how to go about finding what course is right for you, your work schedule, and your interests.

This chapter also discusses how study and training can be an important and valuable part of your personal life, too. Not all courses need to lead to promotions or career advancement – many courses offer study for hobbies that you can enjoy in your spare time.

Gaining Knowledge for New Directions

The idea of staying in one career until retirement age is long gone, with experts generally agreeing that workers born in the 1960s and onwards may experience up to five career changes in their lifetime.

To add even more choice in your working life, a career change doesn't always have to be upwards. Many people, when they decide they can cope with a reduction in income, now choose to downshift to reduce the stress and workload in their lives. Other people have side-shifted several times in order to learn more about a particular field or to work with a company or team that's of particular interest. Side-shifting can also occur with the same employer. For example, you can move to a different department or job.

At stages in your working life, you may want to move further up the pecking order at work or try another career path, only to realise that you require further education or study. For some people, this realisation can be pretty discouraging, especially when you haven't:

- ✔ Left school with enough GCSEs or A-levels
- ✔ Completed a tertiary degree or other specialised course
- ✔ Kept up with new technologies in your chosen field
- ✔ Received good career advice
- ✔ Studied or attended formal training for a few (or many) years

Don't be put off – quite literally thousands of education and training courses are on offer and the courses we describe in this chapter are designed to ease the rusty, the recalcitrant, and the plain reluctant adult into study for either the first time or for the first time in a very l-o-n-g time.

Deciding if you're ready for study

When you decide you're ready to gain new skills and qualifications in your chosen area of expertise, or you want a career change that involves new qualifications, you need to consider these questions:

- ✔ Are you patient and organised? Bear in mind that some courses can take six months to three years full-time. If this length of study doesn't suit you, look around for starter courses or short introductory courses.

- ✔ Can you handle being at the bottom of the heap? If the information you find indicates that you may still only be considered for a position in your chosen field by starting at the bottom, will that be a problem for you?

✔ Does your employer have a policy about supporting the further educational needs of staff and providing assistance such as study leave, financial assistance with course fees, and books or opportunities to study when working on the job?

✔ Are you prepared to do the leg work of finding out everything you can about your chosen qualification level or field from recruitment agencies that specialise in your area of interest, the Internet, and through contacting people already in the industry? Ask them about the best courses, the qualifications that companies and recruitment agencies look for, and how to get the best work experience placements.

✔ How flexible can you be with your studies? Is your preferred course available part-time? Is your contact time (lectures and tutorials) at university available after 5 p.m.? Do you have the time and freedom to study at nights and at the weekends if you can't do any during work time?

✔ How much do you think about the tasks you particularly enjoy and those you

dislike in your current and previous jobs? Are you customer focused or do you prefer to work on a specific project away from the front desk? Do you thrive on research and writing or would you rather be outside or on the shop floor?

✔ What arrangements are you prepared to make to get your foot in the door of your chosen field? On a work-experience (for free, naturally) placement, you can make valuable contacts, and add another highlight to your CV. Work experience can also provide a revealing insight into what a job entails before you leave your job or commit to a training course.

✔ What work/life balance issues are you determined to keep or achieve if you decide to do some training or study? These may include having flexibility to start and leave work earlier to attend course lectures, being given access to the printer and photocopier for assignments, reducing your commuting times, negotiating a salary increase, or negotiating additional leave to incorporate studying for exams.

Understanding Adult Education Courses

If you lack confidence about starting a course or dread the idea of being forced to study after many years, you may find that a Learn Direct course is the ideal way to ease yourself into learning. Learn Direct courses are specifically designed to be informal, achievable, and to involve people who don't like examinations in a competitive and overly structured environment. Over 550 courses are currently available in a whole range of subjects, and the great thing about it is that for most of them, you can choose to learn online, which means at home, at work, or at a specially designated Learn Direct centre.

Short-course study suits busy people

Adult education in the UK increasingly reflects the need for flexibility when delivering courses, with many classes held during weeknights after 5 p.m. or at weekends, or online.

Joanne, a part-time worker and single mother of a 2-year-old, decided, following her divorce, to start a course in Simple Car Maintenance. 'The course ran only for four consecutive Thursday nights and, although it was difficult arranging for my mum to come over and babysit while I

was at college from 6 p.m. to 9 p.m., the effort was worth it,' she said.

Joanne gained so much from the course that she promptly enrolled in another: Beginners' Home Maintenance, and then another: Financial Management. 'Two years later, I'm now half-way through an interior design course that I wouldn't even have considered for a second if I hadn't shown myself what I could learn in the first short course I did.'

Learn Direct centres can be found everywhere, from sports and community centres to churches, libraries, university campuses, and even one or two in railway stations! The centres offer lots of resources for learning, such as Internet access, lending libraries, and desktop publishing facilities. And you can often find cafes, crèches, and good parking to help with the practicalities of fitting it all into your life.

Many Learn Direct courses are structured at an introductory level and include topics such as improving your English and literacy skills, re-entering the workforce after a lengthy break, and developing social skills such as communication, assertiveness, and problem solving.

Learn Direct courses provide an excellent means of road-testing a new job level or brand new career. For example, a short course in public speaking and presentations may give you the encouragement you need to start more formal training in education at university in the next academic year. Training experts say that most people prefer to try a short course, for example, desktop publishing, before deciding to go to do a lengthier course in graphic design.

The full range of courses fall into three categories:

✔ **Skills for Life. Basic literacy in Maths, and English, often leading to a qualification**. Research has shown that something like 80 per cent of the UK population have problems with spelling, even and including many people who are successfully holding down responsible jobs where they need to use effective written communication. In these days of PC spellcheckers maybe that's not a disaster, but increasing numbers of folk are choosing to tackle their gremlin and hence boost their personal confidence.

✔ **Home and office IT**. If you're of a certain age you're likely to have acquired most of your PC skills by trial and error (usually plenty of both!) and although you may get by perfectly well, you may also be very conscious of gaps in your knowledge and that you can always be more effective. Training at work is often available to help you, of course, but when it isn't, a Learn Direct course can help you fathom some of the mysteries of email, the Internet, and software applications. Remember, studying isn't just about learning for work – you may find these courses really whet your appetite to use technology more, and better, for personal hobbies and interests.

✔ **Business and management**. You can find great courses suitable for employed and self-employed people – ranging from start-up skills for new businesses, to customer care, and even one on the lines of the popular TV show 'The Apprentice', to help you brush up on management skills like sales, leadership, and negotiation!

Usually, Learn Direct courses don't require specific entry qualifications, although some vocational or advanced courses (such as apprenticeships or computing) may assume that you already have certain levels of knowledge and skills. For instance, if you're interested in professional development to gain a promotion at work, you can gain management skills through completing short courses in supervising people, accounting, or computing. In addition, some of these courses can be recognised prior learning (RPL) to help you enter more substantial courses at universities and other training organisations. (See the section 'Recognising the Skills You Have' later in this chapter.)

Check out Learn Direct at `www.learndirect.co.uk`.

Adult education can be fun

Adult education courses are available for you to enjoy. That's right, enjoy! Not all training is designed just to get a job, a qualification, or to further your career. You may want to try a course that appeals to you on a personal level.

A great source of training courses that don't just relate to work is Hotcourses (`www.hotcourses.com`), which currently lists over one million courses of varying lengths at colleges, training centres, and universities. You can choose subjects from massage, dance, make-up, photography, the law, computing, business, health . . . almost any subject you can think of is covered on the site.

A key part of achieving your dream of work/life balance is to find a hobby that really interests you. Starting a course in that subject opens more ways for you to enjoy your hobby. Former financial adviser Martin agrees: 'I went to a beginner's woodworking class a few years back and now spend my free time designing furniture, such as media shelves, coffee tables, and entertainment units. Study opened a world for me. My hobby absorbs my attention for hours and provides such an enjoyable break from my "real" job. People now knock first at the shed door when they come to visit me at home.'

Work and play add up to success

A recruiter colleague of mine tells me that 'asking job applicants questions about their extracurricular courses and hobbies is a good way to ease their nerves during an interview and shows their motivation to succeed'.

Another workmate has used his hobby as a black-and-white stills photographer to draw parallels with his work as an engineer: 'Both activities involve concentration and attention to detail and both offer the chance to discover new skills if you're patient and know what you're looking for.'

Make no mistake about it, courses look good on your CV. Therefore, in addition to studying short courses that help improve your communication, time management, and problem-solving abilities, don't discount the courses you've done to further a personal interest or hobby. Learning another language, furniture upholstery, wood-carving, drama, or kite-making all say something about your initiative and motivation. These achievements show employers that you're committed to acquiring more skills and knowledge and have the initiative and determination to take control of your own learning and development.

Accessing Vocational Qualifications

In your search for better work/ life balance you may want to minimise the time you spend actually studying for new skills. Remember that balance is unique to you. You may welcome the extra time you put into an evening or online class because it adds to your enjoyment of life and gives you new inputs to stimulate your creativity. Or you may simply want to increase your employability in order to move up the ladder or secure a job with better working arrangements for you. If you fall into the latter camp, *national vocational qualifications* (NVQs) may be the best way to go.

The principle behind NVQs is to recognise your existing skills and develop them in a structured programme. For example, if you're a customer service advisor already working in a busy call centre, you've already developed loads of communication, negotiation, and influence skills, and you're probably stronger in some areas than others. NVQs are exactly what they say they are – national standards of competence in your job. NVQs assess these standards at five different levels, which can be roughly equated to academic qualifications. Levels 4 and 5 for example, are similar to the standard of HNC, HND, and a first degree. But instead of having to put in hours of study, you focus within an NVQ programme on demonstrating practical skill and competence according to the checklist for that level and occupational area.

It's very possible to gain an NVQ without having to do much 'extra' work, simply because your skill level already matches the national standard. Usually, though, an NVQ highlights many areas of improvement that can be made and because the learning you do to close the gap is practical and vocational, it fits naturally into what you need and want to be doing in your job anyway. Also the process of gathering together a portfolio of evidence can be really motivating as you collect testimonials from bosses, colleagues, and customers in the different areas of your work.

Don't think that NVQs are just for junior level staff. Lots of senior management grades get huge benefit from this practical way of developing skill and it is often an effective alternative to a degree which can mean taking a lot of time out of the business and from family life.

Knowing the skills you need

Believe it or not, around 1,300 different NVQs covering most of the major business sectors are currently available:

- ✔ Business and management
- ✔ Sales, marketing, and distribution
- ✔ Health care
- ✔ Food, catering, and leisure services
- ✔ Construction and property
- ✔ Manufacturing, production, and engineering

Essentially, you can take an NVQ at any age, the only criterion is that you're employed, or are studying with access to a work placement. There's usually no rigid time frame to complete an NVQ – you set the pace yourself. As a guide though, it takes around a year to complete an NVQ at levels 1 and 2 and around two years for an NVQ level 3.

Each business sector includes a range of topics that are directly relevant to the work within that sector. So, for example, if you work in a customer contact centre and you spend most of your time talking to customers on the phone, you would be interested in either the Call Handling NVQ or, if your work is much broader than that, the Customer Service NVQ.

When thinking about the skills you need, consider the balance between getting recognition for specialist skills in a particular industry – as with Call Handling – and undertaking a rather more general NVQ like Customer Service, which has wider recognition outside of contact centres. Keep focusing on your work/life balance goals and why you're doing all this in the first place!

Using NVQs as a springboard

If your first NVQ has given you a taste for new learning you can simply progress up the levels.

And you can also use NVQs as a springboard to other qualifications. Armed with an NVQ level 3 you can go on to do other vocational qualifications such as:

- ✔ Higher National Certificate
- ✔ Higher National Diploma
- ✔ Foundation degree

If you're unemployed and looking to get a break in a new industry sector, you can also consider a government-funded Apprenticeship scheme that incorporates study towards a relevant NVQ. Modern Apprenticeships began life as a way of helping young people up to the age of 19 get their first job; more recently the provision has been extended and there's now no upper age limit. Apprenticeships currently cover 180 different areas spanning more than 80 industries.

Maturing by Degree

Degrees aren't just for school leavers these days. A higher proportion of undergraduates than ever before are 'mature' students, whether full-time (through a career break) or part-time whilst holding down a demanding job. If you still need convincing that graduate qualifications are a valuable addition to your CV, go to www.prospects.ac.uk and take a look at some of the research on graduate employability. Prospects' 1999 report confirmed that more than 70 per cent of graduates had secured a job related to their long-term career plans just three-and-a-half years after leaving university. Most of this population consists, in the main, of new graduates with relatively little work experience, so just imagine the combined power of applying all your existing experience armed with a relevant tertiary qualification!

Having said that, degrees to secure the right job aren't the be all and end all, Most research points to the fact that a degree offers many more benefits than just employability – opportunity for deep self development and enhanced networks and peer groups for example. You need to weigh up the effort that you'll put into getting your degree with the likely benefits – in some cases the degree may not add much to your CV. But if you know that you're going to enjoy the journey of getting there, it can be worth it for that reason alone.

Finding your route into higher education

In the UK, the Universities and Colleges Admission Service (UCAS) manages entry to a full-time higher education course and you can take a look at its website to check up on specific entry requirements for the universities and colleges you're interested in. UCAS uses a points system known as the UCAS tariff to set entry requirements.

For part-time courses you can go direct to a university or college prospectus, most of which are available online.

Remember that each institution sets its own entry requirements for courses so there's a lot of variation. But essentially, if you have some or all of the following you've got a good starting point:

- A-levels
- Higher National Certificate
- NVQs, or SVQs (for Scotland)
- BTEC qualifications
- Key Skills qualifications
- Advanced Diploma qualifications
- International Baccalaureate

And if none of those apply – don't forget any specific specialist or professional qualifications that you've acquired over the years. Some of these may go a long way to fulfilling entry requirements and mean that you've only a few gaps to fill to pass muster.

Having the best of both worlds

Does making a commitment to a degree mean taking a career break? Yes, if that's how you choose to do it. Most first degrees take around three years full-time (a little longer for languages, in which you spend up to a year abroad) and immersing yourself in that world can be a wonderful way of regaining balance in your life as a whole, if you've been able to manage your finances or secure sponsorship to be able to do that.

Realistically though, not everyone wants to, or is able to, make that choice and so part-time study may well be the best option, while you're working full or reduced hours. Here's where you can put your negotiation skills to good use. If you already have a full life outside of work then your part-time degree may take a very long time to complete unless you negotiate some flexible arrangements or other support.

Having the best of both worlds is where your employer really buys into the benefits of your personal and professional development and supports you in gaining your higher qualification. The following sections describe a couple of routes to achieving that.

The Open University (OU)

As the name The Open University suggests, this now venerable British institution began life as a pioneering method of opening up higher education to people who 'missed the boat' in their early careers or who wouldn't otherwise have been eligible for entry to a traditional university because their grades weren't good enough. Even today, its method of assessing the whole person – qualifications and experience – means that entry requirements to many of its courses are less rigid than other institutions. Moreover, it remains the only university fully dedicated to distance learning (or 'supported open learning'), which makes it a highly attractive option when considering how to fit studying into your life.

Qualifications on offer via the OU range from Certificates, which may take around 6–18 months, through to Diplomas (around 18–24 months), and Foundation degrees – an employment-related degree that's highly relevant if you're climbing the career ladder. A Foundation degree at the OU may take around two years to complete and you can apply the credits you've earned from it towards an Open degree (BA or BSc) where you mix and match courses and programmes from the whole curriculum and/or combine subjects. Most people complete an Open degree in five years.

If you then want to turn an Open degree into a full degree – where you get to add 'Honours' to your BA or BSc – you can do a bit more study and gain extra credits. The sky's the limit here and, if you've really got the learning bug, you can go on to do postgraduate qualifications including Masters degrees and doctorates.

There's no doubt that an Open University degree is not an 'easy' option. It takes time, effort, and commitment, not least because its very greatest advantage – distance learning – can be its biggest challenge. You need to be highly self motivated and really make the most of all the resources that are available, which are ample. The OU provides high quality study materials: you'll use audio tapes, videos, DVDs, even the TV – and, of course, the Internet as you download material from the OU website. You're allocated support from a tutor and many courses give you the facility to attend residential weekends or longer events. But the key factor in all of this is your drive and determination to make it happen, so that's an important aspect to take account of when considering how your overall life balance is going to be affected.

Learn Direct's Learning Through Work scheme

For a greater bias towards vocational learning, you can consider this scheme which is gaining respect and popularity amongst UK employers. Like the OU, a Learning Through Work programme offers more flexibility than a traditional degree and is also based around online learning. So you don't need to attend class in person even though you're affiliated to a particular university. As with NVQs, described earlier in the section 'Accessing Vocational Qualifications', Learn Direct focuses on your everyday work projects to form the basis of your assessment. Individual programmes can be tailored by you and your employer to help you get the most out of it and also benefit your business. The more input your employer has to a Learning Through Work programme, the more likely you are to get full support from them financially and in terms of study time.

As with the OU, a credit scheme operates so that you can start at a Certificate level and then put those credits towards a Diploma, Foundation degree, or Honours degree.

Useful sites to stimulate learning

Start your learning by researching the options open to you as a mature student. Here are some great sites that offer you a wealth of options for enhancing your qualifications.

✔ **Department of Trade & Industry** (www. directgov.uk): Go to its education and learning section to find out more about courses available and funding options for adult learners.

✔ **Learn Direct** (www.learndirect. co.uk): Fantastic resource site that signposts you to careers advice, skills and qualifications, as well as loads of courses you can do.

✔ **Open University** (www.open.ac.uk): Take a tour round this virtual campus and get a feel for your options as a mature online student.

✔ **Higher Education and Research in the UK**(www.hero.ac.uk): Provides lots of information about universities and colleges in the UK as well as up-to-date research to help you decide which way forward.

✔ **UCAS** (www.ucas.com): The clearing house for full-time degree applications. You can check out their system for points to see how your own qualifications measure up before considering higher education.

You get involved in a variety of different types of assessment methods including portfolios of work you complete during the course, management reports, essays, practical projects, research, and dissertations.

Learn Direct conducts almost all of these activities online and you interact with your tutor in this way too, although face-to-face tutorials can be built into the process.

Getting the green light from your employer

Broadly speaking, many employers assess an application for study assistance through a variety of guidelines. Make your application stronger by addressing the following key points:

- ✔ Demonstrate clearly that you have the capacity to manage both your work and study loads while maintaining a healthy balance between your work and life needs.

- ✔ Discuss in your application how much of your course work and study can be done remotely or online.

- ✔ Examine in your application the needs of the business and the impact on other staff within the team, and provide suggestions on how continued provision and levels of service and production can be maintained.

- ✔ Provide details on what ongoing work-place support you need to assist your studies, such as access to a computer, fax machine, photocopier, laminating equipment, and so on.

- ✔ Discuss your chosen area of study and its direct relevance to your continuing role within the organisation and how it can enhance your current or future roles.

- ✔ Emphasise your flexibility and willingness to arrange your course to impact on work hours as minimally as is practicable and to regularly review those arrangements.

- ✔ Indicate your willingness to provide informal seminars or in-house talks to your team about what you've learned during your course of study that's relevant to your team's responsibilities and goals.

Many employers, departments, and companies in the UK fully support the lifelong learning needs of their staff members. Smart employers know that they also benefit from your increased qualifications and expertise, which make you a committed and motivated worker who can contribute more to the work place. You may find that your Human Resources (HR) department has a policy on study leave and support that you can access to see if your course of study fits its assistance criteria.

Employers may consider your application for study leave and provide assistance to you through one or all of the following processes:

- ✔ **Financial support:** Some employers may fully or partially pay for your tuition fees or textbooks. Sometimes fee paying is linked to outcomes (after you pass the module, the employer subsidises you for your textbooks and/or tuition fees).

- ✔ **Study leave:** Some employers allow time off for non-contact hours leave (when you're not actively at university attending a lecture or tutorial) to give you an opportunity to study for examinations or prepare lengthy assignments.

Studying for free

If writing essays and sitting exams are never, ever going to be your cup of academic tea, you can study individual subjects at certain universities and colleges for your own personal interest or professional development – for a charge. This plan means that you can attend a course or subject to see whether you think that university study is the right choice for you, and for your work/life arrangements.

As a non-award student, you're permitted to attend lectures and tutorials without the need to submit any work; to just feel free to soak in the knowledge you learn and skills you gain. In some cases, you may also arrange to receive an assessment with the other students who are completing undergraduate degrees. By undertaking this form of study, although you don't end up with a piece of paper at the end of the course, it enables you to demonstrate your learning in many ways. For more information, see the section 'Recognising the Skills You Have' later in this chapter.

From the arts to law – a career and lifestyle change

Straight from school, Mark, now 35, completed an Arts degree, majoring in social work and began work as a disability services officer, looking after adults with disabilities who live in community accommodation. For the first few years, Mark worked day shifts that involved active case management but after the birth of his first child, he switched to night shifts as a carer. This more passive role allows him to sleep over at the community home while being on call for the adults who live there permanently. 'Most nights I get to study and sleep, and having small children, I don't mind the occasional interruption.'

Changing to night-time shifts enabled Mark's partner, Julie, to finish her graduate diploma in Information Studies and care for their children. 'For us, my night duties meant a reduction in salary but Julie started work as a librarian and we've been able to juggle child care and work pretty successfully and we plan our weekends together.'

When Julie settled into her career, Mark decided to study a subject that had interested him since he was 16 – law. Mark began external studies to avoid wasting time commuting to university, trying to find parking, and hanging around between lectures and tutorials. 'Lectures are recorded on audio files that can be downloaded and kept permanently so you can replay bits you miss. Tutorials are live and online. Students log on to a dedicated site that records the name of everyone in the tutorial. We have a microphone or can type in our answers to the tutor's questions. Everyone can hear or see your answer and your name lights up so that the tutor knows who's participating.' Mark has so far passed every subject and is looking forward to working in the legal profession. 'I'm hoping that my relatively mature age and life experience are going to serve me well.'

Recognising the Skills You Have

Recognised Prior Learning (RPL) is an alternative way to get the skills and knowledge that you achieve outside the formal training system to be assessed and counted as a completed training module. This technique is valuable for people who want to gain a qualification but who have not attended a course or received that 'special piece of paper' that shows what experience and expertise they have. Your skills may have been achieved through learning on the job, volunteering, and community work, along with your personal hobbies and interests. All these may be considered for RPL assessment. For example, you may not have qualified for entry to a university course through A-level grades but can be assessed as having the alternative qualifications through work and life experiences, enabling you to participate in the course you want.

The methods used by an assessment team may include:

- ✔ Attending a workshop run by the student that effectively demonstrates the required skills and experience.

- ✔ Assessing specific examples of a student's work (for example, written reports, works of art, trades work, such as welding, electrical, construction, and so on).

- ✔ Examining the student using the same or amended versions of assessments provided to others students at the end of the module/ course/subject.

- ✔ Interviewing the student.

- ✔ Interviewing the student's supervisor, manager, or employer.

- ✔ Linking project results and outcomes to the student's involvement (that is, a safe work place, adoption of a new policy or guideline developed and created by the student, re-engineering a piece of equipment by the student, and so on).

- ✔ Observing the student on the job, in the work place, or in an appropriate social or community setting.

Chapter 13

Doing a 180-Degree Turn: Changing Your Career Completely

. . . .

In This Chapter

▶ Making changes to your career

▶ Refiguring your requirements

▶ Going it alone in your own small business

. . . .

> *The definition of insanity is to continue to do the same things in the hope that those things will miraculously achieve a different result.*
>
> – Albert Einstein

Albert may have been famous for splitting the atom but he was also spot on when he recognised the necessity of change. In your case, if you're feeling resentful and are continually frustrated in your efforts to improve your current job, it's never too late to consider a different career or way to earn your living.

This chapter takes a look into the world of small businesses, ranging from the experience of working from home, to buying a franchise, or setting up your own business, and offers tips on how to prepare for the big leap into the unknown.

In addition, we tell you success stories of ordinary people who've faced their fears of the unknown (without a guaranteed salary) and who are now involved in careers that are nothing like those they moved to from school or university. With good research and planning, and by accessing all the help that's available, you too can take these options.

Knowing Whether You Need a Change

So how do you decide when the time has come to make a dramatic change to your life? Ask yourself these questions (and answer as truthfully as you can):

- ✔ Are you being the parent, partner, family member, and friend you want to be?
- ✔ Are you contributing as much time and energy as you'd like to your community and interests?
- ✔ Do you have enough time for fun?
- ✔ Do you look forward to the working week?
- ✔ Do you love what you do?
- ✔ Does your job still challenge you mentally?
- ✔ Is there something else you would rather be doing?

Your answers can form a picture in your mind of what your ideal career or business venture may be. To make your new career something you can visualise, try going back to your childhood play roots for inspiration. Get a stack of magazines and cut out pictures that appeal to you about ideal jobs, family, home, hobbies, and so on. You may feel a bit silly doing this, but having a visual picture can help you clarify what you're really looking for in work and in life. When your 'art' is done, step back and have a look – how closely does your real life resemble the life that appeals to you?

Still unsure? Refer to Chapter 5 to find out how to do your own brainstorming, visualisations, and checklists to get to know yourself.

Embracing Change

If you decide you need a change (see preceding section), you need to ask yourself if you're ready to make the changes to your employment situation that you need in order to achieve a more sustainable work/life balance. Changing your career can be incredibly worthwhile and can actually make you feel like getting out of bed when the clock-radio starts beeping. But changing your career can also be risky.

Beating a path to the kitchen

After more than 20 years as a police officer, Brett is wearing a different hat – this time a white, puffy one.

Brett had considered becoming an apprentice chef but he was from a family of police officers. 'Being a policeman like my father was what I was ready for at the time.' Two decades later, the desire for police work wasn't as strong as it had been. 'Public support for police and levels of management changed. I saw one of my closest friends go out on stress leave and I decided to leave before it happened to me.'

In his spare time, Brett avidly watched TV cookery shows and read books about cooking. He looked into a Learn Direct course in commercial cookery while still in the police force. 'I was divorced, heading to 40, and unhappy in my job.'

The course completed, Brett now works as a full-time chef and loves the creative freedom. 'It's hard, physical work and you're constantly standing. But it's not as stressful as police work, my work is appreciated, and I get to see people who are happy with my cooking.'

Before you do anything, you need to work out how many changes you're willing to make to your lifestyle – particularly with regard to your finances. Ask yourself the following questions:

✔ Will a new career that fits your lifestyle offer you enough money to live on? For how long do you think that the career you dream of can challenge you?

✔ Are you prepared to work longer hours?

✔ Can you negotiate flexible working arrangements from the start?

✔ How far can you travel?

✔ If you've a partner and children, do they support your desire to change direction and try something new?

Be sure to discuss your plans first with your significant others – anyone who may be directly affected by your decision.

Wanting to change your career and lifestyle because a mate of a mate of your neighbour's cousin's daughter has found a job that earns her heaps of money isn't the reason for you to change. Changing jobs is all about changing for the right reasons. Is money the biggest driver for you to change, no matter what the job title, the hours, or the distances you have to travel away from your loved ones? We thought not. If that's the case, you wouldn't be reading this book about work/life balance and working out how to plan the best possible lifestyle.

Same job, different employer

Doug loved his work as an HR officer but found the culture and low morale at his old department very frustrating. He wanted a change from the sector he was in, but not the actual position he was holding, which he enjoyed. Therefore, he applied for – and won – a position at the same level working for a different government department. 'Some of my friends wonder why I bothered changing employers for the same pay, but the service I contribute to the local community is much more rewarding in my new job.' He also found that he had better work/life balance that showed in his improved frame of mind after work: 'Instead of slumping on the couch and turning on the telly straight away, I now go for a walk before dinner.'

Career counsellors and recruiters find that people wanting a career change are often short-sighted in their goals. For instance, try asking yourself honestly if the reason you're considering this major change is because you don't like your boss. If this issue can be resolved, would you feel satisfied and be prepared to remain in your current job? If this is the case, you may be better off taking a holiday or looking into some short-term training (such as an off-site course of about a week). These strategies give you the break that you need in which to assess your current job and career aspirations more clearly.

Finding out what is motivating your restlessness and desire for change makes your decisions about career change a lot easier.

Some other strategies to consider before taking the plunge include:

- ✔ **Assessing your skills and experience.** See whether you can transfer – and make the most effective use of – your advantages in your new career. Look at your written and communication skills, research skills, selling techniques, and your professional background, for example, finance, science, engineering, education, public service, and so on.

- ✔ **Choosing a job that's related to your existing career.** This may be in the same organisation or department, or using the same strengths, such as teaching, and transferring those skills to training adults in the work place.

- ✔ **Considering a move to a large company.** Find a company that has the resources to provide you with structured internal training and employment opportunities in different teams and departments.

✔ **Finalising your finances.** Seek expert financial advice if necessary. Many career shifters take jobs at the bottom of the ladder and work their way up via experience, in-house job vacancies, and promotions. Make sure that you involve your partner in figuring out what aspects of your lifestyle need to be reined in for you to make the move.

✔ **Investigating what training you may need.** Training can provide you with new skills and qualifications and also help you decide if you're making the right choice. For further information on studying for career and work/life balance, refer to Chapter 12.

✔ **Researching your new career choice.** Look into what constitutes the role (key responsibilities and tasks) and the likely job market before you leave your current job.

✔ **Speaking to someone who already works in your desired career area.** Ask how he got there. What experience and qualifications he has. What makes him stay? What he enjoys about the role. What qualities of the job does he want to change?

A career change doesn't always mean you have to ditch your skills entirely. For example, not all career changes mean that you have to abandon all your background in finance in order to gain new skills. Many opportunities allow you to let your skills blossom in another career – that's maybe right under your nose (see Chapter 11).

New job, different employer

If you work for a large company, you may be lucky enough to secure a different role without having to change employers, location, or to do additional study or training. Danielle knew that she wanted to move from being an administrative officer in the Human Resources (HR) unit to teaching, but instead of leaving and doing her PGCE, she was able to study part-time (supported by her employer) and become an in-house trainer for the government department where she worked.

'My current skills are valued, I keep my long-service leave and accrued annual leave and I can now add "professional trainer" to my CV, she explains. This has renewed my enthusiasm for my job and I'm really enjoying standing up in front of some of my old team leaders and giving them tips on time management.'

Danielle also appreciates being able to work from home occasionally. 'Because my job involves a lot of preparation and course notes, I'm able to decide when it's appropriate to work from home in order to reduce interruptions and focus on the course materials. I do a lot more work on those days because I don't have a 45-minute train trip each way and I feel more refreshed and creative when I am doing the longer days delivering training.

Changing jobs can increase your energy levels

Most career counsellors and recruitment advisers consider that making a career change requires careful research and planning, but the real outcome can be well worth the trouble.

Matt agrees with the experts. The 41-year-old travel agent spent the first 15 years of his working life as an engineer. 'It was what I'd studied at university and seemed to be a good fit in terms of career advancement and salary.'

Eventually his desire to travel overtook his interest in building construction and after some thorough research and preparation, he left his secure job to pursue a new career in travel. 'Before I left, I finally knew the job was no longer interesting to me.'

After planning his downshift to a much lower salary in the travel field, Matt concedes that he and his family have had to make some changes – especially financially. 'I'm much more motivated at work and my two boys can see how much happier I am. My hours haven't reduced much but my energy levels and willingness to be a bit more "hands on" at home have increased. I wish I'd done this earlier.'

Putting a Positive Spin on Downsizing

Not everyone who undergoes or thinks about trying a career change is doing it voluntarily. Even in times of relative prosperity and low unemployment, companies downsize staff and outsource work (manufacturing in particular) to cheaper locations. Despite the increasing recognition of the skills of older workers and the need to retain them for longer periods, some employers remain short-sighted.

Not only school leavers can use career advice – so can you and everyone else. You may feel as though you're in your current career because that's what your family expected of you, or maybe you're there by chance. You may not know how to assess your skills and experience. Therefore, having a professional counsellor assess your professional talents can lead you to a career far more rewarding than your current job. Options to explore include the following:

✔ **Talk to an adviser:** Get on to the Learn Direct free service, at (www. learndirect-advice.co.uk) to discuss a range of issues, from exploring the study options that may be open to you, to dealing with redundancy, or returning to work after a break. Use the online tools to help you assess your skills and interests.

✔ **Find a career coach**: The UK market for coaching is currently unregulated so there is no official listing of coaches, although you can find several good sources where you can access this service. A good place to start is the Association for Coaching (AC) (www.association forcoaching.com) where you can access members who are accredited coaches. You can also ask friends and family for recommendations. The AC's huge database gives you access to occupational information, courses, and industry trends.

✔ **Check out employment agencies and recruitment consultancies**: Many offer free career advice and access to skills tests that can help you. Go to Chapter 11 for more resources, including key websites.

Redundancy, and then what?

At age 54, Trevor was made redundant from an organisation after 32 years. 'It was a very humiliating experience. I had been a department manager for longer than the entire time the HR assistant had been alive and it was tempting to get angry and wallow in the unfairness of it all.'

Instead, he chose to see the situation as a positive. 'The payout was generous enough to allow me to take my wife and kids on an around-Europe holiday and also make me realise that I didn't want to be a weekend dad any more.' With his wife working part-time and his three kids still in school, Trevor decided to go for a 180-degree job change.

For Trevor, the experience of visiting a careers counsellor was refreshing; his skills and experience had not been reviewed since he graduated from university 30 years earlier. 'The counsellor and I had some pretty lengthy discussions and I sat a variety of numerical, word-association, abstract-reasoning, and psychological tests.'

The results led him to high school teaching. Trevor spent a year studying full-time for his PGCE before finding work as a high school science and maths teacher. 'It's bloody hard work, but in a good way. I get the same holidays as my kids do and I'm home by 5 p.m. It's given me a brand new outlook on life, and teaching teenagers has meant that I'm much closer to my own kids these days.'

Seizing Sabbaticals

A *sabbatical* means taking a prolonged career break from your paid employment to fulfil other, more personal goals. Taking a sabbatical can be a good way to give yourself some time to try out a new career or restructure aspects of your personal life and interests. Many employers are becoming aware of the need for workers to take some time out for themselves to pursue other interests or to try their hand at other jobs and career options. Experts believe that offering time off to valued employees is as important as a pay rise. Employees who feel trapped without opportunities to try different work can end up leaving the firm or becoming less effective and enthused about their work.

Often, but not exclusively, taken as unpaid leave, sabbaticals are increasingly being offered as an employee benefit to workers who've been with an employer for a number of years. The longer you've been with a company, and the more valuable your skills are to them, the more likely you are to agree that they support your sabbatical leave by at least some salary contribution, especially if a clear link exists back to enhancing your skills on your return. Sabbatical leave means you still have the security of your paid job waiting at the end of your leave. Here are some typical reasons for sabbaticals:

- Child care
- Humanitarian work overseas
- Paid work overseas
- Research, private study, or book writing
- Travel
- Voluntary or community work

REAL-LIFE STORY

Meditating on a sabbatical

John has qualifications in computer science, and had attended meditation classes at university during his first years of employment. In his fourth year at work, John applied for – and received – twelve months' sabbatical leave. He used his savings to travel across Asia to India, Pakistan, and Nepal to see more of the world and to participate in more complex understanding of meditation.

Several years later, John again took a sabbatical to go into a meditation retreat for the year before resuming his IT work. He considers that having access to career breaks has resulted in his returning refreshed, and in maintaining his interest in computer technology. 'I know that I have freedom to travel and pursue other interests. It's not just my job that defines who I am.'

Working on Your Own

If changing jobs but still 'working for the man' no longer interests you, you may consider going into business for yourself.

Don't take the word 'alone' too literally. Many legal, advisory, and statutory authorities exist to provide you with advice and regulations, not to mention the liaison and effort you need to write up an achievable business plan. These authorities advise on advertising, product development, and any additional training you may need. In addition, you can develop support networks where you meet up with people in a similar position to yourself to share your stories and advice.

Still on a salary, but working from home

Under certain conditions, people in paid employment can arrange to work from home for agreed periods of time or on an 'as needed' basis. Calling this practice *telecommuting* makes it easier to differentiate from owning or running a business from your home. Even though telecommuting is still technically 'working for the man' in that you're paid a salary by someone else, you're being trusted to plan and produce high-quality work using your own skills and initiative.

A lot of proactive employers have working from home or telecommuting policies available, and applications for these practices tend to be assessed on a case-by-case basis. (Refer to Chapter 8 on flexible working options, such as working from home.)

Considerations your employer may use to judge your proposal to work from home may include:

- ✔ How you can establish appropriate methods for monitoring the quality of your work.

- ✔ How your working from home may affect other staff members in your team.

- ✔ The reasons you provide for wanting to work from home (for example, reducing commuting times, having closer access to your children's school and child-care facilities) while still being able to concentrate on detailed tasks at peak times (for example, end-of-month reporting, annual reports, or financial analysis).

- ✔ The type of work you do: it may be that your work doesn't require much face-to-face contact and is more about writing reports or policies, data analysis, or project work.

- ✔ The way your manager can communicate with you, delegate work tasks, and keep updated on your progress.

- ✔ What equipment you need (your home office may need to be checked to ensure that it's ergonomically acceptable and to ensure that it adheres to the relevant occupational health and safety requirements).

- ✔ What home-office set-up you have.

Working from home significantly improves your work/life balance. Not only does working from home increase your motivation and satisfaction (because you know that your employer trusts your abilities to work unsupervised and get the job done), but you also have more family time, which should thrill your partner.

Even when you have to shut your office door and put a 'Working' sign on it, you can still interact with your family. For example, when I (Katherine) am working from home, I may not be able to devote the entire day to my daughter, but I can walk the three blocks to meet her at the school gate, come back hand-in-hand, and have a cup of hot chocolate together at home. She loves having me there and I love hearing her excited chatter and news. All in all, this takes about half an hour out of my work day – pretty well the average amount of time I spend socialising with my colleagues in the work place over a day.

Finding a franchise

Franchising is a business relationship in which the *franchisor* (the owner of the business providing the product or service) gives independent people (you, the franchisee) the right to sell their goods or services, and to use their business name for a fixed period of time. The franchise also provides you with training, operational standards, marketing plans and trademarks, merchandising and business management systems (that is, financials, diary management), and arranges for all referrals and advertising.

Some people fancy the idea of being their own boss and running a business. One way you can do this is to become a franchisee. Franchising appeals to people who are striving for better work/life balance because it gives them choice to plan where, how, and when they work.

Franchising has been around in the UK since the 1970s and is a trend which is gathering momentum. According to the British Franchise Association there are close to 800 franchise systems in operation, accounting for more than

30,000 franchise businesses. The sector turns over almost £11 billion a year and employs close to 400,000 people. That's larger than the whole energy sector and almost as big as the whole of the armed forces! And these figures are expected to rise as more and more people reject the idea of working for someone else and want to be their own boss.

You don't have to buy into McDonalds or the Body Shop to get with the franchise programme. More and more established businesses that offer a staggering range of products and services are recognising the benefits of franchising as they create their growth strategy. It's an ideal vehicle for a business that wants to replicate an already successful business model quickly, and also for the franchisee who wants a turn-key operation and lots of ongoing support.

Franchising experts recommend that you select a franchise that complements your chosen work/life balance goals as well as your skills and interests. For example, getting into dog grooming is pointless when you're allergic to, or don't like, dogs.

The franchise that you choose needs to be consistent with your current or chosen lifestyle. Discuss your choices with your partner and immediate family, because running a business affects them too. Don't forget to also consider the affordability, location (or the 'territory' where you're permitted to run your business), and the likelihood of future growth in earnings and work.

As with any venture into business or any change of financial situation, you need to research the industry thoroughly and seek proper financial and legal advice (see the section 'Finding vital small business links' later in this chapter).

If franchising is for you, then now's the time to start researching the many choices available.

As with any new business opportunities, an Internet search is going to throw up some dubious deals as well as pure gold dust. We recommend that you start your research here:

- ✔ **The British Franchise Association** (www.thebfa.org): This is the voluntary self-regulating governing body for franchising in the UK. The BFA vets all its members against a strict code of business practice and aims to offer impartial advice and guidance. The site provides case studies, links to professional advisers, books, and other resources to help your research. The BFA regularly runs prospective franchisor/franchisee seminars up and down the country which bring all these things to you in person so you can get more one-to-one advice. Check out the BFA Code of Ethics for franchising before you do anything, to be sure that you know what your rights and obligations are likely to be!

✔ **Which Franchise** (www.whichfranchise.com): A real treasure trove of a site stuffed with practical information and support to signpost you in the right direction. You can search for franchising opportunities in your area, zoom in on particular sectors that you're interested in, and check out legal or financial advice that you may need. You can even take an online test to see if franchising really is for you.

For more information about franchising, take a look at Dave Thomas and Michaels Seid's excellent *Franchising For Dummies* (Wiley).

Starting a home-based business

So you're sick and tired of rushing out of the house to catch the bus, or of being stuck in traffic during a long commute. You've had enough of being told what to do and when to do it, and your boss isn't giving you a satisfying existence. A home-based business may be the solution for you.

Home-based businesses are – as their name suggests – small businesses that operate from the business owner's home (usually a spare room or home office). These businesses are very small, with usually just one employee – the business owner – or maybe one or two immediate family members. Being based at home means the business doesn't have a 'shop front', car parking, or signage.

Solo-entrepreneurship is big business in the UK. The Department of Trade and Industry (DTI) reports that around 75 per cent of all businesses in the UK have just one employee – the owner – and that these sole proprietorships and partnerships account for an estimated turnover of around £200 billion per annum. People like to run their own shows and many of these businesses go on to become the backbone of the economy as they grow.

People run home businesses for a variety of benefits, including:

✔ Closer ties with the local community via services, shopping, and business relationships.

✔ Cost savings on rental of business premises.

✔ Cost savings on transport.

✔ Easier availability to care for sick children and other dependants.

✔ Extra freedom to provide some child care or care for an elderly dependant while working or during standard working hours.

✔ Increased flexibility in being able to decide what types of work and how much work to take on.

Figuring out what you can do

People who work from home do pretty well everything you can possibly imagine. A few mouse clicks can reveal home-business sites that advertise for people to run party plans or directly sell make-up, perfume, lingerie, financial services, insurance, gym memberships, secretarial services, data entry, surveys, and collections.

What perhaps is more interesting is that these ingenious *home-preneurs* have developed their own business ideas and ways to engage their services. Here's where the sky's the limit in terms of the sheer range of inventions you can sell – pet clothing and trinkets, swimwear, private investigations, dietary-specific sweets, stationery, website design and maintenance, health care and advice, proofreading and editing, freelance journalism, accounting, and on the list goes.

The list of the many jobs you can take on at home is never ending. Here are a few ideas to give you a start and get you thinking about the type of work you'd like to do from home:

- ✔ **Check out the brainiacs: Visit the British inventors' site at** www. thebis.org for a comprehensive directory that takes you to just about every resource you can ever need, from the Patent Office, to networking groups, to ideas forums, to investment advice. You can even link into inspiring stories of master inventors like James Dyson to increase your motivation about your blue sky idea!

- ✔ **Consider contracting yourself:** Contracting for services is a growing trend in the UK and most recruitment agencies give you plenty of advice on the best way forward for you. It can be a great way for you to control the amount of work you want to do, and can put you in front of different industries that may just spark off a new business idea of your own.

- ✔ **Gear up your skills and experience:** What type of work do you particularly excel in? What have people complimented you most on in your work? What have you always day-dreamed about doing? What drives you crazy at work because you know that you can do it better if given a chance? What service can you deliver that's cheaper/quicker/better/ more creative than what's currently being offered?

 You can make a living in ways that don't involve selling a product you don't believe in or inventing something better than sliced bread. Industries in the fields of research, information technology, finance and accounting, and writing can provide business opportunities – and contacts – that don't have to reside in city office spaces.

Finding vital small business links

If you're thinking about setting up your own business but don't have a clue where to start, you can find a lot of help and advice available to you that's only a mouse click or two away, including:

- ✔ **Business Link** (www.businesslink.gov.uk): Your first stop if you're considering setting up a new business. Business Link gives loads of advice on how to find an accountant, prepare a business plan, and get the skills you need, both online and through free workshops and training.

- ✔ **Chambers of commerce** (www.britishchambers.org.uk): Offer assistance, information, and resources for start-up businesses. You can find your local Chamber and start networking straight away to source help, advice, support, and even potential customers!

- ✔ **Inland Revenue** (www.hmrc.gov.uk): Yes, sadly, you have to pay tax – one day! Check out this site to find out your statutory obligations.

Introducing the virtual assistant

What if you like the idea of working at home but worry that you don't have that unique and profitable idea or the will to work 24 hours a day, seven days a week? The rise of virtual assistants may be an alternative worth investigating.

No, virtual assistants don't live in your computer, they're real flesh-and-blood people looking for work, just like you. Virtual assistants are independent professionals who provide administrative and secretarial support to small and medium-sized businesses. Virtual assistants often offer their services on an hourly or contract/specific project basis and work from home.

Virtual assistants provide ideal help for smaller businesses that don't have the workload or funds to have a full-time employee and only need extra help during peak times. Virtual assistants also provide their own office space, equipment, or cover sick pay or holidays.

Finding the funds

Setting up your own business venture is going to involve some set-up costs, which can range from relatively modest to the size of a mortgage, depending on the equipment and advertising you need. If you haven't yet inherited a fortune or won the lotto, make sure that you get advice from a financial adviser who specialises in small business and tax issues.

Virtually an assistant out of sight

Vicki, a legal secretary before leaving her employer on three separate occasions to have children, has become a virtual assistant so she can work from 9 a.m. to 3 p.m. while her kids are at school. Vicki found her clients by advertising in the local paper and by letterbox-dropped leaflets in the small businesses post boxes in her area. 'I think that some people need administrative services now and then rather than always.'

Vicki types recorded notes, creates and updates spreadsheets, edits documents. and puts together large mail-merge lists for her clients. 'I'm only five minutes away from most of them, so I can pick up work or have it dropped off to me. Another client on the other side of the city communicates by email.'

In the meantime, here are some sources of funding you may be able to access for your new business:

- ✔ **Business loan from a bank:** Assuming that you can comfortably afford the repayments and have sought good financial advice, the advantage of borrowing money this way is that the bank won't have any input into how you run your business. More importantly, the lender won't be entitled to any of the profits you make. But you do have to repay the loan and interest on time. Your tax accountant may be able to show you possible ways in which you can claim some interest as a business expense.

- ✔ **Help from family or friends:** When you have someone close to you who's prepared to lend you money for your business, you're likely to be paying less interest than a bank, as well as no additional monthly loan fees. You may also be able to negotiate lower repayments on longer terms than a commercial bank allows.

- ✔ **Invitations to investors:** You can raise money for your business by allowing trusted friends or family to become part owners of the business with you. The best kind of investors are those who already have proved themselves in business and can give you good advice and help. By choosing this route, you must be prepared to take your investors' interests into account and keep them updated on the progress of your business.

Chapter 14

Simplifying Your Life

· ·

In This Chapter

▶ Defining downshifting

▶ Moving up in your lifestyle – the positives of downshifting

▶ Staying in the city and downsizing

· ·

*D*ownshifting is most simply defined as taking steps to simplify your life by reducing your work demands. This, in turn, gives you more time for family, leisure, and personal fulfilment. Increasingly, people in the UK are thinking about ways to downshift parts of their lives in order to balance their lives better and enjoy their lives more.

The ever-increasing costs of housing, school fees, the culture of long working hours and shrinking free time has seen people change the way they work, the purchases they make, the sizes and locations of their homes, and how much they value family time.

Downshifting doesn't mean moving to the country or seaside, or taking up entirely different careers in order to simplify your lives. It's more about making choices to simplify your existing life arrangements in order to ease the pressure on yourself and enhance your wellbeing and happiness. For more about the big lifestyle changes that involve opting out of the rat race, go to Chapter 15.

Deciding to Downshift Your Life

The term downshifting is a very popular phrase these days. The word was originally coined by US researcher John Drake, who defined it as 'changing voluntarily to a less demanding work schedule in order to enjoy life more'. Since then, downshifting has come to mean a lot more than just making changes to your workload. US researcher Juliet Schor defines downshifting as people 'opting out of excessive consumerism, choosing to have more leisure and balance in their schedules, a slower pace of life, more time with their kids, more meaningful work, and daily lives that line up squarely with their deepest values'. This second, broader definition is the one we're going to follow in this chapter.

Downshifters fall into many sub categories ranging from the very dedicated back-to-nature, self-sufficient, grow-your-own-food types, to people living in the inner-city areas who want to get a bit more out of their non-working lives. Despite the differences between the outcomes wanted by downshifters, everybody agrees that consuming less and contributing more is the way to enjoy life. Whether you want to change your life completely, or just develop new habits that give you more peace of mind, you can fit into the downshifting category.

Discovering reasons for downshifting

Downshifters aim for a more balanced and fulfilled life. The most common reasons to downshift include spending more time with partners and families and being less concerned about accumulating a lot of material possessions and keeping up with the Joneses.

Research here and in similar countries shows that most downshifters make their life changes after a fairly long process of thinking about what is most important in their lives. Others make changes following an unexpected event, such as a severe illness, the death of someone close, or a relationship breakdown.

The Australia Institute's Clive Hamilton has co-written groundbreaking reports on downshifting trends in Australia. In a national survey, he found the main reasons for downshifting were:

✔ **To attain a more balanced life.** Most of the downshifters explained that they no longer wanted the stress of trying to juggle competing demands. In response to a question about downshifting being seen by some others in society as a selfish act, they disagreed. They considered that working long hours and not spending enough time with your children to be a more selfish choice.

✔ **To have their work values more aligned with their personal values.** Many downshifters cited managerial pressures, increased profit seeking, and having to spend the majority of their time and energies working for something they didn't believe in, as major reasons for change. Some downshifters had well-paid professional careers in law, banking, and business and chose to work in the non-profit and community sector as part of their downshifting strategy.

✔ **To improve their health.** Again, this can be related to the accumulation of a range of ailments (for example, insomnia, irritable bowel syndrome, high blood pressure, or depression) due to stress over long periods of time or a sudden 'scare' that is the final undeniable reason to make changes in their lives.

✔ **To search for, find, and develop a more fulfilling life.** This directly relates to the first two reasons to downshift. Downshifters want their family life, work ,and community life to reflect and complement their own value system. This realisation doesn't normally happen overnight, but is something developed over years of experiences.

Escaping the property trap

Traditionally in the UK, many people see home ownership as an ideal way of living, yet first-time buyers are increasingly struggling to get their foot on the property ladder. In times of economic downturn, downshifting isn't always as straightforward as selling up to move to a smaller property, because many other folk are in the same boat, and house sales slow down. *Negative equity* – where you owe more on your mortgage than the current value of the property – can be a real danger.

Most experts suggest that property is a pretty safe long-term bet if you can keep your nerve and hold out through the rough times. As a downshifter, you might want to get creative with your options. If you're sitting in a large house, and you have cash tied up in it that you can't release because no-one seems to be buying, you could investigate whether or not you can let out one or more of your rooms to bring in extra cash. Doing this would enable you to simplify in other areas of your life.

The United Kingdom is sharing downshifting with the United States

A lot of social trends that happen in the UK are also happening in the United States.

✔ A 2004 survey revealed that four out of ten people under the age of 35 in the UK were planning to leave their stressful, high-powered careers and downshift at some point during their working lives.

✔ A US poll in 2004 showed that around 48 per cent of Americans had tried at least one of the following downshifting strategies: cutting back their hours at work; declining or not seeking a promotion; lowering their expectations for what they need out of life; reducing their work commitments; or moved to a community with a less busy way of life.

If you are able to sell your house and release your cash, then you can consider not only investing in a smaller house, but alternatively escaping the property trap altogether and renting the house that you choose to live in. This would leave your capital free for you to invest in other areas, whether that be business opportunities or other wise investments.

All investment carries a risk, including property, so take time to research properly and get good advice.

Downshifting doesn't mean downgrading

The term 'downshifting' does have some negative connotations. When applied to our careers and personal lives, anything with 'down' in it isn't seen as a positive change. Think of phrases, such as being demoted, dumbing down, downsizing, downgrading, and stepping down. Making the decision to downshift requires a great deal of courage, as well as preparation, and goes against our modern society's belief that wealth and acquisition equal success and power.

Talk to people downshifting their lives and you find they don't much like the 'down' part of the word. Maybe they've moved down salary wise, and maybe they've moved down from the big house they lived in to a smaller, less costly home, and maybe they've moved down from the city to the country, but most people who make these moves tell you they've moved up in their lifestyles. And that's what's important to them.

Doing without or doing well

So how do downshifters fare after they make the much-anticipated changes to their lives? Talk to downshifters you may know or chat with them on the Internet and you find some realistic viewpoints. The general advice is not to make a dramatic change to your life until you're fully prepared and ready to do so.

Denise, who left her business analyst position to renovate a cottage with her partner and do contract work from home, says, 'I used to spend hundreds of pounds on the right corporate outfit, not including shoes, leather bags, and designer sunglasses. I now love rummaging through charity shops and I spend far less on simpler, more casual clothes. I don't ever want to wear a suit again.'

The decision to downshift can have implications for friendships. As Mary discovered, 'I found that I hardly had anything in common with my old work buddies, despite having been with them for 12 years. I didn't want to work as hard any longer to have a four-bedroom, two-bathroom house – and they did.'

Don't forget the kids!

When it comes to managing work/life balance, you have to consider the lifestyles of children as well. How many times have you complained – or heard another parent complain – about how much time you spend in your car driving kids to their multiple activities outside school hours? Think about sporting practice, music lessons, swimming classes, drama school, gymnastics, team sports, such as football and rugby, as well as the kid who wants to go to judo because her best friend is doing it.

Several years ago, a work colleague of mine dissolved into tears because she was worried that her 10-year-old daughter wasn't doing well in her academic studies. When I (Katherine) looked at young Annabelle's timetable, why she wasn't performing 100 per cent at school became very clear. She was exhausted. Mondays she had gymnastics, Tuesdays after-school club and then ballet, Wednesdays after-school club, then karate class after dinner,

Thursdays violin lessons and Saturday morning tennis coaching. Thank God for Friday!

And aside from school activities and hobbies, many children lead very full social lives. They have their friends over to play, have sleepovers, go to birthday parties, meet for lunch, watch a film, and so on.

Where and when do we give our children some quiet time? Quiet time – not as time out for punishment for a misdemeanour – but real space so a child can think, read, talk about interests, play, daydream, and simply do whatever she wants to do. What about giving a child an opportunity to simply 'be' with her family without having to rush off to the next activity?

My own theory is this: children need more sleep (up to 12 hours in 24 hours) than adults. Children also need more moderate structured activities in order to rest, have fun, and enjoy being at home with their families.

Stuart says, 'Some of my friends were really supportive and others said pretty unhelpful things like "you must be crazy" and "you'll regret it". Looking back, I think that they were feeling a little bit insulted that we didn't want to live the same lives they were living. I certainly found out who my real friends were.'

Clive Hamilton attributes some of the lack of support by friends and family to *Deferred Happiness Syndrome* and we agree. He defines this as the widespread tendency for people to stay in stressful jobs and home situations while telling themselves one day they'll have an opportunity for happiness. Deferred Happiness Syndrome is not just for workers in their 50s who are concerned about retirement income. Any person who feels trapped and overworked yet stays with the job can be said to be a sufferer.

Another aspect of downshifting is that it can take you down in social status. When success is measured by what kind of car you drive, the size of your house and what suburb it's in, the clothes you wear, the holidays you take, and the schools your children attend, then as a downshifter, you won't make the grade. Downshifters don't use these symbols of success as a yardstick to measure levels of satisfaction.

Ali says, 'I used to be so caught up in the "Where did you go to school?" question, and wanting a groovy car, an inner-city townhouse, and funky clothes. Then I saw that I was striving to impress other people. Now I'm happy to be considered a hands-on parent who helps out at the school, and I'm back studying at college. We don't have much money to throw around but we're getting by on less and place more value on what we can buy.'

My friend Pip told me that her friends (including me) were amazed at how she and her family coped at home without a microwave. I (Katherine) confess to reacting in a similar way when a family of five at my daughter's school decided not to own or use a car. Perhaps friends and colleagues actually experience grudging admiration for those who choose not to work such long hours to pay off a house they rarely get to relax in.

Smart-Shifting City Slickers

Although you may envy your friends' recent decision to downshift and you observe their relaxed lifestyle and increased contentment, you can't assume that everyone's able to find happiness this way. If you enjoy your job and you're challenged by its specialised nature, how would you find working in a simpler job in a small country town? If you moved to the city fringes, would you survive the long commute each day? Would your partner be able to find a satisfying job there? Would your children cope with changing schools and losing friendships? Would you miss the home you're leaving?

Most downshifters don't leave the city to run a tiny B&B in the middle of nowhere, so we're going to give the downshifters who change their lives without dramatically moving location a more positive label – *smart shifters*. To prove the point, here are the four top ways to downshift:

- ✔ Change careers
- ✔ Start up your own (often home-based) business
- ✔ Change to a lower-paying job
- ✔ Reduce working hours
- ✔ Stop doing paid work

If you want to stay put in your job and location, you don't necessarily have to stay stuck in the way you live your life. You can find plenty of ways to add more fulfilment and meaning to your life in less dramatic ways. For ways to change your work hours and gain more flexible working options, refer to Chapters 8 and 9. For tips on how to look after your health, organisation, and wellbeing, refer to Chapter 4.

Downshifting in cities

Most likely you're reading this section because you're interested in finding out how to achieve more of a balance between your work and your personal life but don't necessarily want to throw in your career or head to the hills. Reducing the all-too-readily-accepted culture of long working hours, large mortgages, and the desire to buy more and consume even more can seem like insurmountable challenges. However, many ways exist to counteract these pressures. All it takes is for you to make some small changes in your life.

Stop working long hours

Falling into the long working hours trap is easy. You may start working a little longer each day to show your boss that you deserve a promotion, or you may work longer to finish a time-consuming project on time. The problem is that your working longer hours can turn into an expectation.

A legal friend once said to me, 'I keep trying to tell myself that my high salary factors in those 20 or so hours of overtime that I'm expected to work. But if I start calculating my hourly rate, the argument doesn't look too convincing.' That's the solution: work out how many hours you work, divide your salary by the hours, and then see how much your real hourly rate is. Do you really want to work for that reduced amount? Now calculate how much money you really need to earn in order to be happy, rather than wealthy, and compare the figures to decide your priorities.

The next step is to examine your work values. Is your work of as high a quality when you work long hours as when you work shorter hours and feel more refreshed? Can you do with some help to organise your time and office layout better, so you save some of those extra hours? (If so, refer to Chapter 6 for tips to become as time efficient as possible.)

Medical studies show that continuing to work excessive hours isn't possible without your productivity being adversely affected. People who work regular hours, and have enough time to rest and recuperate, are more productive, more alert, and are able to produce workable solutions to challenging problems. Talk to your employer about working the hours you're paid for, or negotiate an early finish on Fridays or an extra day off as time in lieu, or discuss the option of working part-time if that suits you.

Remember too that you don't have to leave your busy job to achieve more balance. Plenty of dedicated and enthusiastic professionals, business owners, and work-from-home folk put in long days because they love what they do and they care about how their work makes a difference to others.

Step out

Downshifters value additional time in their lives to rest, or just sit still and 'be'. You can gain this sense of calm in a variety of ways:

- ✔ **Meditating:** Try going to a meditation class or buy a CD and meditate on your own. The ultimate aim is to be able to push aside the thoughts and ideas that are annoying you and, if only for a few minutes, relax your muscles, focus on your breathing, and 'sense' rather than think. You can sleep better and value the down time spent meditating as important relaxation and refreshment time.

- ✔ **Sitting outside in your garden:** Notice what plants are growing, what needs tending, listen to the birds singing, watch the dog sleeping or the cat sunning itself, see what colour the sky is. These restful activities seem corny – until you try them. I (Katherine) now have my morning cuppa outside, regardless of the weather. It has certainly made me more aware of the seasons and I now appreciate how many birds are in the neighbourhood.

- ✔ **Walking:** Go for a walk in the mornings before work, or walk at lunch time or just before dinner. If you have a dog, you have the best excuse to walk for at least half an hour every day. Not only do you get fresh air and exercise, you're also making another creature happy.

- ✔ **Willing yourself to try new experiences:** You can find any number of activities to try, some as close as the garden. Try seed collecting to start a veggie garden, tree growing for green groups, delivering pamphlets for a good cause, reading in the garden, writing in the garden, swimming, jogging, bike riding, or coaching a junior team in your favourite sport.

Slim down social stressors

Every Christmas, I (Katherine) used to sit at the table after a long day at work and laboriously write up to 100 Christmas cards to every single person in my address book. It didn't matter that I hadn't seen some of them for years or had never visited their homes or bothered to look them up, they'd still get a hastily written sentence in a mass-produced, poorly designed Christmas card so that I could assure myself that I was a popular person.

My friend Ian said to me, 'Spring clean your friends'. That sounds very harsh, doesn't it? In fact he was telling me that it was okay to honestly appraise which friendships I wanted to continue. This means measuring the worth of a friendship in terms of support, fun, advice, and people whose company you truly enjoy. Another positive attribute of good friendships is that every single person you genuinely consider a friend has at least one quality that you respect, envy, and appreciate. Those qualities alone can be sources of inspiration for your own life.

When your address book has people in it that drain your energy and let you down, get rid of those people. The simplest way to do this is buy yourself a brand new address book and only write the names of your real friends in it. Omit anyone else. Some downshifters find their friendships affected after they make changes in their work and personal lives. Whatever the outcome, whoever is left in your little black book should be the people you really do care about.

Join in the community

Many people downshift in order to live with and be part of a closer-knit community. You don't need to sell your home and shift locations in order to do this, because you already live in a community. Chances are you're too busy to notice and be part of what is right on your doorstop. Allow your eyes to seek and find the many noticeboards in shops, libraries, and cafés. Read your freebie local newspaper for information on events happening in your area rather than automatically throwing it into the recycling bin.

For more information on how to become involved in your community or how to find volunteer work in your local area, refer to Chapter 10.

Discovering downshifting for yourself

One of the goals of downshifting is to simplify your life so that you have time to stop and think about activities you'd like to do. Some of these activities may include good works for others, some may be just to enhance your life. Here are some simple tips to help:

- ✔ **Beat the litter bugs.** Every time you go for a rejuvenating walk, take an old plastic bag with you and pick up the litter that comes across your path. Your local school, property, or park looks much better with a little bit of extra effort.

- ✔ **Book a day off for fun, not chores.** Take time off work and spend it with your partner or best friend. Have a picnic, go for a walk, go to the cinema, or just sit and talk together (about anything except work). Or spend the day by yourself. Take a good book or magazine and read it leisurely – have a nap – take a long walk on the beach, or visit someone in an old people's home.

✔ **Buy charity, not commercialism.** Visit worthy websites, such as Oxfam and World Vision, to donate what you normally spend on those 'people who have everything'. Let your money become productive by helping poverty-stricken communities that need basics such as shelter, crop seeds, anti-malaria tablets, livestock, and rice to help them thrive and prosper.

✔ **Buy in bulk to share.** My friend Pip belongs to a fresh produce and grocery cooperative in the farming community where she lives. She and her neighbours order and buy in bulk and then divide the goods into the amounts needed for each household. You can do this in the city as well.

✔ **Clear out your clutter.** Donate your unwanted clothes, crockery, toys, or books to a local charity shop or refuge.

✔ **Compost your kitchen waste.** Instead of flinging your waste into the rubbish bin and contributing to more landfill, take it outside and make a compost pile. My mother calls compost 'black gold' for gardens.

✔ **Draw a line through your shopping list.** What three items can you do without this week? The new computer game, the item of fashion-victim clothing you won't wear, or the fat-laden takeaway meal? By getting rid of some inessential items, you're not only saving money but also eliminating unnecessary consumption and waste.

✔ **Get into recycling.** Most councils have bins specifically for the purpose of recycling. If they don't, then set up your own bins. You can find recycling depots where you can drop off your paper, cardboard, bottles, and plastics.

✔ **Go green – save water.** Look into getting a rainwater tank and filter. Don't buy bottled water. Use the same, clean bottle, filled from your kitchen tap. And read Sustainable Living For Dummies (Wiley) by Michael Grosvenor, the new guide to living a more sustainable and satisfying lifestyle.

✔ **Look out for locals.** Use dependable work-at-home business suppliers and local businesses for the services you need.

✔ **Manage some 'me' time.** Sign up for a hobby, class or course such as painting, international cooking, wood carving, wine appreciation, sailing – whatever excites and refreshes you.

✔ **Plant vegetables, fruit, and herbs.** Even when you don't have a huge garden, or when you have a completely black thumb like me, planting a fruit tree in your garden or a collection of herbs in pots works.

Besides, you can now use your 'black gold' to increase the chances of your plants thriving.

✔ **Save time by combining commuting with your exercise regime.** Try riding your bike to work on side roads, or power walk your way to work. Leave your car at home and take public transport. Get off two stops earlier and walk the rest of the way. And try taking the stairs instead of the lift for even more fat-burning bonuses.

✔ **Sponsor a child.** Several well-respected organisations use money payments from sponsors and direct the money to a child's community so that everyone benefits. Most also give you the chance to write to your sponsored child and be informed of his or her progress.

✔ **Turning off the telly.** Rest, read, play a board game, or just sit and talk with your family.

Downshifting at work

Having a full-time job doesn't mean that your current job, colleagues, and place of work can't also be part of your downshifting efforts. We're not talking about everyone working four-hour days and having an hour-long company-funded massage every lunch time.

Here are some simple steps you can take to make your work place more relaxed and more productive so people enjoy spending time at work and take pride in their environment:

✔ Adopt a double-sided photocopying and printing policy and use the back side of used paper for the fax machine.

✔ Arrange regular team lunch days fortnightly or weekly by booking the time in everyone's diaries. You don't need to go to a restaurant; just sit in the park with your sandwiches or bring a plate to share.

✔ Ask your local masseuse to come to the office to provide 15-minute, half-hour or hour chair massages at your work place during lunch times.

✔ Avoid printing out anything when you can save the data to a disc, email it to other staff members, or read it online.

✔ Develop eco policies and find out whether your workplace has water-saving taps, eco-friendly heating and cooling systems, and recycling policies (in practice as well as in theory).

✔ Encourage your maintenance and property people to donate unwanted office equipment and furniture to local schools and charities.

✔ Have a fruit basket that everyone helps fill at the start of the week. Set up ten-minute daily morning tea and fruit sessions to encourage breaks and healthy eating.

✔ Arrange for local meditation and yoga instructors to run lunch-time lessons in your work place.

✔ Set up a gym room in a disused office or meeting area with exercise bikes, treadmills, weights (with health and safety guidance), or start a power-walking club at lunch times.

From lecturer to adventurer

Taking control of your life means deciding what you do and when and how you do it, and not having your decisions made for you by the people you work with, your family, your friends, or anyone else who wants to be involved in the life that belongs to you.

Australian mountaineer Duncan Chessell is a great example of a man who controls what he does with his life. Duncan has successfully climbed Mount Everest as well as reaching the tops of the tallest peaks in every continent on Earth. Moreover, he is the first person to have completed a sea-to-summit climb of Mount Vinson, the highest peak in Antarctica.

Notwithstanding Duncan's incredible achievements, they wouldn't have been possible without the support and skills of his wife, Jo Arnold, who's joined Duncan on incredible journeys, including tramping New Zealand, visiting Mount Kilimanjaro, climbing in the Himalayas, walking the Kokoda Track, rock climbing in Australia and the United States, and expeditions to South America.

After graduating as a geologist, Duncan worked in the summers as a mountain-climbing guide in New Zealand to fund his first trip to Mount Everest. Meanwhile, Jo earned her PhD and became a geology lecturer at the University of Queensland. Jo's salary paid the rent, food, and living expenses so that Duncan could prepare to fulfil his goal to climb Mount Everest.

In 2001, Duncan conquered Everest for the first time, and soon afterwards the lure of family, work opportunities, and sponsorship responsibilities led Duncan and Jo to Adelaide. Jo worked for the Department of Industry, Tourism and Resources and helped Duncan launch his mountaineering and expedition company, Duncan Chessell Expeditions (DCXP). When he was away, Jo ran the company, managing the website, answering queries, developing promotional materials and tour guides, liaising with the media about Duncan's progress, and sorting out administration in the evenings. The double-job juggle became too much and Jo resigned her government position to work full-time on their business. In November 2006, she added another job to her CV – mother. For four out of the first eight months of baby Zara's life, Jo was on her own while Duncan conquered Everest a third time and his sea-to-summit feat in Antarctica helped raise valuable funds for the charity, Centacare (a community service agency that provides disability services, supported housing, and AIDS education and counselling). 'Trips like that have to be planned a couple of years in advance, so Zara wasn't even thought of when Duncan committed to these.'

So how does Jo cope with work/life balance? 'I've just started going to a yoga class first thing in the mornings. Duncan looks after Zara so that a friend and I can meet up for the class and then have breakfast together afterwards. I can't believe how refreshed I feel all day.'

Questioning for clarity

The idea of downshifting may interest you for a whole variety of reasons – reducing your workload, reducing stress, giving you more family time, giving you more partner time, improving your health, helping care for older relatives or friends, enjoying hobbies, and so on. You may also be questioning more and more where your place in the world is and why you're working so hard at a job you don't enjoy. Or you may be nearing retirement age and want to start building a new lifestyle outside of working. Understanding about your reasons to slow down and simplify your lifestyle by downshifting is very important.

Downshifting takes a lot of planning and courage to change the way you work, live, and contribute to society. Ask yourself these questions as you think through the possibilities of downshifting:

- Do you have a support network of people interested in downshifting or ways of establishing such friendships?

- Do you want to try a new job or career, or do you want to escape from a job you no longer enjoy?

- How have you planned for your financial future, including superannuation?

- Is now the right time to downshift?

- What key values do you want to live by?

- What do you want more of in your life?

- What do you want to show your partner and your children?

- What is your current financial situation?

- What parts of your life are you prepared to let go?

- What possessions do you want to keep in your life?

- Why do you want to downshift?

If you're thinking about downshifting because you're dissatisfied with your job and home life, make sure that you're not just thinking about it as a way to escape a difficult situation. If conflicts occur at your work, or if problems arise in your relationships, you need to discuss and work through them. (Refer to Chapter 10 for adding the life to your work/life balance, and Chapter 5 for information on making the most of your relationships.)

WORLD WIDE WEB

Smart-living websites to inspire you

Now you're making the move to a more discerning lifestyle, you may enjoy these handy websites that help you downshift from your old life to the new. Instead of circling endlessly on the crazy merry-go-round of work and home commitments, you're going to have time to sit back and consider some new ideas.

- **Deliberate Life** (www.deliberate life.com): Provides information for the more serious, back-to-nature, frugal-living environmentalist and has tips on making everything from brooms to toilet paper; insect repellent to clothes.

- **Downshifting Week** (www.downshifting week.com): General information for National Downshifting Week, the website offers interesting links to many other sites with useful information and success stories.

- **In Praise of Slow** (www.inpraiseof slow.com): Support site for the famous book of the same name by Carl Honoré, who knew that he needed to slow down when he was considering buying 'one-minute' fairy tales to read to his son! He has plenty of good ideas for slowing down outside of work: 'Being slow means doing everything as well as possible rather than as fast as possible.'

- **Self Sufficientish** (www.self sufficientish.com): Creative ideas for urban dwellers who want good results from their back gardens, window boxes, and recyclables. This site has hundreds of tips for self sufficiency, including gardening help, solar-energy saving, and recipes.

If downshifting is for you, you can think about these vital steps before you go any further towards making changes in your life:

- **Family:** You need to consult with your partner and children from the very first stages of your moves towards downshifting. Are they as excited as you are about changing your lifestyle? Are they willing to live on less income? What ideas and advice do they have to contribute? What concerns do they have? What access are you and your family going to have to schools, hobbies, sport, and health services if you relocate?

- **Goods and chattels:** Does downshifting to you mean getting rid of clutter and items you no longer want or use? Does it mean moving to a smaller house? What items do you plan to keep, give away to charity, or sell?

✔ **Plan:** After you and your household decide on what changes you want to make to downshift, write out a realistic plan and time frame. You may find that you're still living your old life (stressful job, city lifestyle, no external interests, and so on) while planning for your new one. Doing everything you need to do may take a few months when buying and selling property is involved, so find hands-on training and advice about moving house, starting a business, studying, or travel. Be easy on yourself and how much you're able to achieve during a busy time of change. And be aware that change can bring uncertainty for everyone involved.

✔ **Research:** Have you found out what finances you need to commence your job shift/return to study/small business or set up reduction to part-time hours? Have you spoken to people who've already downshifted in areas of their lives to find out what worked for them and what didn't? Are you aware of what compromises may have to take place – potential for reduced income, lack of colleagues for support, reduced status, or having to start networking and finding friendships all over again?

✔ **Test runs:** Try dipping your toe in the water before diving straight in. See if you can arrange some work experience to see if changing careers is right for you. Seek proper financial advice about living on a smaller budget and how to save and prepare for changes that you may not anticipate. Consider taking a sabbatical to try your hand at your new lifestyle and perhaps committing to the change. Think about visiting the homes of friends who keep chickens, grow their own vegetables, or are involved in local community groups, to get a taste for what you really like and what you're gladly going to pass on.

✔ **Work:** Will your partner have opportunities to work or participate in the same field and will your partner find fulfilment from a new job? Or, are you expecting your partner to carry a greater load of the financial and familial support?

Chapter 15

Planning Your Moves

*L*ife in our big cities can often feel increasingly stressful and expensive. Increased property values and the risk of rising interest rates mean that the dream of ideal home ownership is becoming less and less achievable if you also want your work, schools, shops, recreation, and health facilities of your choice close by.

Many people in the UK are choosing to leave the traffic, long working hours, crime, pollution, and the lack of family time and community behind and instead gain more control in the way they live. Moving out of the cities and completely changing the way you live and work can be the real dream come true for you – if you plan ahead and do your homework to make sure that it doesn't turn into your worst nightmare. Country living – or beating a rural retreat abroad – might not be all it's cracked up to be, and missing the buzz and convenience of the city can be a major downside. This chapter helps you to make considered decisions based on your needs and wants.

Searching for Lifestyle Heaven

No prizes for guessing that one of the biggest challenges involved in deciding to find a better work/life balance by downshifting is deciding where to live. Your first step is to sit down with your partner and children and make a list of the most important goals that you each believe will give you a better lifestyle.

Don't set your heart on just the one place, or the spot you visited during a relaxing stay several years ago. Do your homework. Your dream location may not have the employment and services you need as a permanent resident. Remember too that when you're moving to a simpler lifestyle, the town may not be quite so simple or quiet when the holiday season means triple the population. Be prepared to compromise – even in sleepy communities the property values for prime locations are expensive. You can move to a house outside the town where you can experience all the benefits of quiet country living and afford your mortgage, and at the same time avoid the worst of the holidaymakers.

Take your list of locations and check out the property prices for a feel of what's currently on offer. Check out too the rental options so that you don't feel rushed to buy a property before you try the location.

Holidaying for homework reasons

You took your car out for a test run before you bought it, so why shouldn't you do the same for your big move? You may have short-listed some places after enjoying a holiday there, or you may have found some ideal spots after clicking around on the Internet. Either way, you need to spend time in those locations with the possibility of living there entrenched in your mind. That's not the *worst* research job you've ever been given as homework, is it?

Make sure that you visit your choice(s) in the off seasons. You may be surprised at how different a cute little market town can be during the darkest days of winter with closed cafés, empty shops, and freezing winds. Although seasons can be variable, knowing whether the climate, services, and facilities suit you for at least two-thirds of the year is very important.

Knowing your needs

While you're doing your homework on location, get out and about to check out the shops, services, recreational facilities, and house prices. Chances are that the lifestyle and services are very different from your current environment (otherwise why would you be moving?). Think about which city comforts you can live without, what facilities you need to make you comfortable, and how you can adapt to other differences in lifestyle. Questions you may want to ask yourself about your new location can range from 'Can you order a pizza for delivery at midnight?' or 'Where do locals buy their clothes?' to more important issues that can affect your work/life balance. Try these:

✔ Are there enough people living in the town who are of the same age group as you and who, like you, have children (or don't have children)?

✔ Are you a gourmet-food lover? Does your town have enough produce and deli-style groceries to make life tasty enough for you?

✔ Are you and your family sports people? If yes, what sports do you like to play and does the community provide them? Alternatively, what sports would you like to start playing?

✔ Are you comfortable with the educational options available to your children?

✔ Are you prepared to get out and make friends?

✔ Can you cope with shopping only on weekdays (not only to avoid tourist crowds but due to restricted hours) and having limited availability to extended shopping hours or a wide range of foods?

✔ Are you willing to get your hands dirty doing jobs yourself around the house and in the garden?

✔ Do you rely on home-delivered fast foods? If the only takeaway option in your rural idyll is a service station that closes at 6 p.m. is that going to be a problem for you and your family?

✔ How far are you willing to live outside the town to commute for school and work?

✔ How important is seeing the latest movies, trying the trendiest restaurants, and attending plays and concerts in the city? Will you be able to commute to the city regularly enough to get your fill of affordable arts, culture, and accommodation?

✔ How important is shopping at boutiques and malls? Can you cope with only shopping in the city a couple of times a year or buying from the Internet?

Making Your Finances Foolproof

If you're determined to go for a big lifestyle change, the money and income issue is your biggest (and perhaps most complicated) hurdle to overcome. Moving location involves many hidden expenses, such as stamp duty, council tax and rates, moving costs, house repairs (to the one you're selling and the one you're buying), travel costs (when you need to regularly travel back to the city), and any future educational costs should your children return to the city for secondary school or university.

Make sure that you appoint an experienced financial adviser to help you plan for your move. The first question a smart adviser asks is: 'What are you going to live on when you arrive in the new location but haven't yet found work or bought a business?'

A professionally prepared financial plan ensures that you know how much income you need to live comfortably, what kind of house and property you can afford to buy or pay off, and what luxuries you may have to live without. If, on the other hand, you're heading towards retirement and don't plan to seek paid employment, you're going to need financial advice to make the most of your superannuation and savings.

Becoming a salaried lifestyle changer

A very important step in making a lifestyle change sustainable for you and your family is to decide what work or business you can do before you move. You need to research what locations can provide you with the income you need: moving to a gorgeous little village on a cliff top is pointless when the entire community flees back to the city during the week.

Write down a list of your work history and include specific job skills, life skills, and experiences and see how they compare to the types of jobs available in the location where you're planning to spend the next part of your life. Carefully consider whether you want to work for someone else and receive a regular salary, or whether you want to buy and run your own business. For information on how to look for employment, refer to Chapter 11.

If employment is your choice but you have highly specialised skills that aren't likely to be needed in a small town, you may want to consider *telecommuting* – working from home (refer to Chapter 13 for more information on dealing with clients from a distance). Alternatively, if you're willing to compromise a little, you may find work using your specific skills in a large regional centre but live further out in a smaller community. The drive may be a bit longer to work but traffic in the country is not like traffic in the city.

If you're interested in finding work and aren't concerned about sticking rigidly to your area of expertise (refer to Chapter 14 for more on downshifting), keep your eyes open for employment opportunities by:

- Grabbing the Yellow Pages and checking local businesses in the area. Do they provide all the services that the location needs? Do they need additional help, such as specialised IT services, copywriting, sales, and so on?

✔ Reading the local papers to check availabilities in the job market. Local businesses often prefer to advertise locally rather than post ads on websites or advertise in city newspapers. Linda found her job by subscribing to the local paper of the area where she wanted to live and reading it every week, even though she was still in Birmingham. 'It didn't take long for an office manager position to come up and it was only advertised in the local paper, not anywhere else. I got the job.'

✔ Using your networks helps because if you have someone who knows someone in the area, you can ask them to be a referee for you. In addition, start your new network by writing an introductory letter to a leading employer or company you're interested in and introduce yourself and your skills. (Have a look at Chapter 11 for tips on covering letters.)

✔ Visiting the local council for more links. Councils often have economic development officers who can highlight the leading industries and businesses, and their employment needs in the area. And ask for details of the local Chamber of Commerce to help you sniff out any other developments.

✔ Walking around the town and introducing yourself in shops, and so on. Country people love this informality. Also, visit the local Job Centre and employment agencies to see what jobs they're offering.

Being your own boss

If you think that running your own business is what you'd like, make sure that you research the economic environment of the location. Many attractive locations rely on the tourism industry and you need to consider if your skills and interests can help you create a viable business amidst the existing competition.

Here are some issues for you to consider thoroughly before making the big leap into small business:

✔ **Always factor in extra costs such as transport.** The goods and services you plan to provide may take longer to be delivered and cost more with the lengthier postal or travel times. Services such as IT help-desk support may be hard to get or non-existent, so the extra times or delays of sending equipment away also need to be factored in. You may want to consider doing some extra training in maintenance so that you aren't negatively affected by breakdowns and delays in getting equipment repaired.

✔ **Always remind yourself of the reasons for your lifestyle change.** If you want to escape the long hours and stress of your city job, then running a small business may not be for you. Many small business owners work extremely hard to establish their customer base, income, and ongoing trade.

✔ **Consider what income you can realistically earn when the trade is largely weekday or weekend related.** Is the income sufficient to cover your lifestyle needs? Consider also the hours you want to work. Do you want to be working on the weekends when your kids want to spend time with you?

✔ **Establish a support system.** Can your partner find paid work to keep the home running while you're establishing the business? Alternatively, are you working the business together to save employee costs? Do you have a back-up plan to sell and seek paid work if the business isn't successful?

✔ **Talk to locals who run their own businesses for hints and tips.** Don't risk alienation by starting a competing business. Explain that you believe that an opening for a different business type exists. Find out how other business owners started, how they built their businesses, and what factors they suggest you consider.

Feathering your nest

Not all remote rural houses are cheap. You aren't the only person thinking about opting out of the rat race, and whatever may appeal to you about a particular location is going to appeal to a lot of other city escapees as well. That's not intended to sound harsh or to denigrate your plans. Instead, this advice is to encourage you to do your sums and look very carefully at what your budget is for buying a house and/or land. However, if you're prepared to live near Millionaire's Row rather than in it, you may find that you have a sum of money left over after selling your home in the city and buying in your new location.

What size and type of home do you really need? Answer these questions:

✔ Are you after a larger house with more bedrooms and mod cons than you can afford in the city?

✔ Are you interested in finding a DIYer's delight as a project to challenge you outside of working hours?

✔ Are you prepared to drive everywhere (public transport may be very limited)?

✔ Do you want a house in a quiet street, on the outskirts of town, or surrounded by open farmland?

✔ Do you want to be within dog-walking distance of the main services?

✔ Do you want to establish a vegetable garden, fruit trees, or have egg-laying chickens, as well as other pets?

✔ Does the idea of a large house sit uncomfortably with you because you want to reduce maintenance costs and consume less fossil fuel?

As with all major decisions, make a list of the things you want in your new home and why you want them. Are you interested in simplifying your life – owning less but feeling richer in experiences and work/life balance? Do you want to be able to afford a better house and lifestyle, and be willing to work hard at your own business or savings plan to achieve them?

Monitoring sales figures

Do your homework in two stages. First, pay attention to recent property sales and auctions in your current area to give you an idea of what equity you may have left after selling and paying off your city mortgage. Second, keep your eyes and ears open for property sales figures in your desired location.

Many banks and financial institutions have loan calculators on their websites that can give you an estimate of how much you can borrow and repay comfortably. From my past work as an assistant bank manager, in the bad old days of 17 per cent interest rates, I (Katherine) recommend that you borrow less than you think that you can pay back to give you more leeway to cope with changes, such as loss or reduction of income due to redundancy, business establishment, maternity leave, and increases in interest rates.

Relaxing your search – and renting for a while

Many experts suggest renting a house and/or property in or near your selected location before committing to selling up your home and jumping into another mortgage. This experience gives you a better idea of property values and takes out the urgency of settling for the first house up for sale. Renting allows you to be selective.

Sussing out schools

Don't forget children's future educational needs – or those of you and your partner. Check whether your local town or regional centre has a local college that provides adult education classes. If your child is ready to attend secondary school, check whether your area has a school that specialises in the subjects your child prefers. Consider whether you're prepared to pay for a private school or send your child to a boarding school in another area. Have you planned for the cost of school fees? Always bear in mind that as your children get older, they may not necessarily want to study and work in your new location. See a financial adviser for ways you can plan effectively to fund any future studying away-from-home needs of your children.

Finding local parents and chatting to them about school options can be very helpful. School decisions also give you a reason to strike up a conversation with someone new. Other ways to find out more about what types of education are on offer include:

- **Schools Web Directory** (www.schoolswebdirectory.co.uk): This lists over 33,000 schools and colleges and links you to over 19,000 individual websites where you can check out stats, facts, and figures on a range of educational institutions. You can search by county, local education authority (LEA), name, or postcode.

- **The Good Schools Guide** (www.goodschoolsguide.co.uk): For an unconventional, not to mention sometimes controversial, stance on the subject, take a look at this site. Started by two parents in 1985, it gives an honest and opinionated account of 100s of schools personally visited by the site creators, and is worth checking out for a parent's eye view.

Heeding your health needs

If you or a member of your family has a health problem or disability that needs specialist medical care or quick access to medical treatment, you need to take these situations into consideration when choosing your destination. You may already have health insurance, but if only one doctor practises in your town, and the nearest hospital or specialist is several hours away, you may not achieve an improved lifestyle for you.

You may not want to think about ageing just yet, but you're wise to include ageing considerations when deciding whether you're going to opt out for a simpler life. Future issues to think about include what facilities support the elderly living at home, community services for special needs, and how many care facilities for the elderly service the area.

Finding Friendships

Chances are, you're going to be moving away from your family and friends. Naturally, you're going to miss them, even if you promise to stay in touch with regular emails, phone calls, and text messages. Your family and friends are going to find your move difficult too, especially those who are used to having you living down the road. You've a lot to consider. Think about the time your children are going to lose with their grandparents after you move. Are you going to have enough room in your downshifted house to have your family and friends visit? You may like to map out a plan for how often you, as a family, can return to the Big Smoke to visit people who care about you.

Most downshifting lifestyle-changers find that when they move more than a couple of hours away from their old homes, friends' and family's visits tend to tail off. As Jenny explains, 'In our first couple of years up here in the Scottish lowlands, we had lots of visits from family and friends. However, later we saw hardly anybody from down south. Once people have made the big trip up they don't want to spend the time and money repeating it every year. They want holidays somewhere different.' What Jenny, her husband Emilio, and their three children do is save for a lengthy holiday down south every second year so that they can visit family and catch up with friends.

Setting up your lifestyle change checklist

If you're thinking about escaping the city or setting off from the suburbs, think about the effect that change has on you. Compiling a checklist of what you plan to do, where you want to go, and how you plan on achieving the work/life balance you're dreaming about, is a good idea. Here are some vital strategies to plan as top priorities on your checklist:

✔ **Don't fluff your finances.** Avoid the temptation to upgrade your new home, property, or business if you've some money left over after selling your city home. Saving or investing the surplus might be a better option, in case finding work or establishing your business is harder than you think. Remember too, that most lifestyle changers experience a drop in income and have to adapt to living a little more frugally. Seek professional financial advice.

✔ **Enjoy happy homework.** Be aware that this step is immensely important. Your homework should involve deciding on what locations or towns appeal to you (and why they appeal to you), what employment options are in the area, whether you know anyone else who has moved to the area who can tell you the pros and cons and what the place is like outside of the warm and pleasant tourist season.

✔ **Have a happy household.** Make sure that the change is also your partner's dream. Make sure that your partner and children are willing and excited about the move. Hold regular discussions about the reasons for the move and discuss what goals you all want to achieve.

✔ **Interrogate internally.** Spend time thinking carefully about what aspects of your work, home, community, and family you value, and what other careers and living arrangements you're prepared to try.

✔ **Open your options.** Don't set your heart on one tiny little town or region to the total exclusion of everywhere else. Instead, compare a number of areas in terms of travel times to the nearest city, the local economy, availability of good schooling, recreation, health care, shopping and cafés, and services, such as home maintenance, mechanical repairs, and banks.

✔ **Work out your work ethic.** Moving to a friendly and laid-back community is pointless when you're still working at your laptop for 70 hours a week, with no time to look at the view out of the window. Check the local papers, Job Centre and websites for available work opportunities.

Understandably, friendships decline if not maintained and you need to be prepared to view this as a natural outcome of the change. For some people, friendships survive because they're convenient, but saving up conversations for planned phone calls or trying to put a months' worth of news into several lines of witty email isn't the right solution for everyone.

You may find that you have to go to your friends rather than the other way around. And when you visit, your friends may expect you to slot back in rather than telling them about your new life. Try to accept and understand their reaction. By choosing to move to a more relaxed location for an improved work/life balance, you may find some friends think that you're rejecting them because of their choices to stay where they are.

Making friends

Do you remember how your mum would grab you by the shoulder and propel you into a group of kids you didn't know and say something utterly embarrassing like, 'Look, here's (insert your name). He wants to be *friends* with you.' Even as an adult, striking up new friendships can be daunting.

Establishing friendships from scratch is an important challenge in your strategy and one that easily can be overlooked. To feel more settled and part of your new community it's vital for you to find social networks and form friendships. That's not to say that you have to abandon your old friends and social networks. But new friends in your local area can enhance your life and help you make the most of your efforts to achieve a better work/life balance. As rural school teacher, Brian, explains, 'It was only when I made friends with a couple of the other teachers that my social life opened up. They invited me to play for their local football teams, which led to meeting more people and rekindling my interest in golf and camping, which eventually led to meeting my future wife.'

Work is often the first way to meet friends, especially in smaller areas where you're not separated by which side of the city you live on or what your postcode is. Small-town living means that you bump into your colleagues at sporting events, in the local shops, and at the annual fair. For partners who aren't in paid employment, it's a good idea to check the council for parenting and hobby groups.

Lewis was completing his studies by correspondence when he moved to a coastal community with his wife, Marie, who found work as a town planner. 'It felt a bit unusual being a stay-at-home dad in a small town. But then I met people through the local playground and being on the nursery management committee. Plus, people I met seemed to know Marie, or their partners or family members knew Marie through her work. A lot of friendships can be made in a small town.'

Helping the community

One of the reasons that people choose a more rural or remote location is the larger role they can play in the community. Big-city living has lost its appeal for many people who live in communities in which streets are lifeless each day when dual-earner families go to work and leave empty houses behind them. Other people find that the demands and long hours at work mean that the little leisure time they have is spent working around the house or trying to recuperate and catch up.

Getting involved

Coastal and inland communities foster their sense of belonging through the contributions of volunteers. Volunteering to be part of a school committee, running a fundraising stall, delivering meals on wheels to elderly residents, or helping revive a conservation area is a great way to meet people and make a difference.

Volunteering is also an excellent way to increase your skills for other opportunities in paid employment. Rosemary told me, 'I had previously worked as a nurse, but being involved in my son's school fundraising committee and doing some work at the care centre for the elderly led to me being employed at the local council. My boss said that he'd been impressed by my organisation, communication, and public-speaking skills, all of which I developed and improved during my involvement in community volunteering.'

Finding Entertainment

Think carefully about how you and your family entertain yourselves and do a test run for a few weekends to see if you can cope without access to trendy restaurants, shopping centres, and cinema complexes. You may daydream of long nights without the television on, playing board games, or reading an engrossing book. But is that the type of cosy night your partner and children enjoy? Don't discount the need to find suitable leisure activities for your family in your new location so that the dreaded, 'I'm bored' from the kids doesn't crop up too often.

Your lifestyle change needs to be for the benefit of everyone in your family. Despite the fact that you and your partner know the reasons why you're making the move to a slower, greener, and less stressful environment, your children may be thinking about what they're leaving behind.

Children don't experience the reasons many adults yearn for a big change – overtime at work, stress, poor health, long commuting times, and so on. Telling your children that moving to the country means having a more fulfilling lifestyle doesn't mean much to them. They're more likely to miss their friends, dread a new school, and be confused about a lifestyle they don't know. Making sure that your kids feel involved and that their concerns have been properly listened to and discussed helps them get ready to participate in your family's new adventure.

 Moving house is a very exhausting time. You're in for a frantic few weeks or months of preparing for open inspections (and herding the family out), disconnecting services, cancelling and redirecting post, and sorting out belongings. De-cluttering and deciding what furniture, clothing, and household goods to take is a stressful task because everyone has different ideas. Travelling between the city and your new location to scout out a new home to rent or buy is also stressful, time consuming, and tiring. You have to investigate kindergartens, schools, child care, health care, recreational facilities, and local employment and business opportunities. And don't forget the cat and the dog. Amongst all of that mayhem, your kids need to feel that they're being consulted and their wishes are followed.

Enthusing Teenagers for the Move

Moving for teenagers can be especially difficult because they've established peer groups, interests, and friendships and most teenagers tend to know where they fit in their group. Some hints to consider to make the transition easier for your children include the following:

- ✓ **Allowing your kids to establish and continue long-distance friendships.** Give the children their own address books and email addresses. With encouragement from you, they can maintain friendships so they don't feel they're leaving their friends forever. Arrange a farewell party for your children and their friends and arrange definite dates for the closest friends to visit. Don't just promise visits one day.

- ✓ **Being patient and being prepared to answer a lot of questions.** You may be very busy, but giving them the attention and discussion time they need to reassure themselves about the move helps them cope better. You and your partner are very likely the ones who made the decision to move and also chose the location, so allowing children to make a few less major choices – like how to decorate their new bedroom in their own style – eases their anxieties and enables them to participate.

✔ **Caring about promises.** If you can't follow through on a promise, don't make it. Deciding that you won't be getting a pet after all can set your kids up to feeling betrayed and resentful, if that was something they were expecting.

✔ **Sticking to a regular routine.** Try to keep meal times regular and healthy even though ordering a takeaway most nights is tempting. Keep your teenagers to their normal times so that their sleep patterns also remain healthy. Having children who are on vegetable withdrawal and cranky because of late nights and bad food isn't fun.

✔ **Talking about the new location.** Don't just tell the children about the fresh air, scenery, and peaceful lifestyle because they're thinking about losing their friends. Instead, talk about the types of sport they can enjoy, the freedom for activities, such as bike riding, camping, and fishing, and the security of a smaller school and a bigger house.

✔ **Visit the area with your children as much as possible.** Drive and walk around the town, showing the kids the attractions of the place (from a kid's perspective – sports centres, skate parks, horse-riding paddocks, farm lands, motorbike tracks, and so on). Walk through the school grounds at the weekends to help make the place seem more familiar when the first day of school rolls around. Show the kids the key natural features of the area and be enthusiastic about why the move is going to benefit them. Your excitement can be contagious.

The sooner children are involved in sporting activities, the sooner they adapt to their new location. Getting a part-time job at the local supermarket also helps teenagers become a part of the community faster. But joining a sports club or getting a job takes time.

Part VI
The Part of Tens

'And of course, the real bonus for George working from home is that he sees the children growing up.'

In this part . . .

This part of *Work/Life Balance For Dummies* consists solely of lists. Lists provide an extremely useful way of putting the most urgent tasks – from tiny jobs (returning a phone call) to major chores (writing a book!) – in order of priority. Lists can help you decide what you have time to do and how you politely say 'No' to work you don't have time to do.

These lists include plenty of leading websites to inspire and advise you, as well as advice on how to influence your work-mates to improve your workplace morale. We also share with you gems of wisdom from real people who've achieved work/life balance. In addition, we reveal how you can teach kids that work can be enjoyable but that work is not more important than life – so you can pass the message on to the next generation!

Chapter 16

Ten Tips from the Experts

Cash rich, lifestyle poor. You leave for work in the dark, and you hit the traffic snarl. You work your nine- or ten-hour day and do the same exhausting journey in reverse and arrive home in the dark. You feel irritable, rushed, and stressed while you hassle the kids to do their homework, or feed your complaining cats, or unpack the dishwasher while you decide what the easiest thing is to make for dinner.

And yes, you feel like a missing person. You're missing out on seeing your kids grow up, on having fun with friends, or cultivating a creative hobby or interest, or even just appreciating your garden and home because they represent more work instead of places to rest and enjoy. Your main source of relaxation is to slump on the sofa with chocolate, wine, and poor television programming until you fall asleep and wake up with the remote control imprinted on your face. The day starts again when you leave for work in the dark.

Now is the time for change. This chapter introduces you to ten ways you, too, can solve the work/life balance dilemma. Instead of us being the experts, we share with you advice from people we've interviewed. These people aren't celebrities with paid entourages, or academic researchers who can't tie their own shoelaces, or lifestyle journalists recovering from last night's premiere hangover. This chapter introduces you to a panel of real-life experts, people who've found ways to improve their work/life balance. Who better to provide tips than people actually living out their decisions to change their lives?

Liberate Yourself from Long Work Hours

You may think that cutting down your work hours is impossible. Certainly, the challenge is a difficult one. Controlling your working hours takes planning and strategies. Here are some stories from our panel of real-life experts who've taken on the working-hours challenge – and won:

- Ian is a general practitioner who often feels pressure to work longer hours. 'How you respond is up to you. When travelling for conferences, I find I work much longer hours because I'm stuck in hotels with nothing to do. Consequently, I keep working on my laptop and mobile when I could have been spending time with my family, even though that's time on the phone. I used to find myself answering endless emails into the night after a day spent training and in meetings. All this achieved – apart from exhaustion and de-motivation – was to let everyone know that it was okay to talk to me and that I was prepared to be on call at any time. It took a heart bypass for me finally to work out what was important. I started cutting back my hours, travelling less, phoning more, and saying 'No'. My mobile is often turned off or not even with me. I'm home with time and energy rather than tired and grumpy.'

- As an IT professional, Richard knows what it's like to have the phone ring at any time from someone seeking IT assistance. 'I think that the time has come for everyone to switch off the computer and go home without the laptop. People on salaries like me are the real mugs because we effectively get paid less for every extra hour we work. If you keep working extra hours, the habit kicks in. I had to work two jobs for six months before my employer decided to replace the manager who'd left and whose job I'd been doing as well as my own. I was tired, stressed, and still in the office long after my boss had gone home. My ridiculous double workload had saved my manager's budget half a year's salary. What did I get for it? Nothing. No extra time off or pay rise. Think about it: tradesmen and wage earners are at least rewarded for their extra hours. I needed to say "No" and I didn't. I do say "No" now and it's made a difference. I'm aware that I have lots of contacts, heaps of skills and experience if I choose to move elsewhere – and my employer has made it clear that he doesn't want to lose me.'

- David is a town planner who loves his job – also his family. 'Yes, I love what I do but I'm tired of having to attend evening meetings that go on for hours without anyone considering those of us with children who've been at work since 8 a.m. I want to be home by 6 p.m. at the latest. I'm being contacted now by other agencies and consultancies because my skills are becoming known, and I intend to follow up any approaches. Make no mistake, I can negotiate a much better work arrangement. I can also work from home part of the week, have earlier start and finish times, and pick up the boys from school sometimes.'

✔ As a health manager, Anne was tired of 12-hour days and 60-hour weeks in her work place. 'You have to put in the hours and then you're not appreciated for the effort. Everybody does it at my work. About three years ago, I decided to change my life in order to get some better work/life balance. I now turn up at 9 a.m. instead of 7 a.m. and leave at 5 p.m. unless a job is really worth the extra time. I now find that I work late only once a fortnight. I can't say that all my bosses are thrilled or that some of the other 60-hour a week wage slaves don't pointedly glance at their watches as I walk out the door, but who cares? I find that I get just as much work done and still generate more revenue than most of the others in the team. That's because I'm not as tired as they are. I now firmly believe that work has the ability to expand to fill the hours you're prepared to allot it. Now that I'm in control of my hours, my life has improved greatly.'

✔ Joel runs his business from home. 'Despite my best efforts, I still find myself buried in work to meet a crucial deadline but that's rare these days. Having two kids and working from home as a web designer pretty much guarantees that. I can say that as I now work fewer hours than I used to, the quality of my work has actually improved. Getting away from the computer and actually having a life has made me more time efficient and a more creative designer.'

Know What Work Should Look Like

When you spend eight hours a day (at least) in your work place, that's a third of every 24 hours of your Monday to Friday life. So you want to be sure that you're happy with the working conditions, the hours, and the job. Here are views from panel members who work in different industries.

✔ Kent is a scientist and father of three: 'We eggheads aren't paid a huge sum to stay working in a government agency but my work is personally rewarding because radiology is making a difference to patients needing the very best medical help. In my previous job, I was researching the effects of radioactive materials on the environment, which I found equally as interesting. To me, what makes a great job is being given the opportunity to do something interesting and worthwhile.'

✔ Dean enjoys his job as a meteorologist. 'A good place to work is one where you're encouraged to participate and contribute to making decisions about specific projects and longer-term stuff, such as setting strategies and work plans. Managers who provide this kind of supportive environment nearly always have committed and happier staff who can understand the purpose of what they're doing and why they're doing it.'

✔ In IT, Richard expects to be appreciated for his skills. 'Being recognised for your individual performance, for team performance, and for any additional or outstanding work you do is essential. Many times I've busted my hump to get a project in on time and at the very best quality and never heard a word of response from my boss. Thankfully, I get feedback from the customers. Now I'm a manager, I make sure that contributions are noticed and recognised. Rewards don't have to be pay rises: I gave one guy, who worked overtime to help me complete a major project, two additional weeks of holiday leave, and another star worker won a weekend away for two.'

✔ Mike's small business means he's the boss but work can still compromise his family time. 'I'm working towards a better balance between work and family time. I'm working fairly long hours to set up the business, but I have planned for this carefully and I'll follow my plan to reduce the hours in a few months' time.'

✔ Anne changed jobs because she wasn't happy with her former working conditions. 'My previous job had no real career paths or genuine ways of getting a promotion. You had to schmooze and put in extra hours to impress, or wait for some old guy to retire. In my new role, I have clear paths to follow plus external and internal education and training opportunities. That says to me that this job offers me a future.'

✔ As a single parent, Cate says she never underestimates job security, even in these so-called prosperous times. 'I've worked in an agency that's been through four restructures in the past six years. I made sure that instead of getting my contract renewed every six months, I was made a permanent member of staff. This has made me feel more settled and a lot more willing to put in the hard work when necessary because they value my skills as a project manager.'

✔ Earning a good salary is important to Rebecca but not the most important aspect of her work as a physiotherapist. 'Whether you like it or not, what you earn is sometimes a measure of your importance and success, especially if you're living in a large city. Cities are expensive. I don't have kids and I enjoy spending my money on concerts, restaurants, and travel. That's why I work.'

Practise Winning Work Tips

One of the best ways to ease your working life and find more time for you is to talk to other people about how they manage this challenge. Discuss with your friends the best ways they find to manage work/life balance and follow their tips. Talk to people you meet at parties or dinners. Work/life balance affects everyone so as a topic of conversation, it's usually a winner. You can start with tips from our panel of real-life experts.

✔ John's winning tip is to put your personal life before work. John's background is in IT but these days he works as the manager of a meditation centre. Quite a contrast! 'Moving from the stresses and pressure of IT work to a meditation environment is a great reality check. I've had to accept that my job isn't my entire life. My personal life is much more important. The job isn't what defines who I am.'

✔ As a financial services worker, Paul says the best tip he can offer is to delegate work to someone else. He used to take work home because he couldn't manage the work in his allotted eight hours. 'Now, when I have to phone overseas at 2 a.m., I make sure that I don't go in to work the next morning until 11 or so. I insist on working only eight hours a day and I'm sticking to that. I made this promise to myself, my wife, and my three kids. My work team members are very skilled, trustworthy, and supportive and I delegate work to them. My staff members know what their roles are and that they're trusted to get on with the job if I'm not there. I meet up with each of them once a week to resolve any problems and discuss ongoing projects. And, like me, they have to work only eight hours. They can then go home, feel refreshed, and live their personal lives.'

✔ Human Resource (HR) managers should be the people who best know how to get on top of work/life balance. Lesley works as an HR consultant and is also a parent. Her tip: run an online diary. 'My diary rules my work day – in a good way. When I'm not available, I block time out in my diary, which is online and available to everyone in the office. That rules out confusion and my staff know when I can't be contacted. Blocked-out times are usually for personal matters, such as picking up my kids from school, doing reading with other kids in their class, or helping out occasionally. By blocking out and reserving chunks of time, I get to balance motherhood with being a professional. I've found out the hard way that work/life balance won't happen unless I actively make it happen.'

✔ Airline pilots spend a lot of time away from home so managing work and life isn't as easy as it may be for the nine-to-five worker. Simon's tip is simple: put the family first. Simon is an airline pilot and a father of three. For him, promotions are not a priority. 'I put the big effort into work when I'm on duty. However, I no longer jump for promotions without considering the impact on my family. That way everybody is happy.'

✔ Cate says her best tip is to be better organised. 'I did a couple of workshops on weekends that were run by a professional organiser. Why? Because I was surrounded by clutter and paperwork. I felt disorganised. I have used ideas from the workshops at work and at home. Being organised helps keep me sane.'

Eradicate the Evils of Email

Technology has taken over your life. But that can be to your advantage. The clue is to ask whether technology runs you or you run technology. What's clear is that technology now plays such a major part in your life that you need to work out strategies to deal with the time and energy it takes. Here, my panel of experts offers technology tactics to make your life easier.

- ✔ Anne believes that controlling your office inbox is the clue to controlling your emails. 'For me, discovering how to control my email inbox – rather than being a slave to it – made a huge difference. I don't automatically stop whatever document I'm working on to check the inbox every time I get that little envelope flashing at the bottom of the screen. I've also turned off the sound to reduce the temptation to have a look and start reading everything else.'

- ✔ Anjali is a researcher which means plenty of time spent on the Internet. 'Never ever let emails dominate you so much that you become inattentive and rude during meetings. If I see someone playing on their PDA or laptop or reading emails during a conversation or meeting, I stop and comment on what's happening. I think that it's as rude as talking on the mobile about something trivial when you're with someone.'

- ✔ As a public servant, Michael also relies on email at work. 'Email used to eat into much of my day and I'd still log-on and check them at night when I got home. Now I make every Wednesday an email-free day. I simply don't read them, don't respond to them, and don't write them. Instead, I concentrate on whatever is the most urgent task on my desk. If I need to contact anyone, I get on the phone or walk over to the other person's desk and speak.'

- ✔ According to Dean, you can avoid all emails that add to the 're' and 'fwd' chain. 'Read the final email from top to bottom and delete the rest. If you have a problem with a project or a person, go and speak to them because sounding accusatory or condemning can be harsher on email than when you're having a real person to person discussion.'

- ✔ Wah Chin works hard as a biological researcher. Her pet annoyance is gossipy emails that waste her time. 'I hate seeing my inbox clogged with emails from people sitting at desks wanting to look busy. I don't reply. This sends a clear message that my time on the computer is to work, not play. I also don't read jokes or silly attachments and believe that people who send these around an office look as though they don't have enough work to do. Again, by not forwarding or replying to these time-wasting emails – which use valuable hard-disk space – I find eventually the emails stop.'

Gain Work/Life Balance for Kid-Free Colleagues, Too

Sometimes, people with families who try to better manage their working and personal lives forget that they're not the only ones who deserve a better work/life balance. Employers can also forget that other people in the work place have responsibilities too – to elderly parents, to study and training courses, and to their personal lives. People without children have to assert their right to work-place arrangements that improve their lifestyles. Here are some tips from the panel for people who have other types of responsibilities that work may affect.

✔ Senti works as an executive assistant in a company that tries to support work/life balance. But the company's efforts don't always cover every-one. 'A lot of colleagues with kids have work/life balance introduced by the executive management team because they also have kids. I used to find it difficult to get a few hours off to help my elderly parents with their medical appointments (Mum doesn't speak English very well). Helping out when Dad was very ill didn't seem to count at work for me. I got around this by making up for lost time skipping lunch breaks and working later, until I was exhausted. Then I did a bit of research about the needs of carers who also hold full-time jobs. It's not only kids who rely on the help of people who work. I made my case and I now have the same flexibility as the parents here do. I feel a lot less anxious because I now don't have to "throw a sickie" and instead can ask for a couple of hours to take my parents to the specialist.'

✔ Study leave is another reason for flexible working arrangements as Bill, an employment coordinator, discovered. 'I don't have kids but work/life balance is getting harder to achieve for everyone these days. I was able to get access to paid study leave because my manager agreed to let me start earlier in the mornings and leave earlier in the afternoons to make it to lectures. This arrangement has made me feel more valued and motivated to do well in my course and to make the most of the time I've got outside of work. With people having less children and the popula-tion getting older, employers that offer work/life balance conditions for everyone are going to benefit in the end.'

✔ In Raoul's law firm, young people without children are expected to work from 8 a.m. to 8 p.m. and come in at least half a day on weekends. 'Everything we do has to be billable to a client so it's all about hours. I could see colleagues that were even younger than me struggling to keep this up day after day and then leaving the firm, or getting out of the legal profession completely. I love my work but I wasn't prepared to have no life outside of my job. I had to re-assess whether I really wanted the city apartment and the flashy sports car, or would prefer a less affluent lifestyle but more free time for golf, computing, and hiking. I ended up pulling back on my hours and feel so much better for it. It even looks as though it's starting to rub off on a few other people too.'

Be a Pro-Active Parent

Having children may well be the most time-consuming, intellectually challenging, and physically draining part of your life. But the rewards are inimitable. Most parents agree that the joys their children bring are well worth the sacrifices. However, in practical terms, having children creates its own particular problems. Here are some experiences and tips from two members of the panel who have pro-actively sought great solutions to challenges.

- ✔ Jo needs family support because she works as a professional city tour guide and is a partner in a small business. 'My relatives aren't readily available at ten minutes' notice if I need a babysitter. However, they are regular visitors – and helpers – and my husband's parents are only on the other side of town. I have also been really lucky in that three very close friends had babies at the same time as me so I can meet up with them regularly. My friends are a great source of support, advice, and laughs.'

- ✔ Simon has experienced the perfect work environment for a dad. 'When our two daughters were very small and hadn't started school, I took a job at a local machinery-hire firm that was never intended to be a long-term career option. The job paid enough while the girls were tiny and not costing us much and – perhaps most importantly – it was only a five-minute walk from home. I was able to go home for lunch and see my family every day and also know that I'd be in that door again at five minutes past five. It was such a wonderful way to be a hands-on father.'

Enjoy Family Time

Family time can include any time you have with your partner, with your children, with parents, relatives, extended family, and close friends. But finding time, with a heavy schedule of work and social commitments, can be difficult. Here are tips for finding family time from our real-life panel of experts.

- ✔ As a business owner and online journalist, Brett can get too busy to remember the pleasure of simply getting together. 'My wife Angela is great at pulling me back into line, and reminding me of when it's time to stop thinking about work and get back into family mode. Sometimes when we're together, she says, "Brett, it's time to be a person". And I know what that means. What she's saying is that work is still in my thoughts, or that it's tiring me out too much. Her words make me aware that I need some time to wind down and enjoy being at home with her. Work can wait until the next day.'

✔ At Philip's home, the television is turned off for dinner. 'We eat together at the table without distractions like the television or radio being on. We also let the answering machine take calls between 6 and 7.30 p.m. so that we avoid cutting into this time with our son. And who wants to waste valuable time on telemarketers? People who know us know that we're available to talk after 8 p.m. if they want to ring then. That's when our son is in bed.'

✔ Lee, who is currently on maternity leave with her second child, believes that anyone who works and has kids doesn't need to see parenting as an end to a career – or, for that matter, as an end to dreams, lifestyle, or goals. 'If you feel that parenting is the end for you, then that will happen. Arrange your time to make sure that you include your needs along the way, even though you have to take life a little slower when you're raising children.'

✔ As a teacher and father, James understands the importance of supportive communities for parents. 'Parents need to have friends and family who can help out. Parents also need to be real partners in the way they juggle their jobs (full-time, part-time, or staying at home) and support each other. We still have our own needs after the bills are paid and the kids are cared for and we make sure that we both allow each other some time off for rest, hobbies, and other social activities.'

✔ For Steve and his wife, having one child meets the standards they set. 'We have a 4-year-old daughter who is beautiful, funny, and incredibly loving. She's also exhausting, demanding, and can sometimes make me want to choose to stay at work a bit late and avoid that witching hour from 6 p.m. to 7 p.m. We have decided to only have one child as we think that it's better to be the best parents we can to the child we've got rather than to try and have another couple of kids just because it's what our families expect of us.'

✔ With a nine-month-old, Joanne is discovering that new mothers can work from home and fulfil their parenting objectives. 'When the baby is down for a nap, I take the opportunity to work. My daughter started child care (two afternoons a week) from six months, and I spend that time working too. I try to make the most of being with her during her waking hours and that seems to work for both of us.'

✔ Simon says going out as a family has been wonderful for his children. 'In the past 12 months, we have been more willing to spend money on meals and activities away from the house. We don't want to be slaves to mortgages, owning lots of possessions or fancy cars. But going out is a priority. These activities really work for us – family bike rides, meeting friends for a picnic, and going camping.'

✔ As a primary school teacher, Nancy works three days a week. 'I'm stimulated and fulfilled professionally without having to work full-time. I'm not run ragged by caring for an active and inquisitive 4-year-old boy every day of the week. Someone else shares the responsibility of stimulating and progressing his learning. Three days work is a great balance because I'm still home more than I am at work. As a mother, I don't feel like I'm neglecting my child by not being there for him every day and I don't suffer much mother guilt with the life we lead.'

Reward Yourself with Relaxation

Relaxation is one of those concepts that people wish for but don't always achieve. How can you relax when you work 60 hours a week, run a home, care for your elderly relatives, and are studying for your next degree? Finding time to relax needs organisation. First step: relax and think about how you're going to find time to relax. Second step: put your new relaxing time into practice. Actively planning your life to have time to relax is a common feature in the following stories.

✔ Ali believes that the answer to relaxation is saying 'No'. 'You get free time when you learn to say "No". For example, when your week is fully booked and you're invited to visit friends on the only night you have free, listen to your instincts, and if they say "don't go" then gracefully decline. If they really know you, they'll understand. I've found that you get as much free time as you allow yourself to have.'

✔ Working as a part-time project officer raising three children leaves Jill with the need to find time to relax. 'I get up at the crack of dawn to walk and that's my time on my own. When I get home, I feel rejuvenated, my head is clear, and the walks keep me fit.'

✔ Philip and his wife enjoy separate social groups and find this independent time away from home relaxing. 'My wife and I have independent interests, which means we have social lives beyond family and work and these give us a sense of belonging in the wider community. Even though we have to plan and negotiate the time to maintain these networks, we both feel a great deal of personal reward from them, and so the effort is worth it.'

✔ Kathy and Jason actively plan their lives to make room for all their needs and interests. Kathy says, 'This doesn't happen naturally. Time needs to be negotiated and arranged with give and take. For example, I may say, "I've got a mums' dinner on Friday night and you've got drinks after work next week so that works." We're also lucky to have family nearby who are happy to mind the children so we can have a night out together every month or so.'

✔ Not everyone relaxes in conventional ways. Steve is a truck driver, he's studying to be a teacher, and he has two children. That takes a lot of time. Fortunately, he also has a sense of humour. 'Sometimes I just spend ten minutes longer in the loo than I have to.'

✔ And from Rick, a word of advice passed on from a professional: 'A doctor once told me the biggest secret medicine for good health, long life, and clear thinking is one of the hardest things for most humans to do. The secret is: discover when and how to stop. Recharging the batteries, smelling the roses, and all that relaxing stuff equals good health. Each day I wake, I consider how lucky I am to see another day, to be given another chance to laugh, and to be with those I love.'

Plan Spontaneity

Doing what you want can be a very wise way to go. When you're working long hours and you feel you need something to help you achieve your goals, then do it. Don't be put off by budgets, advice, common sense, or criticism. After all, only you know exactly how difficult your work and life are. Here are tips from the team to help you make spontaneous decisions, based on your instincts alone, to make your life easier.

✔ Kathy loves outsourcing. 'I think that outsourcing whatever jobs you can, especially the ones you hate, is very important. If you work, it's essential you get domestic help. I have a cleaner once a fortnight, which is fantastic.'

✔ Philip changed his life to work at the pace he felt suited him. 'I'm doing my job by choice, not because I have to do it. It's less high powered than my former job, but I'm now closer to my family, have less than an hour's total commute time each day, and we've become a one-car family.'

✔ Cate has realised she looks forward to her son visiting his father to enjoy some life of her own. 'I've now realised that the custody arrangements that mean my son stays with his father every second weekend also mean that I get that weekend to recuperate. I can go out with friends, see my choice of movie in the evenings, and do those pesky little tasks that can be pretty impossible with a five-year-old.'

✔ If you want some adult time in your life, grab it, says Kathy. 'I am really strict about the kids being in bed at a reasonable time so that we can get some evening adult relaxation time. We sometimes watch junk television or read and try to give each other at least a couple of hours a week of individual time.'

- Jenny has a very simple solution to finding relaxation time. 'I find that half an hour to sit in my bedroom and watch my favourite show on television can be my own personal version of happy time.'

- Simon says his wife helps him to relax. 'I'm lucky in the way I get free time. Because I fly overseas, I get a few days at home to recuperate. Then I'm able to look after our 2-year-old when my wife works – or needs a break – and pick up the other two girls from school. I wouldn't be able to do any of it or relax without the help of my wife, Jodie.'

- According to Nancy, if you have kids, free time can't be spontaneous. 'You need to plan your free time. I work it out with my husband in terms of child-care arrangements.'

  Philip agrees. 'Your needs can be communicated in advance so that babysitting is covered and you avoid double-booking social activities. The reality is that often we need to plan to be spontaneous.'

- Sometimes your partner can help you find time for yourself. Samara says that at her place, when things start to unravel, her husband says, 'Go and have a bath'. She takes a book in for a long soak and that's her way of relaxing and escaping.

- Julie and her partner are another couple who negotiate time off rather than relying on spontaneity. 'We negotiate who needs the time off the most right now and ensure that it happens. After all, we rely on each other to make sure that we earn enough to make ends meet, that study is going okay, and the girls' needs are being met. We both need breaks from work, the kids, and each other and make sure that we schedule that time in.'

- Sonia realised that she and David weren't doing anything together on a regular basis. 'Our annual anniversary dinners out don't count, so we're doing salsa dancing classes once a week now. David's parents live nearby and pick up the boys from day care and school because the classes are straight after work. It's so enjoyable doing something that takes a bit of work to get there and then learn something new. It's also a rather romantic hobby to have.'

- At Rick's place, his daughter is now becoming old enough to take part in her parents' activities. 'Improvements to our family and home life in the past 12 months have given us more priority as a family. Helping each other is important. We're making even more time to spend together rather than separately. We involve our young daughter more now because she's at an age where she can come along to places with us. Spending time with our daughter and her activities has worked, and the bond is even stronger. She tends to listen to us more when we have more together time.'

✔ Angela has the perfect solution. It may not be spontaneous, but it works. 'Brett and I take a week off every three months and we do as much as we can to completely disappear. No mobile phones, no laptops, no email or Internet access, no phone calls to see how things are going at work. We find that by being unavailable, we can really wind down and have a break.'

Test Lifestyle Changes

Making the brave decision to completely change your lifestyle to achieve balance and happiness takes guts and determination. Successful lifestyle changers report that the view of their life from the other side is so much brighter and that many of the perceived sacrifices they thought they would have to make turned out to be things they were happy to let go of. Chapters 14 and 15 help you decide if this kind of radical change is for you and support you to make it. Here, experts on the panel who are trying on big lifestyle changes discuss what has worked for them.

✔ Leaving London for the Scottish Highlands means Peter and his partner spend a lot more time with their kids. 'We earn a quarter of the money we did in London but somehow live pretty well because we don't shell out money every time we walk out of the door. We eat locally grown fresh foods, get to drop the kids at school each day, and have a wonderful caring, friendly, and helpful community. We know everyone and we're not all trying to build a bigger house or get a newer car than our neighbours. We even have other neighbours nearby who have made the lifestyle change too and, like us, they have no regrets or desire to go back to what they had in London.

✔ Michelle's family moved to a remote Cornish coastal town and she finds that lifestyle changing has given her more creative time. 'Moving here has made me realise that wealth is not about a bank balance, but about how much free time I've been given to enjoy my life. Just the difference in commuting means far more time for yourself. What I'd say to anyone considering changing their life is, stop killing yourself by overworking and living in a city full of smog, pollution, and traffic and find somewhere you can stop, sit, and think. Enjoy the good things in your life, and work out what you really want to do. I'm now working on my lifetime dream – my first book – which would never have been possible before.'

- Lifestyle changes don't always mean moving house. Rob left his 'thankless' desk job in the city. 'I worked my butt off for faceless shareholders there. Now I run my own business from home and I have a work space that really inspires me. I know so many people in my community, something I never experienced when I worked in an office. I can pick and choose my clients, my hours, and the types of jobs I want to do. My lifestyle change hasn't involved shifting out of the city but it has completely changed for the better the way I live my life.'

- David threw in his overworked, profit-driven job to find something he enjoyed. 'I work as a masseuse on Monday nights and Fridays and have a second job at a car rental firm on the weekends. I approach my environmental studies like a job – I'm there all day from Tuesday to Thursday and spend every bit of free time between lectures and tutes on reading, researching, and doing my assignments. That way, when I'm home, I'm totally dedicated to time with my wife and our three kids. Changing jobs meant pulling in the financial belts, for sure. However, my environmental studies and work – even helping people in pain through my masseuse skills – has made me feel so much happier because I know I'm making a difference.'

- Retraining can feel like a lifestyle change because it can change the focus and direction of your life. For Samara, distance education is a type of training that suits her lifestyle and family. 'I may be contributing to the coffers by working as a barista at Starbucks when I can fit it in between my studies and looking after our three kids, but distance studies in education is my longer-term career plan. I'm so grateful for the freedom I get to study by correspondence because I wouldn't be able to make structured lectures with a 1-year-old, a 3-year-old and an 8-year-old to care for. At times I can do heaps of writing and assignments. At other times, months pass before I get to do any study at all. We've gone from being a relatively high-income, stressed-out, unhappy household to a much more ramshackle, simpler, and happy family.'

Chapter 17

Ten Things to Teach Your Kids

*T*he demands of work and home often feel as though they're competing with each other, at opposite ends of the long list of responsibilities you have to undertake. If you have kids, you can reduce this conflict for your time and energy by combining family time with genuine opportunities for fun and relaxation instead of housework, nagging, and additional stress. Even if you don't have children of your own, you probably come into contact with nieces, nephews, and children of friends and neighbours. The tips in this chapter give you easy starting points to make the most of family time, to set an example for children, and to pass on your wisdom to the next generation.

Eat Dinner Together

Sharing dinner together gives your family time to find out about each other's lives. And dinner time is when parents can sit back and listen. Prepare the dinner table with all distractions removed – no computer left on, the television switched off, and the answering machine dealing with any phone calls (at meal times it is often telemarketers anyway). This means that you can eat and talk and give your children your full attention.

Genuinely listening to the children during your evening meal assures them that you're interested in them and value their role in the family (refer to Chapter 3 for more on families).

Jill is a university administrator with three children. 'Our family is very busy. We always make sure that we have a family meal around the table in the evenings. Eating together means we have a healthy meal and the food is part of our daily ritual. Without dinner at the table, I think that we'd barely find time to talk, not because we dislike one another but because we're never in the same room at the same time. At dinner, we can concentrate on the food we're eating and on each other. We can resolve conflicts and discuss problems family members may have with the outside world. Dinner is the most important part of my day, every day of the year – and the part I look forward to most.'

Have Fun Holidays

Help kids to enjoy their holidays. After all, they did their homework, completed their projects on time, and helped around the house all year with chores – didn't they?

Holidays are not only times for rest. More importantly, holidays are a chance for a family to spend all day, every day together. These valuable interludes to your busy life are precious for strengthening relationships within a family.

Children change as they grow and busy parents sometimes miss those changes. Holidays give you time to catch up if your work/life balance for the rest of the year isn't quite up to standard. Here's a guide to planning a successful holiday:

- ✔ **Being bored is not a bad thing.** Allow kids to feel bored. When you hear them complain, feel free to tell them to find something to do. Encourage kids to think up activities that they like doing. Get them to make a list and then tick off each activity as they do it.

- ✔ **Encourage hobbies and interests.** Look into what children's summer courses and day programmes are available in your local area. Most libraries, museums, community centres, schools, and sports centres have activities designed to encourage kids to try new experiences.

- ✔ **Get the whole family to decide on activities.** Allowing children to be a part of the decision-making process is a great way to build their self-esteem. Children love making decisions, so use holiday time to give them plenty of opportunities. Of course, you also have to work out the best way to gently replace a not-so-practical decision with another one.

- ✔ **Laze around.** Lazing is okay for kids (and you) when you're on holidays. Like you, kids need some unstructured time to just hang around watching television, playing on the computer, or listening to music. The holiday belongs to them too and they need to rest and refresh themselves.

✔ **Leave information and rules.** When you have to leave older children alone at home during the school holidays while you're at work, give them clear instructions about what to do if a problem arises. Leave a list of phone numbers of people who they can contact.

✔ **Plan ahead and get your diary out.** When you can't take a break during school holidays, look for what child-care options are available in your area ahead of time. Also, see if other parents in your child's class may be interested in scheduling in some days where you can take turns looking after each other's kids for a day or two. Better still, if you can mix some days of your annual leave into the school holidays, plus swap days with other parents and book in some vacation care, you're going to find that the holidays are organised.

Make Family Time a Priority

Dinner isn't the only time when families can get together in a normal working and school week. Kids are natural lovers of having fun, so find times when you can enhance this lovely characteristic and get them enjoying life as much as possible. Here are some positive ways to show the children that you've plenty of time for them.

✔ **Book a day off work once a month.** Even if you stay at home together, this day off can never involve bringing work home, answering the mobile phone, or doing any housework – or school homework for that matter, unless the child wants to use the time to finish a project with you helping. Keep the television and the computer turned off and don't accept any social invitations that day. If you want to get out of the house, try a long drive with a picnic, a day trip to an interesting city, or a visit to a museum or a park. At the end of the day, you all feel refreshed and renewed.

✔ **Plan family outings ahead of time.** The secret to successful, relaxed family outings is to plan ahead of time and not have everyone rushing around at the last minute trying to find walking shoes or beach gear, sunscreen, and something to pack for lunch. Organise what you need the day before, then get out of the house to go to the place you've checked is open, has parking, and so on. Leave nothing to chance to spoil your day.

✔ **Start a family calendar.** Encourage children to keep a diary when they're at an age where they're so busy they start forgetting commitments. Then set up a family diary that everyone can use. Hang the calendar in a prominent place so everyone can see what's happening on particular days.

Turn Off the Television

Spending every night slumped on the couch staring at a square screen isn't going to encourage family conversation or imaginative activities. If turning off the television is difficult in your house, put up a case for a television-free night once a week. That way everyone can decide the night they can do without. If you can't find a common night, you may have to toss a coin at the end, or rotate the day. If you're not in the habit of eating dinner around the table, the television-free night is a great time to start.

Here are some tips to make the dinner-table conversation more fun, whether you're used to eating together or not:

- ✔ **Bring out the board games.** Show the kids how to play any of the hundreds of board games available (they make great Christmas and birthday presents). Do a not-too-hard jigsaw on a board that you can put away and bring out another night after dinner. Depending on the kids' ages, play easy card games, such as Snap or Happy Families. Chances are they're going to love the same games you played as a kid.

- ✔ **Find a shared hobby or project.** Choose a fun activity that interests both you and the child and is something you can look forward to doing and talking about afterwards. Cooking, painting, and walking are three of the most popular choices. You're sure to find the child attracted to one of these activities. You also get to show a child another side of your character when you're concentrating on doing something with him. And you get more opportunities to talk together.

- ✔ **Have a weekly family night.** Schedule one week night for every member of the family to be home in time for dinner. This is especially important with teenagers. Make sure that everyone agrees on the night. You can take it in turns to cook dinner (or do it in teams) and then take it in turns to decide what family activities you can do – go for a walk, take a star chart outside to identify groups of stars, have a family BBQ complete with the traditional umbrella in case of rain – as long as you do it together.

- ✔ **Tell them your stories.** Believe it or not, kids love to hear about what you did when you were their age, especially if the adventures you reveal involve danger, crazy ideas, getting into trouble, or an hilarious ending. Psychologists have found that people tend to emphasise positive emotions when telling a story and you can find it relatively easy to add a moral or happy outcome to your reminiscences.

Be Available

Busy parents have a habit of taking shortcuts when they need to communicate something to a child. Whether the message is positive or punitive, send one clear message – directly from you to the child.

Finding the time to have a conversation with a child is a priority. Remember, when you talk to a young child regularly – discussing positive and negative matters – you're going to find talking to that child when he becomes a teenager much easier, because the pattern is set. This preparation can be quite an advantage with a teenager – especially one of the silent variety.

- ✔ **Communicate directly:** Don't pass messages to your child via your partner. Your child doesn't want to hear it from someone else, your child wants to hear it from you. A few minutes of conversation with you means more to your children than what Mum said that you said to tell them about.

- ✔ **Find 15 minutes:** Every parent can find 15 minutes to spend with their children in the evenings after school and work. This can be cuddle time, walking time, sitting in their room talking just to them, or time to look through their school books.

- ✔ **Help with homework:** Homework time is a great time to show the children that you're interested in their learning and are prepared to spend time helping and encouraging them. Don't ever do the homework for them.

- ✔ **Let your fingers do the walking:** When you're still at work when the kids arrive home from school, or when you're required to travel as part of your work, make a specific time each day to call the kids for a conversation. Stick to that time because the regularity gives your children another opportunity to talk to you about the events of their day at a time that suits you.

- ✔ **Offer one-on-one time:** Being available to a child is not restricted to when you're at home. Taking him out to a café for an ice cream, or out to breakfast with just you, is a nice way to have some time alone together without competing with your partner, other siblings, or dealing with interruptions. Better still, make it a weekly event and stick to it. You're going to find that you both look forward to this outing. This is an ideal opportunity to find out more about what's going on in a child's life.

✔ **Read together:** Education experts have been saying for years that reading to – and with – children not only encourages a love of stories, but also increases their literacy levels and continued love of books. Add to those benefits the fact that reading is a lovely way to get close to children and gives you a privileged glimpse into what interests them.

✔ **Tell them their strengths:** When tucking the kids into bed or getting them up for school, try telling them what you admire about them. Children love hearing about what you value and appreciate about them and respond so positively to praise that it can improve their behaviour and willingness to help you out with manageable tasks.

Keep Fit

My parents, despite trying to raise three children with no additional babysitting or child care nearby, always made an effort to remain fit and healthy through exercise. They ensured that they had time for evening sports activities like running, exercise classes, or early-morning games of golf. Their love of sport rubbed off on all of us children.

Kids who are 10 and older can use their bikes to get to school or friends' houses (with prior arrangement between the parents, of course), giving them (and you) freedom, saving the use of the car, and providing a good source of exercise. Try it for yourself: ride a bike to work instead of taking the bus, or make plans to go for a Sunday morning bike ride in your local area. Many councils are installing and maintaining bike paths in cities and parks to encourage an increase in the number of pedal-powered people. In fact, the UK government has jumped on board, dedicating funds to key 'cycling cities' to lead the way in creating new cycle paths, better facilities, and more training for children in cycle road safety.

Activities you can do to encourage kids to exercise include the following:

✔ **Arrange activities with the parents of your kids' friends.** Go for a regular walk and finish at a café that offers food the kids like.

✔ **Play a sport together.** Try something new, like karate, or perhaps go to swimming classes together. Make this decision jointly.

✔ **Plan active outings for the family such as swimming or hiking.** Take a picnic for afterwards, even if only to munch in the car if it's raining, and you add to the fun factor.

✔ **Set limits on time spent in front of the television and computer.** Few 'activities' drain energy as much as watching the telly and using the computer for long periods. Limiting the amount of time you spend doing this enables your family to focus on enjoying the time you do allocate and then to move onto other things, still feeling refreshed.

✔ **Take your bikes for a ride.** Be active with children. Don't sit on the sidelines. When they see you riding, they're going to want to ride too.

✔ **Walk or cycle to the shops.** Yes, even if it's a bit of a hike! You might not have the time to do this on every occasion but you'll appreciate the boost of energy when you do.

Have a Laugh

'Are you having a laugh?' may be the funny line in the television comedy, *Extras*, but it has very real-life connotations. Kids love humour. You only have to watch them at it. They laugh at a corny old joke book, a classic funny movie, or just larking around at home. Laughter is contagious and an utterly brilliant way for parents and children to connect with each other. A key part of successful and happy families is their encouragement and freedom to explore humour, laughter, wit, and inside jokes.

Recent research at Stanford University shows that laughter is an effective internal aerobic exercise, increasing your lung capacity. Laugher has also been attributed to helping people look younger, improving individuals' self confidence, and reducing feelings of panic. Laughter also helps people to develop closer bonds with each other. Laughter essentially helps to diffuse stress and make you see the funny side of a situation instead of the negative side.

Respect Your Environment

Children are very likely to be learning about how to respect and maintain a sustainable environment in their child-care centres, nurseries, and schools. You have a great opportunity to apply these principles with children at home too. Some activities you can try with your kids include:

✔ **Buying recycled and biodegradable products.** Toilet paper, paper (or use leftover, non-confidential paper from your work place), laundry and dish-washing detergents, non-toxic paints, and furniture that are made from sustainable, natural products, help the environment. Kids who are at reading age love coming along to help you find the right product.

✔ **Controlling the rubbish bins.** Help the kids set up separate bins or boxes for daily recycling (according to your area's recycling policy) – one for paper and cardboard, bottles and plastics, garden compost, and general rubbish. Doing this helps kids discover how much waste a household produces and how much waste you can prevent going to landfill. Not only that, but it makes doing the bins each week a fair bit easier.

✔ **Eating fresh fruit and vegetables in season.** You can show children how to recognise good quality produce from the poorer versions.

✔ **Gardening.** Whether you've only a few window boxes and pots or whether you have a large plot, gardening is a great hobby that allows you to work productively together outside and contribute to your family's needs. To make gardening a fulfilling part of your family lifestyle, include:

- Making compost from food scraps as a natural form of recycling.

- Maintaining a healthy diet. Show the kids how to pick, prepare, and cook fresh meals from food they grew themselves.

- Planning a project garden plot together. Allow each family member to select a herb, fruit, and vegetable they want to plant, grow, and eat from the garden and work out the location, size, seasons, and how the garden is to be watered, composted, and weeded.

- Researching the Internet to discover answers to gardening queries. Kids love to do this part of the job.

- Showing children the importance of water and its appropriate uses. Collect and use grey water from baths and showers, install rainwater tanks, plant drought-tolerant native plants, and so on.

- Working a worm farm. Not every child is going to be fascinated with gardening, or have the patience to wait for the potatoes to grow. Having a worm farm (available in varying sizes) is a good source of mulch for the garden and can be very interesting for kids who love getting dirt under their fingernails and enjoy the grosser aspects of nature.

✔ **Saving electricity.** Setting an example for the children by keeping lights and wall switches turned off when not in use is important. Show them you're actively taking steps to use energy resources wisely and sparingly. Explain to the children why you're turning off electricity switches so they can understand the importance of reducing energy use and waste production. That way they're more likely to adopt the same habits. Easy but significant electricity-saving actions include:

- Closing doors to keep heat in and covering windows to shade the house from the sun.

- Turning off lights when leaving a room.

- Turning off switches at power points.

- Turning the heating down a couple of degrees in winter.

✔ **Turning off taps.** Explain to the kids that approximately 15 litres of water is wasted and washed down the drain if the tap is left on while cleaning their teeth. Wet the brush to start and turn the tap on again to clean and rinse.

See _Green Living For Dummies_ (Wiley) by Liz Barclay and Michael Grosvenor for practical steps your family can take to adapt your home to a more sustainable and environmentally friendly lifestyle.

Help Out

Show children how to do specific jobs around the house so that they can contribute to the family and see the value in helping others. The younger the child, the more supervision is required from you. Look for chances for jobs they can do by themselves and praise them for their efforts. In this age of the dishwasher, not too many children get to dry the dishes any more, but children can help make beds, tidy, sort the washing and hang it to dry, clean the car, and do more jobs around the house.

Set tasks that are to be each child's responsibility. That way the pocket money is genuinely earned. Here are some tasks to start:

- Collecting the mail (including junk mail)
- Feeding and grooming pets
- Getting ready for school by laying out their school clothes and packing their bags the night before
- Keeping their rooms tidy (often the biggest challenge of all)
- Loading and unloading the dishwasher
- Putting school bags, books, toys, and clothes in the right places
- Setting and clearing the dinner table
- Sorting out recycling for the weekly collection
- Trying simple garden tasks, such as watering seedlings, weeding, or picking ripe produce
- Folding and putting away their own laundry

Be Cool about Not Being a Consumer

Peer group pressure can exert a very strong influence on children. However, many popular books, movies, magazines, and other junior and teenage media frequently contain the message that being the person you want to be is better than blindly following what others are doing.

In my day, wearing or even being seen stepping into a second-hand shop was social death. Thankfully, that rule has changed – even A-list celebrities are doing it, although old clothes are called *vintage* now, instead of second-hand. Functional bags and jackets are being creatively made from old sugar bags, advertising signs, and even fruit juice boxes, and the idea of spending money responsibly – instead of irresponsibly – is rapidly gaining social status.

Encourage the children to spend money wisely. Take the kids to browse in your local second-hand shop, and make a point of popping into them on your holidays or Sunday drives into smaller country towns. Even if you don't buy anything the first few times, have a few conversations about how you can use, say, that groovy fondue set for a fun family night, or how your friend who likes to redecorate would love the ethnic tablecloths on sale.

Set an example to the children. If you look hard enough, you can find an item (or several) of clothing that is filled with possibilities. I've (Katherine) found real designer pieces that I've been thrilled to recycle and wear. My daughter has been almost exclusively dressed by the children's charity shop where my mother works because children's clothes are often barely worn before they're too small for the child. Explain to the child that money spent in shops run by charities means the money goes to a good cause. Naturally, shopping there saves money for you as well.

Many parents feel guilty about working full-time, part-time, or not having the amount of free time they'd like to devote to their children. They then buy their kids stuff to show their love and to ease their guilt. This then turns into a cycle of buying more for the kids to make up for the time spent at work, which increases spending and debt, which means they have to work harder to pay for the things they're buying more of, and so on.

The solution? If you go way back, into the mists of time, to your own upbringing, you may remember that a lot of the things you really yearned for were paid for out of your hard-earned pocket money. And very likely you looked after these items because you appreciated how long you'd saved your money for them. Try this approach with your kids. Chat to other parents to gauge what an appropriate amount of pocket money should be, and then stick to that amount. Remind yourself that your children get lots of gifts at birthdays and holiday time, and that they should be able to save or plan for any other additional luxuries themselves.

Chapter 18

Ten Ways to Motivate Your Workmates

*B*osses and trade unions are not the only people who can influence the working arrangements for you and your work colleagues. You can influence them too – individually and as a group.

This chapter looks at the various ways you – as an employee – can research and put together a case to improve working conditions in the place that employs you.

Take Control of Your Workload

Controlling what you do at work isn't as tough as it sounds. Sure you have a boss who has the right to make the final decision on what you do. But how and when you fulfil your tasks is largely up to you. Electronic diary planners are now standard in-office systems and can be used to plan your work day. Some simple steps to making your eight hours at work more productive include the points listed on the following page.

> ✔ **Check email twice a day – maximum.** An entire book could be written about email, but here are a few key tips that have been proven to work. Only check your email after 10 a.m., which gives you at least one hour to work on your top priority for the day before being distracted by 'who left their green umbrella in reception?' and endless 'reply all' emails. After working intently on a big ticket item, book half an hour (or a set period of time that works for you) in the morning to work on your email

and another time in the afternoon. Making two separate times enables you to devote your energy to your messages and provides your busy brain with a bit of down time when reading and responding to emails without wasting time throughout the day. Turn off your sound and icon new-mail notifiers so that you're not tempted to stop what you're doing and have a look in the inbox.

✔ **Embrace online aids.** Make your online diary available to everyone in your team and encourage them to do the same. This may take some paper professionals a bit of getting used to, but this is an effective way to prevent being double-booked for meetings and can be a measure of where you spend your time.

✔ **Gear up to gearing down.** Use your diary to plan your down time from the job as well. Leave a 15-minute gap between meetings to walk back to your office or to take notes or simply wind down. Don't forget to find some time to stretch or have a coffee break. That doesn't mean you need to write 'Coffee break' in your diary. Use a code word for personal entries (such as Project X) so that you're not double-booked by someone else who thinks that your break time is free time. When your energy is at its lowest (after 3 p.m. for me), book time for filing, tidying, or meeting up with someone to discuss an issue at her desk. That way the time is still used wisely and is explained, but isn't as taxing as the two-hour blocks of focused report writing, for instance.

✔ **Know thyself.** Think about when you're at your most productive. Is it mid-morning after the second cup of coffee kicks in or do you feel you're warming up by mid-afternoon? Whatever the time frame, use your 'on' time to block out chunks of time (half an hour to two hours) for working on your priority projects or tasks that need your undivided attention.

Refer to Chapter 6 for ways to use your working hours more effectively.

Leave Work on Time

This can be difficult if you work in a place where leaving at 5 p.m. is like doing the Walk of Shame.

Here's where your timesheet and your electronic diary can be very effective. Use your diary to block out time after 4.30 p.m. My previous boss had no meetings after 4.30 p.m. and blocked out the time to prevent being caught up at work beyond 5 p.m. This was generally respected and adhered to by the staff.

If you're required to keep a timesheet, then grit your teeth and smile through the folk glancing down at their watches when you leave at 5 p.m. and remind yourself that you've done your allotted hours. If you're not required to keep a timesheet, try finding a template on the Internet, or creating your own and using one. Timesheets can be handy to show your manager what hours you're putting in and make you feel more comfortable about leaving on time. If you're unlucky enough to have a manager who doesn't care about all those extra hours you're clocking up, take a look at Chapter 8 for tips to get buy-in. Where all else fails, you may need to start looking around for a new job that does offer you the balance you're after.

Other strategies used by people to make sure that they leave on time, include:

- Being part of a car pool that leaves at a pre-scheduled time each day.
- Being picked up at an arranged time by their partners.
- Belonging to a bike or walking group that walks home at an arranged time.
- Having a particular bus or train to catch (or risk waiting another hour).

Love Your Lunch Break

You've probably read on many other occasions that you need to take regular breaks of at least five minutes each to give your brain and eyes a rest from staring at the computer, complex financial reports, or report writing. However, staying tied to the desk for much longer periods in the hope that getting it all over and done with is worth it in the end seems easier.

Research shows that working without decent break times means that you actually become far less effective. One recent study amongst medics suggested that working 12-hour days was equivalent to driving with a blood-alcohol level of more than 0.08. Fatigue can affect decision making, accuracy, and productivity, and taking ten minutes to go for a walk around the block or sip a cup of tea is not a huge chunk out of your busy day.

As for lunch, try your best to avoid eating over your keyboard. If you must stay inside, use your lunch break to run errands in cyberspace, such as online banking, grocery shopping, finding gifts, and so on. Chapter 7 suggests more ideas on how to make the most of your breaks.

Most importantly, get outside and away from the confines of your work place at lunch time. Eat your sandwiches in a park, go for a walk, meet with a friend, do a five-minute meditation in the sunshine. Chapter 4 offers some suggestions on how you can improve your health and why keeping the body as well as the brain in top condition is important.

Walk and Talk

I'm now going to blush and admit that I've (Katherine) been guilty of this – sending a work mate, who only sits several metres away, an email instead of walking over and talking to her. Many reasons are given for this strange behaviour that's developed in offices since emails came into being – you don't want to disturb your colleague, putting what you want to say in writing is easier, you need to keep a copy of the details in the email, you've passed on a problem to them, and so on.

On the down side, however, sending emails within an office clogs up your colleague's inbox and your sent box, and then your inbox when they reply. Sending emails also robs an office of the camaraderie that's needed for people who work together.

Here's a challenge for 21st-century movers and shakers: how about walking over to your colleague and speaking to them instead of sending an email? I know of several people who set aside one day a week when they don't check or send emails and instead use the phone or actually meet people in person. Meeting people is a far better way of networking than impersonal emailing. And another challenge: turn off your mobile phone when you're walking and talking. Do this and you show the other person that he or she has your undivided attention and that you really value spending some time together. Phone calls can wait. That's why message services were invented.

Take Time Off

Repeat after me: 'I am brilliant at my job and everyone loves me but I am *not* indispensable to the running of the office. I am not a machine; I am a human being who needs to take time off every now and then.' Got that?

We have no doubt that you have some responsibilities that only you can do well or where you know the full story about that particular customer's needs and background. But if you don't go on leave, you're denying someone else the opportunity to have a go and train on the job. You may also be sending the message that you don't trust or value anyone else enough to let go of the reins once in a while.

Time off can be spent at home, away somewhere exciting with your partner and family as a way of re-establishing a connection, or even on your own. In this era of changing jobs more frequently than the previous generation, partners may find that they have different amounts of leave. Taking a break on your own can be a better way of recharging and doing something your partner isn't interested in than hanging around the house, feeling as though you're letting an opportunity for self development pass you by. If you do choose some rest time at home, make sure that your colleagues appreciate that you're still on holiday, so they're not tempted to contact you with 'urgent' queries that they'd have had to deal with if you were less accessible.

Be honest now – you definitely know people who don't take their full holiday leave entitlements each year, citing overwork, fear of emergencies occurring in their absence, and worry that no one else can deal with their work as well as they can, as some of the reasons they stay chained to their desks. If you are one of those people, consider the proven fact that burned-out employees are likely to wind up producing less quality and quantity of work and suffer more health problems. So you are doing no one, least of all yourself, any favours at all.

Create a Brilliant Business Case

If you're interested in reducing your working hours, or working four longer days for a fifth day off (called *compressed hours*), or working from home a couple of days a week, or starting earlier and finishing earlier, then tackle your request as you would any other business manoeuvre. Present your request professionally. Find out what your colleagues use in terms of flexible working options and what workers in other departments in your organisation have in place. Look at similar jobs in similar industries. Often, an organisation's policies and templates can be found on their websites, or you can contact Human Resources (HR) offices.

Collect some relevant case studies on employers and employees, accessing the types of working arrangements that interest you. Two sites provide good examples of how flexible working can increase productivity and employee morale and also reduce absenteeism and recruitment costs:

- Chartered Institute of Personnel Development (CIPD): www.cipd.co.uk.
- Employers for Work Life Balance: www.employersfor work-life balance.org.uk.

For coverage of the whole subject of flexible working arrangements, refer to Chapter 8.

Work from Home

Unless you're like Charlie's father in *Charlie and the Chocolate Factory* and have to be at the conveyor belt screwing on each and every toothpaste cap, you can find many opportunities to work from home (*telecommuting*). As with other flexible working options, how you request to work from home depends on your approach and what preparation you make to anticipate objections, produce relevant examples of how telecommuting works in your work situation, and guidelines that your manager can feel comfortable using.

Go to `www.employersfor work-life balance.org.uk` and search for case studies on home working and telecommuting. You can find many examples of UK companies – BT, Boehringer Ingelheim UK, and KPMG amongst them – who've embraced a whole range of flexible working practices, including working from home.

If you've already negotiated a work-from-home arrangement, here are some quick hints to help you make the arrangement work for you and your employer:

- **Be flexible.** By all means let your colleagues know when you're available to attend meetings in the work place, but try to accommodate their requests for meetings or out-of-agreed-hours work when you can. Being approachable means that you're being flexible.

- **Communicate regularly with your boss.** Let your boss know your progress. This can be a brief bullet-point email that lists the projects you're working on, what stages you're at with each and any key tasks on your 'to do' list. This makes your boss feel informed and able to discuss any work issues or changes with you.

- **Ensure that you're easily contactable.** Be contactable by telephone, mobile, and email for any urgent queries that may arise. Return any calls promptly to assure your boss that you're accessible and following up queries in a timely manner.

- **Make sure that you and your boss agree on what work you're doing at home.** Be very clear about how often you're working from home, which days you're out of the office, and how your performance is to be measured.

- **Set specific times for work and stick to them.** Do this and you avoid the distractions of being at home, such as doing the housework instead of writing a report, putting on a load of washing to avoid data analysis, cooking several meals for freezing to put off creating the new spreadsheet, and so on. Your work time needs to be as structured at home as it is in the office in order to complete your workload.

Lead by Example

Many work places have good work/life balance policies and options for working more flexibly, but still languish under a culture of long working hours and believing that it's a sign of weakness when you take time off. Sometimes working-hour policies exist but no one wants to be the first to step out of the crowd and take up the options. You can be the one: show your leadership qualities by leaving on time and taking your allotted annual leave. And assert yourself by trying the following:

- **Be green.** Become the green god or goddess of your work place by asking people to recycle discarded printer paper and use the other side for notepaper. Put in recycling bins for glass, paper, and plastics. Try low-energy light bulbs and move towards greener office products. For many ways you can make a difference, see *Green Living For Dummies* (Wiley) by Liz Barclay and Michael Grosvenor.

- **Have an interest or hobby outside work.** Have you ever held a conversation with co-workers more senior than you and discovered that they've run the London marathon three times, or have built their own loft extension? Often, highly successful people have fulfilling interests outside of work that not only help reduce work stress but also provide some self-development and personal satisfaction. It can also be a way of extending a side of yourself that you rarely get to use in work. Dean is a meteorologist and as such focuses his energies at work on logic, analysis, mathematics, physics, and programming. In the evenings, he creates gourmet meals that are delicious to eat, is learning the piano, and has set up his own gym. He says, 'These activities help me use some of my untapped creative side and I really look forward to them.'

- **Have breakfast with your family.** Why have a stale muffin and an over-priced coffee over your laptop when you can spend 15 minutes in the morning having breakfast with your kids? Jill and her partner get up earlier and make coffee. That quarter of an hour allows them to plan the rest of the day together before things get really crazy when the kids wake up.

- **Outsource to increase your free time.** Talk to your workmates and find out how many of the team have help at home. If they spend most of their time in the office doing 10-hour plus stretches, then logic says that no time's left for household chores. Cleaners and gardeners come fairly cheap. The difference is that when you hire them to keep your home in shape, you lose all that stress of worrying about when you're going to have time to do the work. Dozens of franchise industries cater to working people in the fields of ironing, maintenance, dog walking and grooming, pre-cooked healthy meals, and personal fitness training.

Men are supposed to enjoy gardening but Karl told me he hated spending half of his weekend in the garden so he and his wife decided to pay someone to do the work and then they can enjoy the ambience of the garden at weekends. It means Karl gets more time with the kids after a busy week at work.

✔ **Your bike or walk to work.** Riding a bike is so good for you. Your health and fitness benefit, your mental health improves (nothing like a good half an hour outside in the fresh air to help you solve a nagging problem), and the planet has less fumes to deal with. You may find that a workmate who lives near you may also decide to join you.

✔ **Value your health.** The best times to exercise are often first thing in the morning before breakfast, at lunch times, or straight after work before going home. Refer to Chapter 4 for more ideas on how to incorporate exercise into your life.

Be Nice

Don't whinge about what's wrong at work; that only makes your work place seem even more miserable. Be proactive and think up solutions or new ways of doing things instead. Make a time to meet up with your boss and provide some ideas for changes instead of just complaints.

You know that answering the phone with a smile or approaching a client with a smile always works – well, almost always. Psychological studies find that by choosing to approach a task or the day in a positive way, you contribute a great deal to your inner sense of optimism. As you get out of bed in the morning, try asking yourself, 'Am I going to choose to feel grumpy and sorry for myself, or smile and look forward to the good things that can happen today?' Corny? Maybe. True? Yes.

Other tips you can try include:

✔ **Acknowledging the contributions of others in your projects and tasks.** Nothing is sourer than seeing your immediate boss or colleague take the praise or promotion for something without acknowledging your efforts in their work. Make sure that you thank and acknowledge the co-workers who help you. Not only is offering credits an important relationship builder but those people are going to be prepared to work with you on future projects.

✔ **Avoiding participating in office gossip.** You don't necessarily have to butt in and shut it down, but don't put in your own ten cents' worth. It is destructive and unprofessional, and rumours can get wildly out of hand and into the wrong ears.

✔ **Being an active listener.** Don't fiddle with your SMS screen or tap at emails when someone's talking to you. Turn off your mobile so you can give them your full attention.

✔ **Being on time with your work.** If you have agreed to produce work by a certain due date, stick to it. You risk letting others down as well as yourself when you don't fulfil your side of the bargain.

✔ **Contributing at team meetings.** It's disconcerting when people who sit in silence during meetings then gripe later on. You don't have to chat during a meeting when you've nothing to offer, but it's important that you raise an issue that concerns or interests you.

✔ **Picking your passions.** When you disagree with the decisions made, choose one or two of the most important to discuss. When others arise, leave them for another time. When you challenge every decision made at every meeting, you end up being shunned by your team and ignored as a drama queen (oh, and men can be drama queens too!). Decide which events may be potential catastrophes, and which you can live with.

✔ **Sharing your ideas.** You never know what others can contribute in terms of work or advice until you discuss your work with them. Build up a network in your office and offer suggestions in return for accepting suggestions from your colleagues.

Be a Genuine Team Member

Everyone says in their job interviews that they like working in teams and are team players. The way to prove that you are a team player is to show your support for your colleagues. Being approachable and offering to participate in a group project, or helping complete a priority task before a deadline, is an invaluable way of contributing towards the larger goals and targets of your work place. This shows the boss that you're prepared to work hard when it's required of you.

Being mindful of the needs of new employees with flexible working arrangements, or those who return to work after taking time off to raise children, is another way to help out. Ask a new colleague if she would like to shadow you (sit with you and work together) until she's up to speed on the relevant procedures and computer programs. Help provide on-the-job training to colleagues who need it.

Keep communicating with your teammates. It is very frustrating to miss out on important news or feedback because a colleague hasn't passed the information on. Keep your workmates informed via a brief email or verbal update on what tasks you have on your plate and where you're up to on each of them (it also helps them if you have an unplanned absence due to illness or emergency so that they can pick up where you left off).

Other ways to contribute include:

- ✔ Avoiding use of the 'Reply all' email or sending unimportant emails to busy team members.

- ✔ Laughing. Times are when a well-timed joke or a laugh work better than an 'I told you so'. Laughing decreases stress and tensions in the work place. Refer to Chapter 3 for more information about using laughter to improve your health.

- ✔ Offering to mentor a more junior colleague.

- ✔ Setting up a lunchtime walking group or yoga class for interested staff.

- ✔ Sharing your lists of contacts and networks with your teammates to help them in their work.

- ✔ Organising team morning teas, lunches, and family days.

- ✔ Volunteering to work on an inter-departmental project or committee to get to know more people outside of your specific unit.

Index

• E •

• *N* •

Notes

Notes

FOR DUMMIES

Do Anything. Just Add Dummies

UK editions

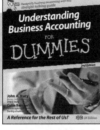

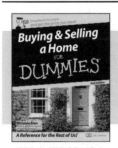
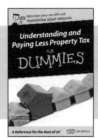

FOR DUMMIES®

A world of resources to help you grow

UK editions

SELF-HELP

978-0-470-01838-5

978-0-7645-7028-5

978-0-470-75876-2

HEALTH

978-0-470-69430-5

978-0-470-51737-6

978-0-470-71401-0

HISTORY

978-0-470-99468-9

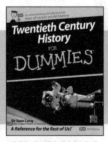

978-0-470-51015-5

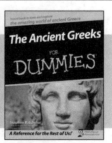

978-0-470-98787-2

Inventing For Dummies
978-0-470-51996-7

Job Hunting and Career Change
All-In-One For Dummies
978-0-470-51611-9

Motivation For Dummies
978-0-470-76035-2

Origami Kit For Dummies
978-0-470-75857-1

Personal Development All-In-One
For Dummies
978-0-470-51501-3

PRINCE2 For Dummies
978-0-470-51919-6

Psychometric Tests For Dummies
978-0-470-75366-8

Raising Happy Children For
Dummies
978-0-470-05978-4

Starting and Running a Business
All-in-One For Dummies
978-0-470-51648-5

Sudoku for Dummies
978-0-470-01892-7

The British Citizenship Test
For Dummies, 2nd Edition
978-0-470-72339-5

Time Management For Dummies
978-0-470-77765-7

Wills, Probate, & Inheritance Tax
For Dummies, 2nd Edition
978-0-470-75629-4

Winning on Betfair For Dummies,
2nd Edition
978-0-470-72336-4

Available wherever books are sold. For more information or to order direct go to www.wiley.com or call +44 (0) 1243 843291

13902_p2

FOR DUMMIES®

The easy way to get more done and have more fun

LANGUAGES

978-0-7645-5194-9

978-0-7645-5193-2

978-0-471-77270-5

MUSIC

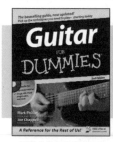

978-0-7645-9904-0

978-0-470-03275-6
UK Edition

978-0-7645-5105-5

SCIENCE & MATHS

978-0-7645-5326-4

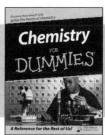

978-0-7645-5430-8

978-0-7645-5325-7

Art For Dummies
978-0-7645-5104-8

Baby & Toddler Sleep Solutions For
Dummies
978-0-470-11794-1

Bass Guitar For Dummies
978-0-7645-2487-5

Brain Games For Dummies
978-0-470-37378-1

Christianity For Dummies
978-0-7645-4482-8

Filmmaking For Dummies, 2nd
Edition
978-0-470-38694-1

Forensics For Dummies
978-0-7645-5580-0

German For Dummies
978-0-7645-5195-6

Hobby Farming For Dummies
978-0-470-28172-7

Jewelry Making & Beading For
Dummies
978-0-7645-2571-1

Knitting for Dummies, 2nd Edition
978-0-470-28747-7

Music Composition For Dummies
978-0-470-22421-2

Physics For Dummies
978-0-7645-5433-9

Sex For Dummies, 3rd Edition
978-0-470-04523-7

Solar Power Your Home For Dummies
978-0-470-17569-9

Tennis For Dummies
978-0-7645-5087-4

The Koran For Dummies
978-0-7645-5581-7

U.S. History For Dummies
978-0-7645-5249-6

Wine For Dummies, 4th Edition
978-0-470-04579-4

Available wherever books are sold. For more information or to order direct go to
www.wiley.com or call +44 (0) 1243 843291

13902_p3

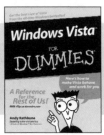
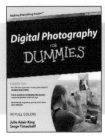

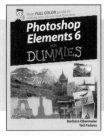